301.5

The
Military
and
American
Society

THE MILITARY AND AMERICAN SOCIETY

Essays & Readings

EDITED BY Stephen E. Ambrose

 James A. Barber, Jr.

The Free Press NEW YORK

Collier-Macmillan Ltd. LONDON

The Free Press
A Division of The Macmillan Company
866 Third Avenue, New York, New York 10022

Collier-Macmillan Canada Ltd., Toronto, Ontario

Library of Congress Catalog Card Number: 77–163236

printing number

1 2 3 4 5 6 7 8 9 10

Contents

About the Contributors

MARTIN BLUMENSON, formerly of the Office of the Chief of Military History, is Ernest J. King Professor of Maritime History at the Naval War College. One of the country's most prolific military historians, Blumenson is the author of numerous books on the military in World War II and after.

VINCENT DAVIS, Professor of Political Science at the Graduate School of International Studies, University of Denver, served as Executive Secretary of the International Studies Association from 1965 to 1970. A specialist in American foreign policy and national security policy, he has published several books on these subjects, including the important *The Admiral's Lobby*.

ELIZABETH B. DREW, in her position as Washington editor for *The Atlantic Monthly*, and as a regular columnist for that journal, has been a consistent critic of the armed forces. Since the time this article was published in *The Atlantic Monthly*, several steps have been taken to redirect the activities of the Corps of Engineers, including the decision to stop construction of the half-finished Cross-Florida barge canal, which had been under attack by conservationists. At the time of this writing it appeared that a series of changes may have put the Corps well on the road to becoming a primary agency of environmental repair, rather than part of the problem as represented in this article.

DWIGHT DAVID EISENHOWER, the thirty-fourth President of the United States, was the tenth General to be elected President, but the only one to be so chosen in this century. The phrase "military-industrial complex" was used for the first time in his Farewell Address, a portion of which is reproduced in this book.

JOHN KENNETH GALBRAITH, Professor of Economics at Harvard University and former American Ambassador to India, has long been active in politics as a liberal. During the 1950's and 1960's he published a number of volumes in which he provided a provocative analysis of the American economic system and argued for a reordering of national priorities.

JAMES M. GAVIN, Chairman of the Board of Arthur D. Little, Inc. and former American Ambassador to France, is a retired Lieutenant General who won great distinction in World War II as a paratroop commander. At the time he describes in this section of his memoirs, *Crisis Now*, Gavin served directly under the then Army Chief of Staff, Matthew B. Ridgway.

SAMUEL PHILLIPS HUNTINGTON, of the Institute of War and Peace Studies in New York, is one of America's leading conservative political scientists. His specialty is civil-military relations. His books include the classic *Soldier and the State*, and *The Common Defense*, a trail-blazing work on current strategic problems.

MORRIS JANOWITZ, Professor of Sociology at the University of Chicago, is generally recognized as the leading American military sociologist. He published his classic study of the American military officer corps, *The Professional Soldier*, in 1960. Since that time, he has continued to publish important books on military and political sociology, as well as to prod the academic field of sociology into more thorough and rigorous attempts to study the social roles of military organizations.

CHARLES C. MOSKSOS, JR., Professor of Sociology at Northwestern University, has written widely on such problems as modernization and social change. In addition to numerous articles, he has published *The Sociology of Political Independence* and *The American Enlisted Man*.

JACK RAYMOND for the past thirty years has written as a foreign correspondent for the New York *Times*. His interview with Djilas in Yugoslavia precipitated the former's first trial. In addition to his writings as a foreign correspondent, Raymond has also written *Power at the Pentagon*.

BRUCE RUSSETT is presently Professor of Political Science and Director of Graduate Studies at Yale. His recent research efforts have been largely directed to the attempt to bring empirical tools of political science to bear on the problems of achieving stable world peace.

I. F. STONE is a radical journalist of the old muckraking school, with an impressive and enviable reputation for honesty and accuracy. In addition to writing numerous books and making regular contributions to *The New York Review of Books*, Stone is both editor and publisher of *I. F. Stone's Weekly*, which is carefully read in official Washington.

CHARLES WOLF, JR., is a senior economist with the Rand Corporation, a firm specializing in contract research, much of it for the government. Wolf has published several books on economic aspects of foreign policy, and on national security policy. His article in this book originated as a talk to the faculty of the Air Force Academy in Colorado Springs, and was later published as a Rand Corporation paper.

The
Military
and
American
Society

PART I

An
Overview

The Military and American Society: An Overview

STEPHEN E. AMBROSE

In 1939, as Franklin Roosevelt began his sixth year as President, the United States had an Army of 185,000 officers and men, with an annual budget of less than $500 million. The troops were scattered in small posts throughout the country and in America's colonial possessions. Except in Washington, D.C. (where the officers, by order, wore mufti to reduce their visibility), the public seldom saw an active duty soldier. Officers were isolated from the main stream of American life, partly by personal choice, partly because the public wanted nothing to do with them, but primarily because they were physically separated. Most enlisted men were unmarried, long-serving regulars who had even less contact with the public than the officers. America on the eve of global conflict remained as firmly opposed to conscription as it had been in the nineteenth century; young men knew that only in the event of a true national emergency would they have to serve in the Armed Services, and even then they could take comfort in knowing that almost everyone in their age-group would also be conscripted. Except for some relatively small ship-building yards, no American industry was dependent on military orders for its existence. The country and its citizens had a multitude of serious problems, but the impact of the military on American life was not among them.

The insignificance of the military was a reflection of American foreign policy. In 1939 the United States had no military alliances and no troops stationed in any foreign country. Except on the high seas and within North America, the nation had no offensive capability at all. The overwhelming sentiment within the country was isolationist, which in its turn was a reflection of geography.

No power in the Western Hemisphere could mount anything resembling a serious threat to the United States and no European power could project enough force across the Atlantic Ocean to challenge American security. After World War I the United States unilaterally disarmed, as it had after all its nineteenth century wars, for reasons that had nothing to do with morality but which nevertheless allowed Americans to feel morally superior to Europeans. The Versailles Treaty added to the isolationist sentiment, for most Americans felt that their country had been cheated by the European powers and they were determined that never again would they be dragged into European disputes.

The single most important fact about American foreign policy in January, 1939, was that the great bulk of the American people felt little need to become involved in foreign wars. American security, the *sine qua non* of foreign policy, was assured, not because of American alliances or military might but because of the distance between America and any potential enemy. As a result, the Army and Navy were among the least important of all national institutions.

One generation later, the Armed Services were by any measurement among the most important of all national institutions. The United States had a standing Army of well over one million men, with an Air Force and a Navy almost as large. The budget of the Department of Defense was almost $80 billion, a figure that did not include the cost of the world-wide espionage organization maintained by the Central Intelligence Agency (CIA). The United States had military alliances with 48 nations, had 1,517,000 soldiers and sailors stationed in 119 countries, and had a military capability sufficient to destroy the world many times over. Vast segments of American industry were totally dependent upon military orders for their economic health and almost ten per cent of the gross national product went into arms. The Department of Defense employed, directly, over 1,000,000 civilian workers, while millions of others worked in industries dependent on the Department for orders. Conscription had been a permanent feature of American life for two decades. All young men planned their lives around the draft; a large percentage spent two or more of the most productive years of their life in the Armed Services. The military was deeply involved in, and had an incalculable impact on, every aspect of American life, including foreign policy, the economy, the allocation of resources, college and university programs and funding, the black revolution, civil disorders, the environment, basic education of millions of non-high-school graduates (and thousands who had graduated), and most of all the general tone and quality of contemporary life.

America had developed some of the features of Laswell's garrison state, not because of a conspiracy by the Armed Services, not because of a triumph of the militarists in the inner councils of the government, not because of the machinations of the military-industrial complex, but rather because of a fundamental shift of revolutionary proportions in the way American political leaders—and the public—viewed the nation's relationship to the world. In one generation, Americans had changed from a people relatively unconcerned with events outside the Western Hemisphere to a people deeply involved in developments everywhere in the world.

An historic change of this magnitude cannot be brought about by one man, or even by powerful groups of men. The forces at work are complex and difficult to describe separately, much less in their interaction. But if any one man had to be singled out as the most responsible individual in creating the shape of the world today, and America's role in it, that man would be Adolf Hitler. It was Hitler who forced Roosevelt, his successors, and the American people generally to adopt a new foreign policy, Hitler who upset such balance as had been attained at Versailles, Hitler who threatened to create a world-power in Europe that potentially could mount a successful military challenge to the United States, Hitler who opened Eastern Europe to the Soviet Union, previously hemmed in by capitalistic nations, Hitler who created a vacuum in Western Europe and elsewhere in 1945 into which American power could flow. Most of all, Hitler was the personification of irrational evil, the madman who would, if he could, destroy the world.

After the war the American people and their leaders found it relatively easy to transfer the image they had of Hitler—an image that was rooted in reality—to the man they chose to regard as Hitler's successor, Joseph Stalin. Technological change, especially in military weapons, gave added impetus to the process. For the first time in history, the United States could be threatened from abroad. High-speed ships, long-range bombers, jet aircraft, atomic weapons, and eventually intercontinental missiles all combined to endanger the actual physical security of the United States. Previously, those who tried to unite Europe by force, such as Napoleon or the Kaiser, threatened to some extent the economy of the United States, but not its basic security. By the late thirties, however, this situation was being transformed, and by the early fifties the process was complete. The combination of the new weaponry and irrational, evil rulers like Hitler or Stalin terrified many Americans.

The process of transference of attitudes toward Hitler onto others gained in popularity as time went on, until by the mid-sixties it could be applied even to those who did not have modern, sophisticated weapons. Secretary of State Dean Rusk frequently made an analogy that linked the leaders of tiny North Vietnam with Hitler. Whatever the historical faults (and they were many) of Rusk's comparison of any move toward peace in Vietnam to the appeasement of Hitler at Munich, it had the virtue of arousing a built-in reaction among large segments of the population, especially those over 45 years of age (which included most of America's leaders in the sixties) who had fought in World War II. Hitler's legacy cannot be ignored. Much of the modern world and American foreign policy testifies to his lasting influence.

Everything that the United States did in the generation after 1939, obviously, could not be traced to the reaction to Hitler. There were other forces at work. At the conclusion of World War II, America was in an enviable position. Her power was such that it invited comparison with Imperial Rome. In all the world, only America had a healthy economy, an intact physical plant capable of mass production of both heavy and consumer goods, and excess capital. It seemed obvious that America would finance the reconstruction of a war-torn world, which carried with it the implication that American leaders would decide what form the reconstruction would take, even to the point of influencing the nature of the governments rising from the smouldering ashes. American troops occupied Japan, the only important industrial power in the Pacific, while American influence was dominant in France, Britain, and western Germany, the industrial heart of Europe. The Pacific and the Mediterranean had become American lakes. Most of all, the United States had a monopoly on the atomic bomb.

Yet despite the nation's preeminent position in the world, America's leaders in the summer of 1945 feared the future. There were three fundamental reasons. The first was the possibility of the emergence of another Hitler, a role Stalin seemed already to have assumed. The second was technological. The atomic secret could not be kept forever (scientists estimated Russia would have the bomb within three to ten years) and the German development of rocket weapons clearly demonstrated that once missile technology was more mature, the United States would never again be invulnerable.

The third fear was economic. The shadow of the depression loomed as ominously over the decision-makers' shoulders as did the shadow of Munich. There was an almost universal feeling in Washington that in the postwar era America could slip—or plunge—into another depression, which would lead to a revolution at home. Whether the political right or left triumphed made little difference, as leading figures in the Administration saw it, for the result would be the same either way—an end to the American system.

American foreign policy in the crucial years from 1945 to 1950 can be understood only in reference to the widespread fear of another depression. To oversimplify, most men at most times expect the future to resemble the past and, just as the Truman Administration (and its successors) used the increasingly irrelevant example of Hitler and Munich as the touchstone for American relations with Stalin and the rest of the non-capitalist world, so did the Administration believe that a return to prewar economic conditions would spell a return to depression.

How to avoid depression became the great concern. Government spending could help, but not much—the New Deal had obviously treated only symptoms and had not provided a cure. In 1945, almost no one believed that in peacetime Washington could spend anything like enough money to keep the economy booming, unless the nation adopted some form of central economic dictation. The trouble with extensive central planning and control, however, as the men of 1945 saw it, was that it would evolve into either a government of the right or one of the left, each of which was repugnant.

The solution to the problem of another depression, as most of the policy-makers in the Truman Administration saw it, was a continuation of the New Deal (renamed Fair Deal) and, far more important, greatly expanded foreign trade. What America needed above all was foreign markets in which she could sell the products pouring out of her factories—and, as some realized, access to raw materials to feed the factories.[1]

The trouble with expanded foreign trade as a preferred solution to America's economic dilemma was that much of the proposed market place was closed, nationalized, or both. Americans

[1] Expansion of the market-place was, of course, a traditional American program that merely took on new, and more active, forms after 1945. For a discussion of expansion in the nineteenth century, see William A. Williams, *The Roots of the Modern American Empire* (Random House, New York, 1969).

feared that their manufacturers would be unable to compete with foreign industries that had all the resources of the state behind them. If the rest of the world nationalized its basic industries and/or closed its markets, America could avoid over-production and a resultant depression only by nationalizing industry itself. American foreign policy after 1945 had as one of its guiding stars, therefore, the prevention of these evils—or, put positively, the creation of an open door everywhere. To insure these conditions the nation prepared to use her economic might (as in the 1946 British loan and the 1948 Marshall Plan) or her military muscle (as in Greece, Korea, and elsewhere). The leaders believed that free, private enterprise was essential to a free, open, democratic society, and they would save it at home by imposing it abroad. Truman described the program most succinctly in March, 1947. "The whole world should adopt the American system," he declared. "The American system can survive in America only if it becomes a world system."

The villain was the Soviet Union, which had closed the East European market and seemed to be extending its closed system elsewhere. Given American assumptions and Soviet actions, conflict was inevitable. Even had the American economy not required foreign markets, outlets for investment, or access to raw materials, however, the ideological differences between the Soviet Union and the United States would have fed an arms race, for each side was deeply suspicious of the other—with good reason. Nuclear weapons and the missiles to deliver them became the pivot around which much of the cold war revolved. Each time one side developed a new bomb or built an additional missile, the other side followed. The growth of the Armed Services and their suppliers—the military-industrial complex—gave generals and admirals and industrialists new sources of power (in Russia as well as in America), leading to a situation in which Americans tended to find military answers to political problems. The President and his chief advisors frequently accepted the military solution precisely because the United States did have so much power. No people or nation, it seemed, could stand against the American Armed Services, and one of the best things about inaugurating military action was that when the shooting was over the Americans could make the political decisions unilaterally—assuming they won. Not until the late sixties did large numbers of Americans learn the painful lesson that the power to destroy is not the power to control.

The United States of the cold war period, like ancient Rome, was concerned with all political problems in the world. The loss of this or that country to communism, therefore, while not in itself a threat to American physical security, carried with it implications that officials in Washington found highly disturbing. They became greatly concerned with trends, with the appearance as well as the reality of events, and there was much talk of dominos. Who ruled the Dominican Republic, for example, was of concern to one or two American corporations only, and clearly nothing that happened on that island posed the slightest threat to American security. But the State Department, the White House, and the CIA were certain that if the communists won in the Dominican Republic, they would soon win elsewhere. In the early sixties, few important officials argued that South Vietnam was essential to the defense of the United States, but the attitude that "we have to prove that wars of national liberation don't work" did carry the day, aided in no small measure by the argument that if Vietnam went, all Southeast Asia would soon follow. Then would come the Pacific islands, and finally the fight would be on America's West Coast.

The attitude that what happened anywhere in the world was important to the United States was a far cry from the American outlook of 1939. One additional reason for the change was the astonishing growth of America's overseas military bases. The American Armed Services flowed into many vacuums at the end of the war and once American troops were stationed on foreign soil, the soil was included in the list of America's "vital interests."

But America's rise to globalism was by no means mindless, just as it was not exclusively a reaction to the supposed communist challenge. During World War II Henry Luce of *Life* magazine spoke for most political leaders as well as American businessmen and soldiers when he said that the twentieth century would be the American century. The politicians looked for areas in which American influence could dominate; the businessmen looked for profitable markets and new sources of raw materials; the military looked for overseas bases. All found what they wanted as America after 1945 inaugurated a program of expansion that had no inherent limits.

Americans who wanted to bring the blessings of democracy, capitalism, and stability to everyone meant just what they said— the whole world, in their view, should be a reflection of the United States. Americans launched a crusade for freedom that would be complete only when freedom—as they defined it—

reigned everywhere. Conversatives like Senator Robert Taft doubted that such a goal was obtainable, and old New Dealers like Henry Wallace argued that it could only be achieved at the cost of domestic reform. But most politicians and nearly all businessmen and soldiers signed on as crusaders.

While America was creating her empire, while her business-men and soldiers and politicians moved into Latin America, Europe, Southeast Asia and nearly everywhere else, her leaders scarcely wondered if there were limits to American power. The disorderly expansion and the astronomical growth of areas de-fined as constituting a vital interest seemed to Washington and Wall Street and the Pentagon as entirely normal and natural. Almost no important public figure argued that the nation was over-extended, just as none could suggest any attitude toward communism other than that of unrelieved hostility. The idea that the Third World would resent and eventually struggle against American domination was hardly considered.

Only the ultimate military reality put limits on American expansion. At no time after 1950 was the United States capable of destroying Russia or her allies without taking on totally unacceptable risks herself. The crusade against communism, therefore, soon took the form of containment rather than overt attack. Containment, with its implication of an acceptance of a permanently divided world and thus of a limit to American expansion, led to almost intolerable frustration. But no alterna-tive to containment was seriously considered. As she moved into the 1970's, America remained determined to hold to the empire she had won, whatever the cost. The revolution in attitudes, policies, and methods that began in 1939 had gone too far to be easily reversed.

The military did not make the policy, but it surely benefited from it, emerging from its historic subordination to become a significant and powerful element in American society and social institutions. In sheer size alone the military dwarfed all other institutions. In 1962 the *Statistical Abstract of the United States* estimated the worth of the real and personal property of the Department of Defense at $164.8 billion, a figure widely re-garded as an underestimate since much of the property was listed at its purchase, not current, value. Also, since the build-up of American forces following the war in Vietnam, and with infla-tion, the figure has probably more than doubled. But it is only when military assets are compared with those of the giant corporations that one gains some perspective on the magnitude of military holdings. In 1958, the Air Force estimated that its net assets were in excess of $70 billion, which meant that the Air Force alone exceeded in worth the combined value of the 55 largest industrial corporations in the United States.

More than half the federal budget each year since 1951 has gone to the Department of Defense, which in turn spends one-third of its income on material procurement (with less—about 28 per cent—on salaries). The military budget is a factor of basic importance in the economy. Allocation of natural resources, capital, and labor are all directly affected by the needs of the military. Hundreds of industrial concerns survive solely because of military contracts, while others, including some of the very largest, continue their high levels of production only because of military purchases. By the sixties, some economists seriously doubted that the United States could ever return to a true peacetime, non-expansive economy without immediately suffering a severe depression. And no one could deny that the key civilians and soldiers in the Pentagon had greater power over the economy than any group outside the government.

The impact of the military knew almost no bounds. Before 1940, for example, there had been two basic types of institutions of higher learning in the United States, state universities and colleges and private schools. The private institutions were supported by endowments and fees, the state schools by state taxes and to a lesser extent fees. Neither type had much if any direct contact with the federal government. By the sixties it was more nearly correct to speak of state schools on the one hand, and federal universities on the other, for the private schools —especially the elite ones on the east and west coasts—drew the major portion of their support from federal funds, with by far the largest share coming from the Department of Defense. It is usually forgotten that President Eisenhower, in his Farewell Address (made famous by his warning about the military-industrial complex) also warned against the intrusion of the federal government into the affairs of America's universities. "The free university, historically the fountainhead of free ideas and scientific discovery, has experienced a revolution in the conduct of research," Eisenhower said. "The prospect of domination of the nation's scholars by Federal employment, project allocations, and the power of money is ever present—and is gravely to be regarded." Still, the trend continued, until by 1970 one out of every five of the top 500 defense contractors were educational institutions.

The most direct effect the military has on American society is in the allocation of resources. Savings on the Department of Defense budget could, at least in theory, be directly applied to restoring America's urban areas, anti-pollution measures, poverty, and other pressing domestic needs. But savings from the Pentagon are hard to come by, for two fundamental reasons. The first is the threat, over which the Congress, the White House, and the Pentagon have little direct control. While it is true that the United States, by increasing its own military, can force the Russians to respond in kind, thereby creating a self-fulfilling prophecy, and also true that the brass tend to over-estimate the threat, since their concern is primarily Russian capabilities rather than Russian intentions, and finally true that by limiting access to information the Pentagon can paint a picture of the threat that outsiders cannot challenge for lack of information, it still remains a fact that the threat itself is mounted outside the United States and must be met.

The second reason it is difficult to squeeze the Pentagon for savings is the nature of the beast. When the Secretary of Defense, speaking as the deputy of the Commander in Chief, says that the nation needs an anti-ballistic missile system (ABM) to insure its security in the seventies, Congressmen find it difficult if not impossible to argue with him. The Armed Services spend millions of dollars each year on publicity to demonstrate their efficiency and the need for the new programs or weapons they demand. There is no organized counter-propaganda campaign, nor any possibility of one on the scale mounted by the Department of Defense. Few Congressmen are courageous or strong enough to face a charge of neglecting the national defense, nor do those who have stood against the Department of Defense have the information available to dispute the Pentagon's claims about what the national defense requires. In the reverse situation, when strong elements in Congress want to buy more military hardware than the administration says it needs, the public tends to support the hard-liners. Nixon lost the 1960 Presidential election in large part because Kennedy convinced millions of Americans that the Republican Eisenhower Administration had allowed a missile gap to develop and had thereby endangered the nation's security. Kennedy's victory was a sobering lesson to all politicians who had been tempted to try to cut down military appropriations.[2]

Most of all, in any struggle over appropriations (i.e., allocation of resources) between domestic and defense needs, the military has a favored position because it is already there. Its bases are established, and local economies revolve around them. Its contracts have been granted. In an inflationary period, it is almost impossible even to hold the line on defense spending (because of necessary pay increases and the mounting costs of procurement), much less cut down. As the largest single employer in the nation, by far, the Department of Defense has millions of voters directly and indirectly dependent upon it for their daily bread. There are ten times as many military personnel as there are physicians and surgeons in the United States, or than there are clergymen or lawyers. There are over half as many persons involved in the services as there are farmers. There are nearly a million more servicemen than there are teachers. None of these figures includes the civilians working directly or indirectly for the Department of Defense. By 1970 it seemed clear to many economists and politicians that the most the nation could hope for was marginal savings from the defense budget, plus increased efficiency, but not a massive reallocation of resources.

It would be a mistake, however, to assume that because the Department of Defense is so powerful, generals and admirals now run the country. Every Secretary of Defense, with one exception (George C. Marshall, who served less than a year) has been a civilian. The major decisions on procurement in the Pentagon are made by deputy and assistant secretaries, all civilians. The professional soldiers can and do give advice on what to buy, or on where to build or shut down a base, but they do not decide. The Pentagon can and does overwhelm Congress with figures and statistics on the threat and on America's needs, forcing most Congressmen to throw up their hands and admit they cannot possibly understand such a complex subject. But within the Pentagon, especially since Secretary Robert S. McNamara and his "whiz kids," the tendency is for the civilian staff

[2] Goldwater's defeat in 1964, on the other hand, came about partly because he was widely regarded as an adventuristic militarist. This should not be taken to indicate a shift in the public's attitude toward defense, however, for it was hardly possible to charge Johnson with neglecting the needs of the Armed Services.

in the Office of the Secretary of Defense to overwhelm the soldiers with figures and statistics. Civilian control of the military is as complete as it could be; from the congressional point of view, the trouble is not that the soldiers are running the economy or foreign policy through the Pentagon, but rather that the executive branch of the government is in such total charge that neither the Congress nor the soldiers can effectively challenge it.

A similar phenomenon pervades the making of American foreign policy. Military men, in general, act as advisers to and agents of the executive branch, but not as decision-makers. Soldiers have never forced the executive into a military action against the will of the civilian leaders, nor is it likely that the Armed Services would be able to do so. Obviously, the advice the military gives is important, and on occasion crucial, but historically there has been no single military point of view on fundamental questions, so the President has been able to pick and choose from among various options. In a crisis situation the President is far more likely to turn to civilians outside the chain of command than he is to the military for advice, as Kennedy turned to his younger brother during the Cuban missile crisis or as Johnson turned to McGeorge Bundy and Walt Rostow during the Vietnamese build-up. Dean Acheson had a much greater impact on Harry Truman's foreign and military policy than did anyone in uniform.

The Armed Services play a role in the economy and in foreign policy, although not a decisive one. The military does have a direct impact on millions of Americans, however, an impact that with the exception of the public schools and possibly the churches is greater than that of any other institution. Nearly 30 million males, or more than one in four from the entire male population, are veterans. These 30 million constitute the heart of America's productive labor force. At the top, most members of elite groups, especially in the colleges, manage one way or another to avoid the draft and escape the service (or, in periods of full mobilization, such as World War II, become officers through special programs designed especially for them), while at the bottom the military rejects hundreds of thousands for physical or mental shortcomings. The percentages vary according to current needs; in World War II, when the demand was great, the Army still rejected nearly 50 per cent of the blacks it examined. As a result, those who do serve in the enlisted ranks, in general, later make up the labor force. In 1970 the head of the construction unions in New York City estimated that 95 per cent of his union members were veterans.

In the service, these men learned obedience, respect for authority, and discipline—traits which are indispensable in an industrial society. The disciplining process begins in the public schools, to be sure, but it reaches a culmination in the services. The entire military experience helps break down the values to which Americans like to give lip service, such as equality, freedom from restraint, individual worth and individualism, and democracy, teaches the rewards of staying within the rules, and punishes the deviant. In so doing, of course, the military is not creating new values, but rather reinforcing those imposed by or crucial to other institutions in the society. The prospective employee who has an honorable discharge can present to employers what amounts to a guarantee that he will not be a trouble-maker.

Although the Armed Services, in theory, are only concerned with an efficient use of their personnel, socialization has in fact often been a major goal. The Army prides itself on offering a "second chance" to those who for one reason or another did not learn essential skills or proper behavior in the public schools, and much of the recruiting program revolves around the promise of an opportunity to learn skills that can be transferred to civilian life. It is not at all uncommon in the United States for judges to give convicted young criminals a choice between a prison sentence and enlistment in the Army, which speaks volumes about the view the judges have of the military.

Following WW II, Truman tried to sell his Universal Military Training bill (UMT) on the grounds that military service would improve the quality of America's youth. "The military phase was incidental to what I had in mind," he admitted. The President said his main interest was "to develop skills that could be used in civilian life, to raise the physical standards of the nation's manpower, to lower the illiteracy rate, to develop citizenship responsibilities, and to foster the moral and spiritual welfare of our young people."

Truman's presentation may well have hurt rather than helped UMT's chances in Congress, where politicians displayed a healthy skepticism about using the Army to teach citizenship and moral and spiritual values. Nevertheless, the military has persisted. There has been a steady stream of pilot programs (some of considerable size; in 1970 the Army was carrying out a program involving 100,000 young men) designed to meet some of Truman's objectives. The services take men who would ordinarily be rejected on grounds of functional illiteracy and create special programs to teach them to survive in modern society. In terms of increased reading capacity, productivity, dependability, and so on, the programs have enjoyed impressive successes. The theoretical problem remains—is socialization a proper function of the Armed Services?

In the area of racial integration the military has—or at least once believed that it had—conclusively demonstrated its unique ability to move society forward. Before the Korean War, almost all blacks in the Armed Services served in segregated outfits. The military justified segregation on the usual grounds—blacks wanted it; blacks would not serve effectively with whites; whites would resent the presence of blacks and morale would break down if they were integrated; blacks were inherently incapable of performing at the same level as whites; and on and on. Truman ordered integration in July, 1948, in response to political pressure from black leaders. Despite dire predictions, the military integrated with amazing speed; within less than ten years the process was virtually complete. The military had rooted out official prejudice, going far beyond the accomplishments of even the most socially conscious corporation or university.

By every available measurement, integration was a success. Blacks performed better than they had in segregated units; whites accepted them. Old stereotypes broke down, or at least it seemed that whites had adopted a more realistic view of blacks.

The integration of the Armed Services was one of the most far-reaching social and racial experiments in American history. In the late fifties and early sixties pundits could claim that the military had eliminated all overt and most subtle prejudice, and argue that what the Army had accomplished, society could also. The Army would lead the way. By the late sixties, however, it was no longer so clear that the military had resolved the fundamental dilemma of American democracy. Black draftees complained that their personal relations and official position in the services were little if any better than in the outside, civilian world. Both in the United States and in Vietnam, the Army and Marine Corps had to contend with race riots. While the military was certainly using its black personnel more efficiently than it had before 1948, it had by no means overcome racism within the services, much less in the civilian world.

That even the military—where orders, once given, are obeyed —could not provide true equality for blacks and other minority groups illustrated not only the depth of racism in the United States, but also the limitations under which the military operates. Draftees, after all, are Americans first, soldiers second. So are the officers. They respond to the same stimuli as the civilian population and hold similar prejudices.

These limitations were most obvious in the utilization of women personnel in the military. American society expects women to play the roles of wife, housekeeper, and mother or, if they hold an income producing position, to be secretaries, teachers, telephone operators, nurses, or other "traditional" female positions. Military service is far from being an approved role for women, an attitude the Armed Services have done virtually nothing to combat, even though other societies (Israel and Russia, for example) have conclusively demonstrated how great a contribution women can make in the military, and even though the overwhelming majority of jobs in the services could be performed as effectively by women as by men. There are some efforts going on in the military to provide equal opportunities for women, two members of the Women's Army Corps do hold the rank of brigadier general, and it is probably true that in the services career women, like blacks, can go higher than they could in the civilian world. But as an agency to promote social change, or even to use personnel efficiently whatever the prevailing attitudes toward proper roles may be, the military is obviously limited. However great its impact on American life, it is not enough to overcome deep-seated social mores and prejudices.

In nineteenth-century Prussia it was said that the nation existed to support the army. Things have hardly reached such a state in America. The military is of—not outside—society, so much so that it even makes its contribution to pollution through nuclear testing and leaking nerve gas. Military officers are a part of the mainstream of American thought, holding political and social attitudes similar to those of young executives and corporate managers. Retired officers move easily into the academic as well as the business world, where their administrative abilities are much in demand. The military is a readily available force to control civil disorders and is so used often enough, but it always acts at the direction of civil authority, in support of widely held goals or values.

The United States has created the most powerful Armed Forces the world has ever known. The military has reached a

size and has an influence on American society far beyond anything anyone dreamed of before 1938. It has a direct and deep
impact on all Americans and it is apparently here to stay. But
it is neither a Leviathan nor an alien force in the land. The military reflects the society from which it comes. The really remarkable thing is that America has managed to create an
institution of such staggering size without being swallowed up
by it. For important as the military is, it does not dominate our
lives, establish values, or dictate our foreign and domestic
policies.

The "McNamara Monarchy"

"The Navy, the Air Force and Army must work as a unit. If I had my way they would all be in the same uniform."—General Dwight D. Eisenhower

"I do not believe that the head of the proposed Governmental colossus . . . will ever have more than the most superficial knowledge of the Department."—James V. Forrestal

The first Secretary of Defense, James Forrestal, used to say that he was not so much interested in an organization chart as in the names of the men in the little boxes. It was a good point. Organizations are made of men. There is no substitute for their quality. Nevertheless, Paul Hammond correctly pointed out: "Men in Government—at least in the American Government—do not last. The things that last are the institutional arrangements which impart continuity to policy and meaning (however valid) to process, and the modes of thought which made both significant." Thus, regardless of who runs the building, the Pentagon's organization is itself an influential factor in its performance.

The unification of the armed forces in 1947 has been described as the most extensive reorganization of the military establishment since George Washington assumed command of the Continental Army. It separated the Air Force from the Army and established three military departments—Army, Navy and Air Force—all within a single military establishment. The name Department of Defense came two years later. The Secretary of Defense was at first regarded merely as a coordinator

Reprinted by permission of Harper & Row, Publishers, and William Heinemann Ltd., Publishers, from pp. 277–93 and 347–48, *Power at the Pentagon*. Copyright 1964 by Jack Raymond.

with rather ill-defined powers of "general authority, direction and control" over the military departments. On the military side, the chairman of the Joint Chiefs of Staff did not command any troops, nor was he the "superior" of any of his colleagues. He was responsible mainly for the agenda of their deliberations. The JCS staff was specifically limited to one hundred officers as a protection against undue military power accruing to the chairman, whose title was intended to underscore his managerial rather than command function.

Nevertheless even this relatively mild centralization was strongly opposed, particularly by the Navy and its supporters. Secretary of the Navy Forrestal, warning that such a mammoth military element might be dangerous, once testified: "I do not believe that the head of the proposed Governmental colossus . . . will ever have more than the most superficial knowledge of the Department." As much to mollify the Navy as to assure others who worried about the new element of military authority in the government, President Truman appointed Forrestal the first Secretary of Defense. Moving into the Pentagon, Forrestal remarked: "This office will probably be the biggest cemetery for dead cats in history." Before the year was out he sought more powers. In 1949, on his recommendation, amendments to the National Security Act removed the term "general" from the phrase "general authority, direction and control" to be exercised by the Secretary of Defense, and relieved the service secretaries of their Cabinet status. The Joint Staff was raised from 100 to a maximum of 210. Forrestal did not live to see the Defense Department functioning under the more centralized setup. The years of government service, unceasing administrative struggles with the great problems of the postwar period, wore him down and finally broke his mind. The official Pentagon statement said his condition was "directly the result of excessive work during the war and post-war years." He took his own life May 22, 1949.

The mood of the office of the Secretary of Defense has varied according to the men who have held it. Forrestal's worried tenseness about the fate of the world communicated itself to the men around him, who worshipped him. His successor, Louis Johnson, a wily politician, held his cards closer to his chest. General Marshall was already an elder statesman when he took over; most of the job was done by Robert Lovett, his deputy, who also became his successor. Lovett generated an atmosphere of quiet wisdom. Charles E. Wilson exuded "big business." Thomas S. Gates worked quietly, effectively, unobtrusively.

Yet regardless of their individual personalities the sudden growth of American responsibilities around the world and the inevitable untidiness of the technological explosion in weaponry gave the impression that no man, just as Forrestal feared, could really get on top of the Pentagon job, as though confusion, waste and stubborn resistance to change were part of the price of maintaining the world's most powerful military-industrial complex. Somehow the hallmark of the Pentagon became indecisiveness and inaction, qualities that invite disaster on the battlefield. The grim decisions that lead to war or peace appeared to be tangled in a miasma of interservice rivalries for roles, missions and spending money. Personal feuds were dressed in the obfuscating language of high policy and military tradition.

When President Kennedy took office in 1961, he was handed a report by one of his pre-inauguration task forces on government that called for another sweeping reorganization of the Department of Defense—the fourth since it was created in 1947. The report said:

> Throughout all proposals, past and present, to make more effective the Defense Department organization, has run one central theme—the clarification and strengthening of the authority of the Secretary of Defense over the entire United States Military Establishment. There are some who believed even prior to the 1958 amendment of the National Security Act that existing legislation provided ample basis for the Secretary's authority. Others took a contrary view. It is the conclusion of the committee that the doctrine of civilian control will be compromised as long as doubt exists on this point.

Robert Strange McNamara, the new Secretary of Defense, lost no time in erasing the doubt. Within a couple of years, he was under sharp attack for exercising too much control at the Pentagon. He was accused—accurately—of forcing the armed services to "speak with one voice"; of establishing superagencies to take over certain functions that had been handled separately by the individual military services; of downgrading, ignoring and by-passing the military chiefs; of submerging the service Secretaries as well as the uniformed chiefs beneath a hierarchy of Assistant Secretaries under his direct supervision; of overriding the voice of professional experience and "substituting a military party line"; of establishing what Hanson Baldwin described as "the McNamara Monarchy."

Historically, the country has been alert to the dangers of military domination. But under McNamara, in the Kennedy

Administration, there were widespread complaints—against a
background of praise by those who favored it—of what Mark
Watson, another military commentator, described as "the Pentagon's trend toward constant further depreciation of the military
as essential advisors—not on political issues, but on strictly military issues." In a colorful and pertinent observation, still another
military writer, Jerry Greene, described McNamara as a "civilian
on horseback," who had mounted the horse from the offside
while the Congress has been concerned with preventing the rise
to the saddle of a general on horseback.

Thus there developed considerable discussion whether one-
man civilian rule over the military establishment was not just as
dangerous to American democratic precepts as rule exercised
by a man in uniform. As Baldwin put it:

The "unification" of the armed services sponsored by Secretary of
Defense Robert S. McNamara poses some subtle and insidious dangers
—creeping dangers that are political, military and administrative. And
they could present, in their ultimate form, almost as great a threat to
a secure and free nation as the attempted military coup, envisaged in
the recent novel, "Seven Days in May." For the kind of "unification"
being practiced and preached today has ominous overtones. It is
dangerous to the nation's political system of checks and balances,
dangerous to the continued development of sound military advice, dangerous to managerial and administrative efficiency.

On the other hand, others said McNamara had merely righted
a military-biased tilt in what was supposed to be a civilian-con-
trolled enterprise. Over the years, according to this view, the
military chiefs had turned most of the Secretaries of Defense
into "patsies." Until McNamara came along, one of his admirers
said, "civilians could be briefed, flattered, outwitted and finally
absorbed by generals and admirals who systematically study all
leadership patterns among men from Red Square to Wall Street.
By the end of the Eisenhower Administration, control of American strategy lay not in the hands of civilian leadership, but in
the hands of the uniformed chiefs of staff."

This attribution of overwhelming shrewdness to generals and
admirals when dealing with civilians is ludicrous. It resembles
the attitude that Right Wing extremists adopt when they picture communists outwitting supposedly naïve Americans. Moreover, it flies in the face of the titanic struggles that have ensued
in the Pentagon and have forced the departure of many high
officers. But as a stereotype of the military, consistent with con-

spiracy theory of war, it has had wide acceptance. Anyway, when McNamara took office, there was a feeling that he had come along in the nick of time to knock the rival generals' and admirals' heads together and "keep them in line."

McNamara, the man who came along, did not meet the criteria for the job laid down by the experts—although neither did most of his predecessors. Ideally, the Secretary of Defense is supposed to be policy- and strategy-minded, one who commands the admiration of the public, a man of experience, possibly having moved up from other posts in the Department of Defense or some equivalent branch of government; a man who, according to Samuel P. Huntington, probably should be concluding his career and thus not be in a position to use it as a stepping stone. McNamara had virtually no experience either in the military or in government. Far from being ready to conclude his career, he had just risen, at forty-five, to the presidency of the Ford Motor Company. When he was named for the post of Secretary of Defense, it took the country by surprise. Most people in Washington had never heard of him.

McNamara was born just outside of San Francisco in an almost country-like community in the bay area. High school friends almost without expection recall his excruciating neatness. He was the boy in the class who wore jackets, ties and white shirts while the other kids dressed in sweaters and jeans. He was a good student and became editor of the yearbook, president of the French club, a member of the glee club and a member of the board of student control. He was popular despite his odd addiction to tidiness. He went to the University of California, where he made Phi Beta Kappa in his junior year. He shipped out on merchant vessels in the summers. He went to Harvard Business School on a partial scholarship, worked with an accounting firm for a year, married his University of California sweetheart and returned to Harvard as an instructor.

McNamara's specialty was statistical control. At the outbreak of World War II, he taught specially selected Army Air Force officers the techniques of calculating the thousands, millions and billions of people and things that went into military logistics. He joined the Air Force as a captain and rose to lieutenant colonel. He reportedly was so serious about the official order to save scarce paper that he did his calculations on the cardboard backs of writing pads. When the war was over, he and nine other "stat control" officers sold themselves as a management team to the Ford Motor Company. They were so successful that they became known as "whiz kids," and McNamara himself was named president of the company on November 9, 1960, one day following the election that named John F. Kennedy President of the United States.

McNamara did not fit the image of a millionaire industrialist. He was an aloof "egghead" at Ford, preferring to live in a comfortable old house in the college community at Ann Arbor rather than in the wealthy Grosse Point suburb peopled with auto executives. He was regarded as a Republican but had been known to support Democrats, including John F. Kennedy, for public office. He was an elder in the Presbyterian Church. When he arrived in Washington, he immediately sent two of his three children to a Quaker school in the District. With his slicked-down, thinning black hair and rimless gold spectacles he gave the impression of a brash college professor.

His relations with the Joint Chiefs of Staff started abrasively as he ignored them on certain issues, sidestepped their recommendations on others and demanded speedy, deadline responses to some fundamental old military quandaries. In an official memorandum, within two months after the new Secretary took over, General Lyman L. Lemnitzer, then chairman of the Joint Chiefs, complained that the Chiefs had not been given a "full opportunity to study carefully" space weapons assignments, "which have far-reaching military implications."

McNamara ordered four major studies in military policy and strategy. These were not assigned to the military, as in the past, but to the new civilian aides at the Pentagon. The basic study on nuclear war strategy, for example, was assigned to Charles J. Hitch, the Pentagon controller, a former official at RAND. The Defense Secretary delved into all details of operations instead of abiding by the military practice of giving out assignments, demanding results and leaving details to others. He seemed determined to disprove Forrestal's warning that one man could not do the job.

Lemnitzer, an experienced hand in Washington affairs, did not frontally counterattack the civilian assault on what had been regarded in the past as the military area of responsibility. A good soldier, he remained discreetly silent. But shortly before he was transferred from the Pentagon in the fall of 1962 to command the Allied forces in Europe, he expressed his feelings in a speech that received little notice in the press but must have been carefully read in the Secretary's office. Lemnitzer's subject was leadership and his audience the graduating class of the Command and General Staff College.

"We all recognize in the abstract," he said, "that it is simply a physical impossibility for the leader of a higher organization to provide personal leadership at all places where it is simultaneously required. This is why such concepts as the chain of command and span of control have been devised. It is the foundation stone of our whole organizational system. This does not mean that you cannot impose your personality on your unit. Indeed, unless you do so—unless you make yourself the recognized symbol of command—your leadership will be ineffective. But to employ the chain of command concept and to make the organizational system work most effectively, an implicit requirement upon the higher commander is to delegate authority to his subordinates. This obvious requirement—with which everyone promptly agrees—is extremely difficult to achieve in practice. A battle group commander who occupies himself with the internal details of the operation of his companies may be showing how much he knows about being a company commander. But he is also showing how little he knows about commanding a battle group. He is doing an injustice to the ability and conscientiousness of his captains. He is failing to take advantage of the great asset they represent for carrying out the mission of the organization as a whole. Finally, he is displaying his own lack of confidence in his own ability to do his assigned job."

When McNamara assumed control of the Pentagon, much of the wartime glory of the military had receded. Whatever prestige the military incumbents of the Pentagon high command had left was dealt a devastating blow in the Cuban invasion fiasco of 1961. In the immediate aftermath of the Bay of Pigs affair civilians of the Kennedy Administration sneeringly cast the blame for failure on the Chiefs. Newsmen were called into the White House and told that the Chiefs of Staff had selected the beaches for the invasion. A story, apparently inspired at the White House, appeared in the Washington *Post* hammering home the charge that the Chiefs were responsible for the failure in Cuba. On May 19, 1961, Senator Albert Gore, Democrat of Tennessee, called for the removal of all the members of the Joint Chiefs of Staff after hearing secret testimony as a member of the Senate Foreign Relations Committee. The Senator called for "new, wiser and abler men."

Neither the President nor Secretary McNamara spoke out for

a week. The President, in fact, told a group of newsmen privately that he could have managed the military responsibilities of the Bay of Pigs affair better than his military experts. McNamara, when asked about the Senator's attack on the Chiefs, shrugged his shoulders and said he had decided against making a public comment, following consultation with General Lemnitzer. However, he telephoned some people on Capitol Hill to assure them of his confidence in the Chiefs. General Lemnitzer, as usual, kept his public silence. To a private visitor he said angrily that he had been on a tour in Southeast Asia when the seemingly high-placed insinuations of incompetence were being launched against him and his colleagues, "and I can assure you they did not help the United States very much."

Even when, at a news conference ten days afterward, McNamara ended the Administration's silence on the Chiefs, he did not deny the allegations against them. He finessed a question on the subject with a reply that he, as Secretary of Defense, was responsible for "the actions of all personnel in the department, both military and civilian" and that he accepted that responsibility. If any errors were committed, he said, they were his errors, and he looked forward to a "long and pleasant association" with the Chiefs.

The Chiefs at that time were Lemnitzer, General George H. Kecker, of the Army; General Thomas D. White, of the Air Force; Admiral Arleigh A. Burke, Chief of Naval Operations; and General David M. Shoup, Commandant of the Marine Corps. Within a year, all but Shoup were gone. General Maxwell D. Taylor, who was brought out of retirement and given an office at the White House to review United States intelligence, paramilitary and guerrilla warfare activities, as military representative of the President, eventually was named chairman of the Joint Chiefs of Staff. Lemnitzer was transferred to succeed General Lauris Norstad as commander of Allied forces in Europe. Admiral Burke, who had served an unprecedented series of three two-year terms, retired and was succeeded by Admiral George W. Anderson. General White retired and was succeeded by General Curtis E. LeMay. General Decker retired and was succeeded by General Earle G. Wheeler. General Shoup, appointed to a four-year term, retired in January 1, 1964.

Admiral Anderson lasted two years, and his experience in the Cuban crisis of 1962 was perhaps the outstanding illustration of the low regard in which the Service Chiefs were held. First there was an incident on October 6. The Defense officials decided they wanted to send a squadron of Navy fighters from Oceana, Virginia, to Key West, Florida, and to put the squadron tem-porarily under Air Force control. Deputy Defense Secretary Gilpatric, without going through channels, ignored the Chief of Naval Operations, and called directly to Admiral Robert L. Dennison, the Commander in Chief, Atlantic, at Norfolk, Virginia, to give him the order. Admiral Anderson's bruised feelings, shared by many officers in the Pentagon, soon became well-known.

As the crisis grew worse, the United States undertook a naval quarantine of Cuba. Secretary McNamara began spending time in the Navy's Flag Plot, or operations center. This room, under Marine Guard, contains visual materials locating the position of every ship. It also has communications links with ship commanders. McNamara insisted upon making decisions on the spot. He wanted to call ship commanders directly on the voice-scrambling, single-side-band radios. Admiral Anderson tried to dissuade the civilian official. The Navy uses formal, stylized voice communications with coded names going through the chain of command. McNamara was inclined to ignore or belittle these techniques. He pointed to a symbol for one ship at sea and demanded of Admiral Anderson, "What's that ship doing there?" The Chief of Naval Operations replied, "I don't know, but I have faith in my officers."

Admiral Anderson, like General Lemnitzer, expressed his feelings on the subject of the exercise of authority when he spoke to the Navy League, May 3, 1963, at San Juan, Puerto Rico. "Without respect flowing both ways between juniors and seniors we have little hope of doing the jobs we will be called upon to do," he said. Three days later the White House announced that Admiral Anderson, who had testified against McNamara in the TFX dispute, had been dropped as Chief of Naval Operations, to be succeeded by Admiral David B. McDonald, a relative unknown. Anderson was named Ambassador to Portugal, apparently as a sop. After he left the Pentagon, Anderson made another speech to the National Press Club, decrying the lack of "confidence and trust between the civilian and military echelons," but his post-mortem caused hardly a ripple.

During World War II and for many years after it, the Service Chiefs were well-known, heroic figures. They even participated in a variety of political and administrative roles. The chairmen of the Joint Chiefs of Staff in the postwar era, General Omar N. Bradley and Admiral Arthur S. Radford, operated in the continued glow of victory in war, but were impressive in their own right as well. Huntington described them as true "samurai," military statesmen rather than military experts. Their successors, General Nathan F. Twining, an Air Force officer who had risen from sergeant in the National Guard, and General Lemnitzer, who was caught in an administrative changing of the guard, had good war records but were bland, passive men in Washington. In the meantime, civilians came to the fore, especially during the Kennedy Administration. These civilians spread the notion that they had studied the military posture of the country and had found it wanting. "General," one young new Frontiersman was quoted as saying at Strategic Air Command headquarters, "you don't have a war plan. All you have is a sort of horrible spasm." McNamara himself made the charge, consistently denied during the Eisenhower Administration, that there were no unified strategic military plans at the Pentagon before he came along.

As military heroes have receded from the public view, civilians have flourished. Theodore White, author of the classic *Making of the President*, noticed something about the Kennedy team at the Pentagon. They were, with few exceptions, an Ivy League team designed to be a direct descendant of the wartime Ivy League team of Lovett, McCloy, Patterson and Forrestal. "All through the Kennedy Administration runs the most intense, if unrecognized, desire to attach itself to the older traditions of American Government," White observed.

McNamara's first Deputy Defense Secretary, Roswell L. Gilpatric, was a familiar headliner in the press. He had been an Under Secretary of the Air Force in the Truman Administration. Tall, nattily dressed, urbane, a New Yorker, he was considered a suave, tempering balance wheel for McNamara's reputed impolitic way with Congressmen as well as generals and admirals. But, like so many other high civilian officials, he "could not afford" to stay in government and returned to private life in January, 1964. Gilpatric's membership in a famous law firm, education at a good prep school—Hotchkiss—and scholastic honors at Yale made him a member of "The Establishment," that roster of distinguished public men to whom all Administrations turn for helpings of prestige.

Other Ivy Leaguers at the Pentagon are Cyrus R. Vance, of Kent School and Yale, Gilpatric's successor as Deputy Defense Secretary; Eugene M. Zuckert of Salisbury Prep and Yale, Secretary of the Air Force; Paul H. Nitze, of Hotchkiss and Princeton, Secretary of the Navy; Stephen Ailes, of Scarborough and

Princeton, Secretary of the Army; and William P. Bundy, of Groton and Harvard, Assistant Secretary for International Security Affairs. . . .

What irritates many of the military men at the Pentagon under McNamara is the implication that computer calculations, operational analysis and abstract theories somehow have greater weight in the decision-making process than the voices of experience and the recorded lessons of history. The picture of young smart-alecks invading the precincts of military responsibility was drawn by Retired Air Force Chief of Staff General Thomas D. White when he said that, "in common with other military men I am profoundly apprehensive of the pipe-smoking, trees-full-of-owls type of so-called defense intellectuals who have been brought into this nation's capital." Military men in the Pentagon argue, like General White, that civilian aides are making decisions without responsibility. That is, they safely and arrogantly propound various theories of strategy without having the responsibility of command.

And some of the high-ranking civilian officials, no less than the military brass, find McNamara a difficult boss. Many of the civilian officials, including but not limited to the career civil service, criticize the Secretary for delving into the details of management and making many minor decisions himself. In preparing the 1965 budget, he is said to have made more than 500 decisions.

Elvis J. Stahr, who was Secretary of the Army for a little over a year under McNamara, said after quitting to become president of the University of Indiana:

McNamara is certainly the ablest man I have ever been closely associated with. But he has a tendency to overreach in exercising control and intrude in small details of administration. The Defense Department is too big to be run by one man and there are just not enough McNamaras. The machinery of administration ought to be flexible. I, personally, favored most of the administration unification measures undertaken by the Defense Secretary, but I'm afraid there is a tendency to neglect the accumulated wisdom and responsible toughness of the career officers.

President Kennedy was most emphatic in his support of McNamara, however. During one particularly virulent battle between the Secretary of Defense and the military, President Kennedy said: "We have a very good, effective Secretary of Defense with a great deal of courage who is willing to make hard decisions and who doesn't mind when they are made that a good many people don't like it." And President Johnson's endorsement has been no less emphatic. After his assumption of the Presidency placed him in a new, more intimate and more difficult relationship with the Defense Secretary, Johnson let it be known that he had found the "myth" of McNamara's excellence to be not a myth but "the truth."

The resistance to "McNamara and his band" has been ineffectual. Even General Curtis E. LeMay, an early antagonist, faded into silence although he was reappointed Air Force Chief of Staff in 1963 for a single year instead of the customary two. LeMay had created the all-powerful Strategic Air Command, but the new strategic forces of computer-minded missiles had no place for a crushed-hat bomber pilot. LeMay's retirement in 1964 was inevitable.

One high officer of the age of combat heroes has remained. He is Maxwell Davenport Taylor, the vindicated author of *The Uncertain Trumpet*, whose strategic arguments—all rejected by the Eisenhower Administration—were adopted by Kennedy. Taylor is something special in American military history—a fighting hero, an acknowledged intellectual and a keenly political person with no apparent personal political ambitions. He runs counter to the prevailing image of professional soldiers as inarticulate men of narrow interests, men who are technicians and traditionalists with conceptions of patriotism drawn from textbooks. According to this image, they are fighting champions on the battlefield but helpless without plans of action off it. They are given to bellicose "habit of command" and unchallenging obedience to superior rank except when, like Billy Mitchell, they fight for a "cause" against higher authority.

J.P. Marquand once wrote that "Many generals appear to civilians like deceptively simple men. Most of them possess, from a civilian point of view, an unworldly character. . . . Debate, when protracted, makes [the professional officer] impatient." But General Taylor, who won his high school debating championship, does not fit this image. The son of a Keyesville, Missouri, railroad lawyer, he finished high school at sixteen. He was fourth in his class at West Point in 1922. The class yearbook called him the "most learned" of the graduates. The pre-World War II years took him to China and Japan as a military attaché and to various European and Latin-American capitals on similar semidiplomatic assignments. As a paratroop commander in World War II and leader of the Eighth Army during the Korean War, he covered his tunic with combat laurels.

Fluent in several languages, he also received eight honorary engineering and law degrees from leading universities. Instead of the tough-talking bellicosity of the military stereotype, Taylor has been impressive for his soft-spoken suavity. During the Eisenhower Administration he did not immediately do battle for his "cause." Indeed, many Army officers felt that he had not pushed his ideas vigorously enough as Chief of Staff. When he finally did speak out, his retirement followed swiftly. Like General Matthew B. Ridgway before him, he could not persuade Eisenhower, a former Army Chief of Staff, that strategic air power, even with nuclear warheads, was a false god.

The return of Maxwell Taylor to the Pentagon is no mere personal drama, however. It has been significant also in terms of his administrative role. "A Secretary of Defense needs a strong chairman to direct the work of the chiefs, to keep their noses to the grindstone, and to extract from them timely advice and recommendations—preferably of a kind which can be accepted and approved without embarrassment," General Taylor wrote in his book criticizing the Eisenhower Administration. . . .

General Taylor wrote that as any Army Chief of Staff he had found himself repeatedly outweighed by Chairman Admiral Radford. To prevent continuance of this situation, he urged a drastic reorganization of the Joint Chiefs' setup. But when he returned as chairman, he did not press for reorganization. He silently proceeded to exercise the powers of the chairman that he recognized so clearly, as "a sort of party whip, charged with conveying the official line to the chiefs."

Taylor, true to his conception of his role, has proved a valuable adjutant to McNamara, although they differ on some fundamental issues. Together, without the legislation that was so often recommended, they have centralized the authority over the armed forces in the offices of the chairman of the Joint Chiefs and the Secretary of Defense, although many of their measures actually were proposed by predecessors. The transfer of authority over the unified and specified commands from the military departments of the Joint Chiefs of Staff was accomplished in the reorganization during the Eisenhower Administration. The creation of the new Strike Command, combining much of the Air Force's tactical aircraft with Army assault troops, was initiated in the Eisenhower Administration. Secretary of Defense Gates began the practice of sitting with the members of the Joint Chiefs to nip disputes in the bud. Gates ordered the formation of a single Defense Intelligence Agency in order to reduce conflicts in intelligence estimates. McNamara's predecessor also ordered the creation of a single defense communications to unify the long-distance networks that were operated separately by the services. Most important, perhaps, of all, Gates forced the services to adopt a single strategic targeting system. Each of these actions, however, although debated vigorously within the Pentagon, became sources of public friction when carried out in McNamara's uncompromising manner.

Much of the unification of the Services—and thus centralization of authority—has been made inevitable by the technical changes in weaponry and the consequent changes in force structure. Indeed, General Eisenhower told West Point cadets in 1945 that if he had his way the Army, Navy and Air Force would "all be in the same uniform." That power has been centralized in the hands of a civilian Secretary rather than in a single "Prussian-style" Chief of Staff is due largely to the historical and legal barriers against military dominance that exist in the United States. But does that make one-man rule over so vast an establishment any less dangerous? The question has been asked repeatedly as McNamara realigns the administrative channels into a rather monolithic instrument of government. Critics of the centralization of authority fear that it silences the possible voices of dissent and reduces the arguments that must be offered and heard. In 1947 the Defense establishment was created with a single Secretary of Defense who was regarded primarily as a coordinator, aided by three specialist assistants. Now, the civilian hierarchy directly under the Secretary of Defense includes a Deputy Secretary of Defense, a powerful Director of Research, seven Assistant Secretaries, a General Counsel, a Deputy General Counsel, two special Assistants and five Deputy Assistant Secretaries. The acknowledged excellence of a McNamara should not divert us from traditional precautions against centralized military authority outside the White House, whether exercised by a man in uniform or in civilian clothes. It is not the character of the man but the power he wields that should concern us.

The Political Roles
of the Joint Chiefs

SAMUEL HUNTINGTON

Political Roles: Substantive and Advocatory

The political involvement of a military leadership institution such as the Joint Chiefs may take two different forms. The military leaders may espouse or recommend policies which are derived from nonmilitary sources and which are unrelated to or contrary to the professional military viewpoint. In this event the military leaders assume a substantive political role. Alternatively, the military leaders may play an active part in the public defense or merchandising of policies (irrespective of their content) before Congress and the public. The political involvement in this case stems not from the substantive views of the military leaders but rather from the place, manner, timing, and effects of their expression of those views. This is an advocatory political role. . . . These roles are of course not mutually exclusive: military leaders could assume both at once by publicly urging a nonmilitary policy.

Although the Joint Chiefs in the postwar years retreated somewhat from their World War II heights of power and glory, they still continued a high level of political involvement. The most striking aspect of this period, however, was not the degree of their involvement, which it was to be expected would remain at a high level, but rather the differing forms which it took. During the Truman Administration the views of the Joint Chiefs on pol-

Reprinted by permission of the Belknap Press of Harvard University Press from pp. 374–87, *The Soldier and the State: The Theory and Politics of Civil-Military Relations.* Copyright 1957 by the President and Fellows of Harvard College.

icy coincided to an astonishing extent with the professional military ethic. In many respects their attitudes would have done credit to the German General Staff in its heyday of professionalism. In view of the extent to which the Chiefs had deviated from the ethic in World War II, this return to the traditional military line stands out as all the more remarkable. On the other hand, the Truman Chiefs quite obviously did become involved in an advocatory political role as the proponents of policy before Congress and the public. In the first two years of the Eisenhower Administration, on the other hand, the reverse tended to be true. In many important instances the views on national policy of the Eisenhower Chiefs, as reported in the press, showed significant departures from the professional military viewpoint. Although thus assuming a substantive political role, the Eisenhower Chiefs were considerably more reticent than their predecessors in the public exposition of their views. It would be erroneous to overemphasize this difference between the Truman and the Eisenhower Chiefs—both to some extent assumed both political roles —but it would be even more unfortunate to ignore it. Each pattern of behavior was in its own way an effort to ease the tension between the professional military leadership institution and the political environment in which it operated.

What caused the differing tendencies in the political roles of the two sets of Joint Chiefs? The reason cannot be found in organization. The Defense Department was reorganized in 1953, but it had also undergone a more significant reorganization in 1949. Neither reorganization fundamentally altered the position of the JCS in the government. While difference in organization may have been a contributing factor to the differences in behavior, it can hardly be rated as a decisive one. Nor can the change be explained by shifts in the fundamental national attitudes toward the military. Throughout the period these remained basically liberal. The answer must be found in the more specific environments created about the Joint Chiefs by the two Administrations, their political leadership, their dominant interests, and their policy viewpoints. The Joint Chiefs operate immediately and primarily in a governmental framework. Inevitably they must be affected by the attitudes and behavior of the policy makers and statesmen with whom they are in constant contact. These immediate surrounding circumstances, the "governmental environment," have a greater immediate influence on the Joint Chiefs than the more basic but also more remote national environment. In the long run, of course, the latter is decisive, but in the short run the two may differ. The differences between the Truman and Eisenhower Chiefs of Staff derive from the differences between the governmental environments of the Truman and Eisenhower Administrations.

The Joint Chiefs in the Truman Administration

Duality

The reasons for the behavior of the Truman Joint Chiefs may be found in one of the most striking characteristics of the Truman Administration: its split personality between foreign affairs and defense, on the one hand, and domestic affairs on the other. In many respects it was two Administrations in one. In domestic affairs the Administration pursued a policy of liberal reform which was formulated and executed by one set of officials. In foreign affairs the Administration followed a policy of conservative containment which was formulated and executed by a different set of officials. The contact between these two halves was almost minimal. In fact, the only place where they were really linked together was in the President himself. . . .

The final source of the foreign policy conservatism of the Truman Administration was, of course, the military themselves. Along with Marshall, the Joint Chiefs returned to the professional ethic. But the return was possible only because the wartime union of foreign policy and domestic liberalism had been split asunder. The political outlook of Truman and the top civilian leaders plus the new conservative realism of the State Department furnished a sympathetic environment. The civilians led the military back home. With respect to force levels and the military budget, the Truman Chiefs fairly consistently represented the military needs of national security. As a result, their strategic thinking was frequently divorced from political and economic reality. Their budgetary demands were normally drastically cut. At times, to be sure, they did integrate into their analysis an estimate of what the "country could afford," but subsequently, General Bradley, at least, recognized that in so doing they were abandoning their proper roles. With respect to the employment of military force the Truman Joint Chiefs similarly pursued a cautious, conservative line. In 1946, when the Yugoslavs shot down some American planes, the State Department wanted to

despatch an ultimatum backed up by a show of force; the Joint
Chiefs pointed out the limitations of our military resources and
urged moderation. With respect to Korea the State Department
again urged intervention and the Joint Chiefs played a passive
role. In their recommendations regarding the expansion of the
Korean War, Israel, the Japanese peace treaty, German rearmament, and organization and arming of NATO, the Joint Chiefs
similarly reflected a paramount concern with military security
and a desire to avoid adventurous forays until the United States
had strengthened its defenses. General Bradley's entire outlook
with its emphasis on the impossibility of quick and easy solutions,
the necessity of basing policy on enemy capabilities rather than
intentions, the desirability of a pluralistic strategy embodying
many and varied types of force, and the transcendence of political goals over military ones, was an almost perfect formulation
of the professional military ethic. In their views on civilian con-
tral, the Truman Chiefs likewise espoused the traditional military
viewpoint.

Implementation

The ability of the Truman Administration to carry out its conservative foreign policy depended upon the extent of popular in-
difference to foreign affairs, the extent to which foreign policy
decisions could be removed from popular control, and the extent
to which the people could be won over to the Administration's
viewpoint.

A key factor favoring the Administration was the relative in-
difference of its supporters to foreign policy. The interests of
the Democratic Party coalition were numerous, varied, conflicting—and essentially domestic in nature. The Administration was
returned to office in 1948 by appealing to those interests in an
election fought primarily on domestic economic issues. Consequently only on those issues was it politically committed. The
political stalemate among the interests of the coalition, moreover,
insured that there would be no overwhelmingly dominant group
to insist that its viewpoint prevail on both domestic and foreign
policy. The largest bloc of Administration voters, in any event,
was drawn from the poorer economic classes, who typically are
indifferent to and fatalistic toward foreign policy. Consequently,
the Administration was left relatively free to pursue a foreign
policy derived from unpopular and professional sources. At some
points, of course, such as Palestine, conflicts arose between do-

mestic interests and the conservative line, in which case the latter
normally had to give way. But in general the Democratic interests had little concern with the foreign policy carried out on
their behalf by the bankers, diplomats, and soldiers.

The Administration also attempted to isolate as far as possible
foreign policy decisions from congressional and public control.
Ironically, the tradition of executive leadership and decision-making developed by Roosevelt to implement a popular domestic
policy and a liberal wartime foreign policy was invoked by the
Truman Administration to carry out an unpopular and conservative foreign policy. The sense of sweeping, dynamic leadership
which had been so present under Roosevelt was lacking with
Truman because the latter asserted the presidential prerogative
not as a Jacksonian "tribune of the people" but rather as a Bur-
keian virtual representative of the nation. Roosevelt embodied
the popular will; Truman escaped from it. For nonlegislative
matters the typical pattern was for the decision to be made first
and then to be publicly announced, and debated, ratified, or
modified in Congress. Virtually all the great congressional debates on foreign policy in the Truman Administration took place
after the executive had committed the nation. The decisions on
the Berlin airlift, the hydrogen bomb, Formosa policy, the
Korean War, the proclamation of national emergency, the troops
to Europe, the firing of MacArthur all tended to follow this pattern. In effect, the Administration so far as possible adhered to
Locke's federative power theory that control over foreign policy
does not belong to the legislature but instead should be in the
hands of those who can better use it for the public good. This
theory was, indeed, restated by Kennan, who, in almost Platonic
terms, argued that foreign policy was no place for mass opinion
and that the public should be guided by the judgement of professional experts there just as much as in law and medicine.

At times a serious gap existed between the policies demanded
by the external affairs side of the Truman Administration and
the policies which were politically feasible for it to put into practice. This was perhaps best illustrated by the history of "NSC
68": the plan for the extensive build-up of American armed
strength developed in the winter of 1949-1950 as a reaction to
the Soviet explosion of an atomic bomb. The conclusions of NSC
68 were in general vigorously supported by the State Department
and by the military echelons of the Defense Department. Louis
Johnson, Secretary of Defense, was somewhat less sympathetic
toward the expansion program, and the Budget Bureau was

definitely opposed to it. The President approved the general
principles of NSC 68 in April 1950, subject to the development
of the detailed implementing programs and further consideration
of their cost. Thus, in the spring of 1950 the Administration, in
effect, had two defense policies: a public one embodied in the
$13 billion defense budget recommended for the next fiscal year
and a private one embodied in NSC 68. This duality was ended
only by the outbreak of the Korean War which permitted the
Administration in the summer of 1950 to go ahead with the
build-up of forces which had been urged the previous fall by
the supporters of NSC 68.

As the history of NSC 68 indicates, Congress and the public
could not be excluded from many of the most important decisions on foreign policy. The principal area of continuous legislative participation was, of course, appropriations for defense and
foreign aid. Here the policies of the foreign affairs side of the
Administration ran into the interests of the domestic agencies
pushing the claims of their programs and the ever-present demands for economy, a balanced budget, and reduced taxes. Consequently, it was in this area that the conservative foreign policy
was left incomplete. In the long run, no foreign policy was
feasible which did not have legislative and popular support. The
Administration had to supplement its other efforts by salesman-
ship.

The merchandising of containment to the American people,
however, was far beyond the scanty political resources of the
Truman Administration. The President himself did not command
the prestige and respect necessary for the job. The State Department had always suffered from the lack of a domestic constituency. It was, furthermore, under increasing partisan attack. Its
personnel were labeled as incompetent or disloyal, and it became
the symbol of popular frustration with the course of foreign
affairs. Mr. Acheson, moreover, had at times a somewhat cool
disregard for the sensitivities of public opinion; by 1951 even
most Democrats in Congress favored his dismissal. As Republicans or conservative Democrats in what was normally regarded
as a liberal Democratic Administration, the civilian leaders of
foreign affairs were in effect politically sterile. New Dealers and
party-line Republicans both had their suspicions of a Lovett or
a Hoffman.

The Administration consequently was forced to turn to the
military professionals to explain and justify its policies before
Congress and the public. To a considerable extent this was done

by appointing men such as Marshall to civilian posts. Reliance was also placed upon the Joint Chiefs themselves. The Joint Chiefs still retained much of their World War II prestige. They commanded attention as a professional, disinterested body, and the complete aloofness of their members from public affairs prior to 1940 made it impossible to associate them with radicalism or any other form of sordid politics. Thus, although it was the existence of a special conservative foreign affairs environment which permitted the Chiefs to return to their professional outlook, it was also the existence of this special environment which forced them to become its public advocates before the country. Within the foreign affairs side of the Administration the tension between military professional and civilian statesman which had characterized American civil-military relations for seventy-five years evaporated in a unity of outlook as real as that of World War II but far different in substance. Given the prevalence of liberalism in the American mind, however, this tension reappeared along the line between the foreign affairs sector and the rest of the political community. The military became the principal ambassadors of the former to the latter. They pleaded for foreign aid appropriations, urged the ratification of treaties, defended the assignment of American troops to Europe, justified the dismissal of General MacArthur, defended the conduct of the Korean War, and explained the Administration's decisions on force levels and budgets. Generally speaking, they did not relish this role, but they were drawn into it by the needs of the Administration. Before both congressional committees and civic groups they acted as political advocates. Symbolic of their activities was General Bradley's famous talk before the Pasadena Chamber of Commerce on March 20, 1952 in which he castigated the "Gibraltar theory" of defense advocated by Hoover and Taft as "selfish" and "defensive," and urged a policy of balanced military strength without overweighting of air power. As Hanson Baldwin acutely pointed out at the time, Bradley's views were simply "military common sense," yet he had no business adding them to the rising tide of a presidential election.

For a while the Joint Chiefs were a success in their advocatory role, capitalizing upon the combined prestige of military hero and technical expert. Congress listened to Bradley when it ignored Acheson. Eventually, however, the military currency began to lose value. The unpopularity of the policies which they were advocating lowered the personal and institutional prestige of the men who were advocating them. Although they still adhered to their professional views on the substance of policy, the Joint Chiefs inevitably opened themselves to partisan criticism by ardently defending that policy in public on behalf of an Administration which had adopted it as a political course. This mounted rapidly after the outbreak of the Korean War and intensified with the firing of MacArthur. "I have come to the point where I do not accept them as experts," Senator Taft declared in the spring of 1951, "particularly when General Bradley makes a foreign policy speech. I suggest that the Joint Chiefs of Staff are absolutely under the control of the Administration. . . ." In more restrained terms the Republican foreign policy spokesman, John Foster Dulles, also criticized the role of the military in foreign policy. By 1952 their persuasiveness had largely been dissipated.

The carrying out for half a dozen years of a conservative foreign policy on behalf of a fundamentally liberal nation was, in a sense, a considerable political achievement for the Truman Administration. But, inevitably, it could not last. Just as it had been impossible for the military to remain conservative in World War II, so also was it impossible for the combined military-civilian foreign policy agencies to maintain a conservative policy in the Cold War. The issue came to a head over the conduct of the Korean War and subsequently was a major element in the Democratic defeat of 1952. A critic might say that this simply proved the Lincolnian dictum that you can't fool all the people all the time. But that is unfair. That the conservative policy lasted as long as it did is a tribute to the ability of the Administration to make the best of scant resources. That it came to an end when it did is a tribute to the vitality of American democracy.

PART II

The
Military-Industrial
Complex

The Military-Industrial Complex

JAMES ALDEN BARBER, JR.

In his farewell address to the nation on the 17th of January, 1961, President Eisenhower warned against "the acquisition of unwarranted influence, whether sought or unsought, by the military-industrial complex." This was the first use of the term, and although the idea received little attention at the time, in the past few years it has become a matter of serious and widespread concern.

Although the term "military-industrial complex" itself is a relatively new one, suspicion of the military has a long history in American life. The Founding Fathers themselves had a healthy suspicion regarding standing armies, and the Declaration of Independence charged King George with having "kept among us, in Times of Peace, Standing Armies, without the consent of our Legislatures." The Constitution itself contains a provision prohibiting the Congress from appropriating money for raising and supporting armies for a longer term than two years. In the nineteenth century, hundreds of thousands of immigrants streamed into America, many of them to avoid conscription into Europe's standing armies. In the 1930's the congressional investigation under Senator Gerald P. Nye of the influence of the munitions manufacturers generated public attention almost equal to the current outcry.

As with most fashionable phrases, particularly those with pejorative meaning, the term "military-industrial complex" does not have a very precise meaning. Eisenhower's speech suggests that he means the military services and the armament industry. Definitions used by others have ranged from very narrow ones to those that encompass virtually all of organized society. Senator

Proxmire, for example, suggests that what he is talking about when he assails the military-industrial complex should really be called the "military industrial-bureaucratic-labor-intellectual-technical-academic complex."

Any attempt to describe the military-industrial complex is likely to resemble the fable of the several blind men who tried to describe an elephant: the description depends pretty much on which part you get hold of. It is true, for example, that defense procurement has been plagued by chronic huge cost overruns on virtually every major weapons system contracted for by the military. It is also true, however, that defense contracting is not a particularly profitable business, and many firms are reluctant to take on defense contracts. Comparative figures on profit rates between different industries must be interpreted with caution, because of variations in accounting procedures, but one of the most careful studies to date has shown that defense contracting profits are now running somewhat below profits on commercial business. A report released in 1970 by the Logistics Management Institute compared profit rates of 41 defense contractors with those of 217 firms doing mainly commercial business. In the most recent year for which complete figures were available, calendar 1968, the average before tax profits on defense sales were 3.9 per cent, compared with profits of 7.6 per cent on the same firm's commercial sales, and a 9.3 per cent profit earned by commercial durable goods manufacturers. When profits were calculated as a percentage of total capital investment, they were 12.8 per cent before taxes on defense contracts, 16.3 per cent on defense contractor's commercial business, and 19.5 per cent for the commercial durable goods firms.[1]

By virtually any measure, defense is the biggest single business in the United States, with total outlays of almost $80 billion a year in each of the last several years. Yet the general impression that defense expenditures have been growing at the expense of other sectors of the economy is false. Although still far above the share of the national product devoted to military expenditure in the years before World War II, military expenditures as a percentage of the gross national product have shown a relatively steady decline from more than 13 per cent at the high point of Korean War expenditures in 1953 to a projected 7 per cent in 1971, as shown in Figure 1. Actual dollar expenditures have in-

[1] "Facts for Critics of the 'Military-Industrial Complex': Defense Contract Profits 25 Per Cent Below Commercial Business," *Armed Forces Journal,* April 18, 1970, pp. 2–3.

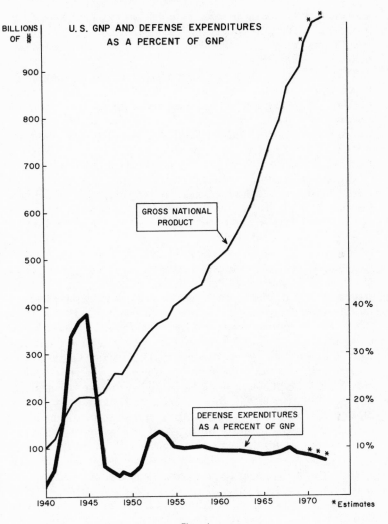

Figure 1

creased sharply during that same period, but because the total of goods and services produced in the United States has increased even more steeply, relative expenditures on defense have declined.

Much the same thing has been true in terms of manpower. From a post-World War II low of just under one and one half million men in 1950, the number of men in military service more than doubled during the Korean War, to a high of three and one half million in 1953. Although subject to fluctuation, the total number of men in military service has declined somewhat since then, at the same time that the national labor force has been growing. As a result, the proportion of the nation's work force in the Armed forces has declined. In percentage terms, military manpower amounted to 4.8 per cent of the nation's workforce in 1951; 4.7 per cent in 1960; and a projected 3.5 per cent in 1971.

A frequently heard statistic is that at the peak of the Vietnam War the United States was spending almost as much every year for military purposes as in the most expensive year of the all-out effort of World War II. In raw dollar terms this is an accurate statement. In the fiscal year 1945 United States defense expenditures amounted to just over $80 billion, and in fiscal 1969 they fell just short of that figure. What is omitted, however, is the change in the value of the dollar that took place in the interim. Year by year inflation has chipped away at the value of the dollar, with the result that in 1969 a dollar bought considerably less in the way of military hardware and manpower than it did twenty-four years earlier. In Figure 2 are plotted military expenditures in terms of both raw dollars, and in terms of constant dollars, as stated in terms of 1958 values. When replotted in terms of real values the picture changes greatly, with the World War II peak looming proportionately much higher, and the Vietnam peak dropping to about the same level as the peak of the Korean War.

It is also frequently asserted that demands for military expenditures have prevented the Federal Government from pursuing more important programs of social welfare. This is true to the extent that within the relatively inelastic limits of the federal budget alternative claimants must compete for resources, and in the past the military services have often seemed to enjoy unfair advantage in the competition. Yet the argument tends to neglect the fact that cutting military expenditures is still a long way from getting Congress to vote funds for any particular social program. It is useful to assess the relationship between defense

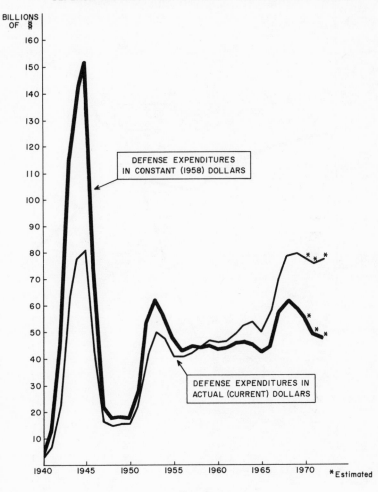

DEFENSE EXPENDITURES IN CURRENT AND CONSTANT DOLLARS

Figure 2

DEFENSE SHARE OF FEDERAL BUDGET

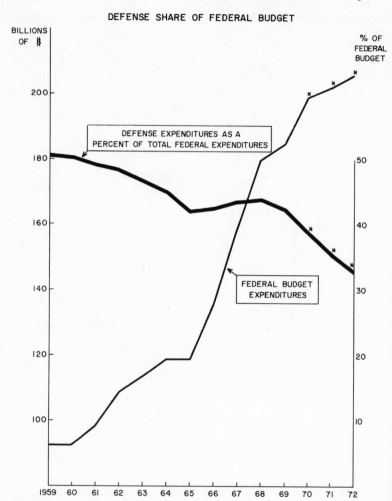

Figure 3

* Estimated

expenditures and the federal budget. This is done in Figure 3.
Because total federal expenditures have increased even more
rapidly than military expenditures, defense money has become
a smaller portion of the total federal budget. From somewhat
more than half of all federal expenditures in 1959, the Pentagon
is scheduled to spend only slightly over a third of the federal
budget in 1971. The defense establishment is gigantic, but the
impression that it is expanding and encroaching further and
further upon the rest of the economy is erroneous. By virtually
any measure defense expenditures are becoming relatively less
important.

Characteristics of Defense Contractors

The phrase "military-industrial complex" implies that there is a
specific sector of industry with special interest and influence in
military procurement. It is true that a relatively few firms account for the majority of defense contracts; in a typical recent
year, the 100 companies receiving the largest dollar volume of
defense contracts accounted for two-thirds of all contracts let.
Through subcontracts, however, defense dollars are spread more
widely, with an estimated 100,000 firms receiving some kind of
defense related contract.

For most of these firms, defense contracts constitute only a
minor portion of their business. Of greater interest are those few
large firms which tend to specialize in defense business. Contrary to frequent assertion, the giants of American industry do
not dominate defense contracting. The giants, firms like American Telephone and Telegraph, Standard Oil of New Jersey,
General Motors, Ford, Texaco, and United States Steel, account
for only a relatively small proportion of defense contracts.
Among this group only AT&T does more than about 5 per cent
of its total business in defense contracts, and even AT&T does
less than 9 per cent of its business with the Defense Department.[2]

The limitation on defense business by the giant firms is often
a matter of company policy. A typical statement is that made
by the Chairman of AT&T, Mr. H. I. Romnes, at the company's
annual meeting in April, 1970:

[2] Ralph E. Lapp, *The Weapons Culture* (New York: Norton, 1968),
pp. 186–187.

The Bell System does not seek out military work and we do not seek to expand the amount we have. Over the years, we have scrupulously refrained from any statement or action that could be construed as promoting military business. . . . The final point I want to make in connection with this work is that profit is not our motivation for undertaking it. This should be clearly apparent from the fact that our sales to the military accounted for something less than four cents of the $4.00 per share we earned in 1969. Why then do we accept military contracts? Because—and simply because it is a responsibility we owe our country. Where military work is concerned, we respond to the country's needs, not as we construe them, but as they are defined by the responsible agencies of government.[3]

This viewpoint is not shared among the true defense specialists, many of whom appear in the next group in size: the near-giant corporations.

These near-giant corporations are interesting for two reasons: not only do they get the largest portion of defense contracts, but they are also the most dependent upon them. Such firms as Lockheed and General Dynamics actively seek government contracts, and they frequently lobby on behalf of a continued high level of defense spending. Large firms which do more than half of their business with the government include AVCO (75%), Collins Radio (65%), General Dynamics (67%), Ling-Temco-Vought (70%), Lockheed (88%), Martin-Marietta (62%), McDonnell Douglas (75%), Newport News Shipbuilding (90%), Northrop (61%), and Raytheon (55%)[4] These firms are the real industrial core of the military-industrial complex.

The list of major defense contractors is not particularly stable. A comparison of the one hundred largest defense contractors now with a similar list of thirty years ago show that only about one-third of the original list have survived. During World War II automobile manufacturers held 25 per cent of procurement contracts, but now account for only 4 per cent. During the same period aircraft companies have increased their share from a third to more than half.

Somehow, despite the clearly excessive cost of many weapons systems, and accusations that some defense contractors have made exorbitant profits, as has been indicated, defense business does not on average seem to be very good business. The Logistics Management Institute survey cited earlier computed the

[3] AT&T, "Share Owner's Quarterly," Summer, 1970, pp. 2–3.
[4] Lapp, *loc. cit.*

profits of the 46 largest defense contractors as averaging 25 per cent below the profits of 217 firms doing comparable commercial business.[5]

The High Cost of Defense Procurement

If defense contracting is not a high profit business, then what accounts for the high cost of defense procurement? Virtually every major weapons system contracted for by the Pentagon in the last decade has, in the end, exceeded estimated costs by a large amount. To make matters worse, rising costs are often accompanied by late delivery and poor performance. Judged by almost any standard of efficiency, the defense procurement system does not work very well, at least for major weapons systems.

There is no single reason which can by itself explain the inefficiencies of the military procurement process. Portions of the blame belong to Congress, the Department of Defense, the individual services, and to the defense contractors themselves.

One of the explanations most often offered in defense of cost increases is that inflation drives up costs. In some degree this is so, but it is certainly an inadequate explanation for cases where costs exceed original estimates severalfold, and such cases are frequent. In any event, inflation has been a fact of life for a sufficiently long time that it should not come as a complete surprise to anyone charged with estimating costs, and should properly be taken into account in making the estimates.

Perhaps even more detrimental from a cost standpoint is the tendency of the services to tinker with designs after a contract is negotiated. Building a weapons system is much like building a house in this regard: changes after construction has started cost a great deal more than if they had been incorporated in the design in the first place. The argument is always that the proposed change will improve the system, and in most cases this is true, but the cost increase is often disproportionate to the improvement. We sometimes suffer from a failure to realize that the law of diminishing returns also applies to military systems.

A related factor which drives up costs is the almost invariable tendency to "push the state of the art" in specifying performance characteristics for weapons systems. The attempt to achieve the

[5] *Armed Forces Journal, op. cit.,* p. 2.

ultimate in performance by doing things that have never been done before often has two detrimental effects: 1) it drives up costs, since it is almost impossible to estimate accurately the cost of achieving technological breakthroughs; and 2) it leads to system unreliability when the expected technological advance turns out to have flaws. Examples include the problems of the "swing wing" assembly on the F-111, the problems with the rigid rotor technology on the Cheyenne helicopter, and the problems encountered by the Army with the new-design ammunition for the Sheridan tank. The pressures of the arms race may explain the effort to get a jump ahead of an opponent by means of a technological breakthrough, but when the result is greatly increased cost and an unreliable product, the gain is questionable at best. In an attempt to overcome some of these problems, Deputy Secretary of Defense David Packard announced in 1970 a Defense Department "fly before you buy" policy, designed to insure that new systems meet acceptable standards before they are ordered into production.

The Relationship between the Government and the Contractors

The relationship between the government and the major defense contractors differs greatly from the classic relationship between customer and private entrepreneur. For the defense specialist the government may be his only important customer, and from the government's point of view there is often only a very limited selection of potential contractors to undertake complex projects. As a result the relationship is frequently closer to that between a monopolist producer and a single consumer than to the classic free market.

Traditionally government procurement has been through a process of sealed bids. The government sets the specific requirements for a product, advertises for bids, and awards the contract to the lowest bidder judged capable of meeting the requirements. There have been deviations from this policy in time of war, as for example during World War II, when the "cost plus" contract became commonplace. During the Truman Administration an executive order was issued permitting exceptions to the competitive bidding process in certain cases. By now the exception has become the rule, with less than 20 per cent of defense procurement being through formally advertised contracts. Instead, there has been a tendency to use individually negotiated contracts, often emphasizing research and development aspects more than costs. In many cases, contracts have been written in which the higher the costs, the higher the dollar profit to the contractor. The predictable result has been high cost to the government.

Another factor which makes final costs a great deal higher than original estimates is the tendency for both the Pentagon and the contractors to minimize cost estimates in order to "sell" a program to the Congress. The rationale is simple: the Pentagon wants the new system, the contractor wants the business, and both are more likely to get what they want from the Congress if the initial price estimate is low. It is always easier to go back later for more money once the project is fully underway. Thus there is a strong incentive to minimize cost estimates in order to get programs authorized. This has led to a situation in which the average weapons system costs three times the original estimate.[6]

Yet another source of inefficiency and higher costs lies in the nature of the relationship between the defense contractors and the government. The major defense contractors have lost much of their independence in the process of military specialization. What products are produced is determined by the government, not by the producer. In many cases the source of capital is regulated by the government, and often government facilities and equipment are provided. Finally, and probably most detrimental, the contractors are subject to elaborate and detailed supervision of almost every facet of their operation. Each aspect of the detailed supervision, accompanying red tape, and horrendous documentation requirements tends to seem reasonable when viewed in isolation. It is not hard to make a case for requiring that contractors meet government safety standards or that they hire specified numbers of employees from minority groups. Very rarely considered, however, is the cumulative impact of such detailed regulation on company initiative, imagination and efficiency. The result seems to be a markedly lower level of managerial performance by defense contractors—with the inevitable result of higher cost and poorer system performance.

[6] Merton J. Peck and Frederick M. Scherer, *The Weapons Acquisition Process* (Cambridge: Harvard University Press, 1962), p. 24.

Congress and the Military-Industrial Complex

Every cent spent on defense must be authorized by Congress. It is within the Congress that national priorities are determined, in the very fundamental sense of how much federal money is to be spent on what programs. With regard to defense spending, the Constitution of the United States provides that "The Congress shall have power . . . to raise and support armies, but no appropriation of money shall be for a longer term than two years; To provide and maintain a navy; To make rules for the government and regulation of the land and naval forces." No examination of the military-industrial complex could hope to be complete without examining the role played by the Congress.

For several reasons, Congress has not until quite recently tended to be as critical of military programs as it has been of other programs competing for funds. Senator Gaylord A. Nelson commented in 1969:

> In the brief period of six years that I have been in the Senate, no military budget has been subjected by the Congress—or by the public, either—to really critical evaluation. We have passed $70 billion budgets with ten minutes or an hour of discussion, and whenever some of us attempted to do something about modest amendments to the military budget, it was a foregone conclusion what the result would be. We defaulted—the Congress and the public—in all matters of judgment on the military budget, on the theory that the military knew best and that we really were dealing with purely technical military matters and not with political matters. This has been our greatest mistake.[7]

One reason Congress has not been more critical in the past has been that it is hard to be against the idea of defense, and the idea that "nothing is too good for our boys" has tended to prevail. Further, Congress has not been well equipped to effectively criticize and evaluate military programs for two reasons: 1) the increasing complexity of military technology has made evaluation of proposed programs more and more difficult, with the result that congressmen have been forced to rely on the expert testimony provided by the Pentagon; and 2) the unification of

[7] Senator Gaylord A. Nelson, "Congress is Waking Up," *The Progressive*, June, 1969, p. 12.

the services under a single Secretary of Defense has largely prevented competing viewpoints from reaching the Congress.

Military weapons systems have become increasingly complex
and sophisticated, involving long lead times and depending upon
the most advanced technology—even to the extent of frequently
depending upon anticipated technical developments not yet out
of the laboratories. Proper evaluation of proposals in such eso-
teric fields requires a degree of expert knowledge not usually
available to a congressional committee other than through testimony offered by the Pentagon, whose witnesses are often constrained to support administration proposals. Part of the solution
to this problem has been to develop alternative sources of expert
testimony. For example, during the controversy over the anti-
ballistic missile in 1969, opponents of Administration proposals
mustered an impressive array of experts outside of the Defense
Department who provided testimony and articles in opposition
to the program.[8]

The problem of getting both sides of the question from military officers constrained to support administration proposals is
a persistent one. At one time Congress itself prohibited officers
from making any estimate or requesting any appropriation which
differed from administration budget proposals.[9] This is no longer
the case, but military officers testifying before Congress are still
expected by the Administration to support Administration proposals. Huntington, for example, notes that during both the
Truman and Eisenhower Administrations an attempt was made
to "define as broadly as possible the obligation of military officers
to support Administration programs before Congress."[10] Under
Secretary of Defense Robert McNamara restrictions became even
more severe. In 1965 a Defense Department memorandum signed
by Deputy Secretary of Defense Cyrus Vance stated that if an
officer testifying before a congressional committee was pressed
for his own opinion, he would, in addition to providing his own
opinion, defend the official position and make clear "the consideration or factors which support the decision."[11] The result
of these restrictions has been that it is hard for the Congress to

[8] Abram Chayes and Jerome B. Wiesner (eds.), *ABM: An Evaluation
of the Decision to Deploy an Antiballistic Missile System* (New York:
Harper and Row, 1969).

[9] Budget and Accounting Act of 1921.

[10] Samuel P. Huntington, *The Common Defense* (New York: Columbia
University Press, 1961), p. 188.

[11] Sec Def Memo, January 11, 1965.

adequately discover and develop the counter-arguments to administration proposals.

A third reason Congress has not been fully effective in evaluating military programs is the classic problem of self-interest. I. F. Stone, in a subsequent article on the TFX [F-111], reports on one way in which politics can distort the process of defense procurement. Although members of Congress by and large attempt to avoid waste, inefficiency and duplication in military spending, there is a strong tendency to become parochial when issues are at stake which affect the Congressmens' own districts or states. Congressmen are almost invariably quick to protest loudly the closing of any base or facility within their districts, no matter how unnecessary the installation may be. Military installations are often of great economic importance to a community, and it is usually in a Congressman's political self-interest to fight to keep them open.

Politics often works in a similar way on contract awards. In June of 1970 the Navy announced the award of a long-term contract for the construction of destroyers to Litton Industries, to be built in their new automated shipyard in Pascagoula, Mississippi. The Navy was immediately subjected to both public and private pressure from New England Congressmen demanding that a portion of the contract be given to the Bath Iron Works of Bath, Maine, despite the Navy's contention that splitting the contract would substantially increase the costs.[12] Supporters of a split contract were successful in the House of Representatives in passing an amendment to the Military Procurement Bill which would have required the Navy to use at least two supply sources for the new class of destroyers, but the requirement was later defeated in the Senate. Thus in this case, the Navy, with Senate support, did manage to stick to the more economical single source procurement. Of interest, however, is that less than a month after the award of the $2.1 billion contract to Litton, Bath received a $19.3 million contract to modernize three Navy guided missile destroyers.[13] The two contracts may very well have been unrelated, but the timing made the second award appear to be a response to political pressure.

Few Congressmen are willing to see their own districts get less than their "fair share" of the defense budget. Since Congress is the source of all funds, the Pentagon is careful to avoid un-

[12] *Boston Herald*, June 25, 1970.
[13] *Providence Evening Bulletin*, July 16, 1970.

necessarily antagonizing members of Congress, so that decisions are often affected by political considerations completely unrelated to genuine defense needs. The result is usually higher cost and lower effectiveness.

The Place of the Military-Industrial Complex

There is danger of distortion in focusing on the defects in any system. A classic retort to criticism of the serious flaws in democratic government is that it is indeed the worst of all possible systems of government, with the exception of all of those alternative systems which have been tried by men from time to time. The problem of political interference, for example, is probably inherent in a system of civil control of the military, where representatives are responsible to the people who elect them and liable to being voted out of office. It is difficult to imagine a system which would remedy this flaw without introducing more serious problems in its stead.

Many of the problems in defense spending are inherent in bigness. Any large bureaucracy invariably creates rigidities, inefficiency and red tape—yet we do not know of any way of accomplishing things on a large scale without also organizing on a large scale.

The present world political situation contains most of the elements which have led to armed conflict in the past. The United States has treaty commitments throughout the world which carry a military obligation. We have in the past tried the alternative of virtual unilateral disarmament, and it has not been successful in keeping us out of war. Most Americans now seem to believe that armed strength is a necessity. A standing military establishment and a large defense budget are therefore likely to be with us for some time.

The idea of the citizen soldier who could make the transition from the plow to the rifle on a moment's notice has been an appealing one for Americans from before the time of the Revolutionary War. The idea of rapid conversion from peacetime to wartime employment has been applied to men and to industries alike. In the past this has worked satisfactorily for two reasons: 1) in the days of simple weapons the conversion was relatively easy for both men and machines, and 2) our entry into war has frequently been sufficiently delayed so that time for conversion was available. The ability of Singer Co. to change its production line from sewing machines to machine guns and Ford Motor Co. to change from passenger cars to tanks was accepted as a matter of course. The time factor received little or no publicity until the sobering experiences with weapon shortages at the beginning of World War II.

World War II first presented this country with serious evidence that the minute-man concept has become untenable. The nation was unprepared for the magnitude of the transition from a peacetime to a wartime economy because of what James McKie has called the "M-day delusion":

For some years prior to World War II there was a myth, cultivated by popular magazines and even subscribed to by some responsible officials, that the gigantic resources of the United States could be instantly converted to war production if an emergency arose. On Mobilization Day, previously prepared orders which had lain dormant in the files of the procurement agencies would go forth to every plant in the country whose facilities were usable for defense production. . . . When the emergency did strike, of course, an almost unparalleled state of confusion replaced this attractive picture. Not many had anticipated the immensely difficult problems involved in mobilizing industry, and almost two years elapsed before the country was in a passable "attitude of defense."[14]

Since World War II, the conversion from peacetime to wartime manufacture has become many times more difficult. The design and manufacture of guided missiles, nuclear submarines and supersonic aircraft requires a degree of knowledge, skill, experience and physical plant which cannot be obtained through hasty conversion. It is this reality to which President Eisenhower referred in his Farewell Address when he said "we have been compelled to create a permanent armaments industry of vast proportions." Of necessity the military-industrial complex is going to be with us for a long time. The real question, in Eisenhower's words, is how to "compel the proper meshing of the huge industrial and military machinery of defense with our peaceful methods and goals, so that security and liberty may prosper together."

Constitutionally, it is Congress that must play the major role in ensuring the "proper meshing" of security and liberty. After a lengthy period in which Congress was relatively uncritical of

[14] James W. McKie, "Controlling Production for Defense," *Economics of Mobilization for War*, ed. by W. Glenn Campbell (Chicago: Irwin, 1952), p. 47.

military programs and of foreign commitments which entailed obligations, a reaction has set in. The military budget and proposals for new systems have recently encountered more searching examination and vigorous criticism, and Congress has been casting about for ways to more effectively influence foreign policy. The controversy, lengthy debate, and close vote on the anti-ballistic missile is but one example. The best safeguard against unwarranted or inefficient expenditures for military purposes is careful examination of the Defense Department budget by a critical Congress. Any detailed discussions of needed reforms is impossible here, but four changes should be sufficient to permit effective congressional control. These are: 1) adequate staffing of congressional committees to permit competent independent appraisal of proposed new programs, to avoid exclusive reliance upon testimony by Pentagon experts, as was done effectively during the ABM hearings; 2) a measure of decentralization within the Department of Defense to reduce its monolithic aspects, and to permit competing views to reach Congress; 3) a concerted effort both in the Department of Defense and the Congress to avoid systems which attempt to radically or unnecessarily advance the state of the art, coupled with rigorous controls over changes after a program is underway; and 4) an increased emphasis upon sealed bid competition, where possible, and fixed price contracts. This should enforce realistic pricing at the time a system is being considered, and provide Congress a more realistic basis for evaluating programs.

The dangers of the military-industrial complex for democratic institutions are real, but at least for now are more latent than actual. The famous labor leader, Samuel Gompers, reputedly once answered a reporter's query as to what it was that the labor movement really wanted, with a single word: "More!" The same answer would probably serve if the defense contractors or the military services were asked the same question. Like any other businessman, the defense contractor would like to increase his sales, and no military man ever feels that his forces are entirely adequate to meet all foreseeable contingencies. No malevolency is involved, but it would be unreasonable to expect either defense contractors or military officers to initiate military budget cuts. It is in the Congress that competing claims for resources must be resolved, and defense is one of the imperative needs that must be balanced against other pressing claims for resources. The important thing is that the Congress be properly equipped to assess competing needs properly. Many have argued for drastic cuts in military spending in the belief that this would release resources for their favorite project, whether it is pollution control, rebuilding the inner city, public transportation, a guaranteed annual income, or whatever. But it is important to understand that it is a long way from military cuts to affirmative programs, and that politically popular tax cuts compete for congressional favor along with spending proposals. It is Congress that must weigh the competing demands and allocate national resources.

As shown in the graphs at the beginning of this section, the trend is toward reduction in the relative amount of military spending. This means that the relative influence of the military-industrial complex is also being reduced, as defense spending takes a smaller part of the national wealth. There can be very real dangers to democratic institutions from a standing military and a permanent arms industry, but for now the trend appears to be away from that danger. Trends can change, however, and we must look to the political process to ensure against the military-industrial complex gaining at some future time the "unwarranted influence" against which President Eisenhower warned.

The following essays are selected to represent both critics and defenders of the military-industrial complex. Critics are represented by an excerpt from John Kenneth Galbraith's *How to Control the Military* and by I. F. Stone's essay on the F-111. Charles Wolf offers a defense of the existing system in his article "Military-Industrial Complexities." In the final essay of this section Bruce Russett tries to avoid the role of either critic or advocate, and attempts to present a balanced assessment. Preceding these essays, however, is an excerpt from President Eisenhower's farewell address in which the term "military-industrial complex" was used for the first time.

From "Farewell Address to the Nation," January 17, 1961

Throughout America's adventure in free government, our basic purposes have been to keep the peace, to foster progress in human achievement, and to enhance liberty, dignity and integrity among people and among nations. To strive for less would be unworthy of a free and religious people. Any failure traceable to arrogance, or our lack of comprehension or readiness to sacrifice would inflict upon us grievous hurt both at home and abroad.

Progress toward these noble goals is persistently threatened by the conflict now engulfing the world. It commands our whole attention, absorbs our very beings. We face a hostile ideology—global in scope, atheistic in character, ruthless in purpose, and insidious in method. Unhappily the danger it poses promises to be of indefinite duration. To meet it successfully, there is called for, not so much the emotional and transitory sacrifices of crisis, but rather those which enable us to carry forward steadily, surely, and without complaint the burdens of a prolonged and complex struggle—with liberty the stake. Only thus shall we remain, despite every provocation, on our charted course toward permanent peace and human betterment.

Crises there will continue to be. In meeting them, whether foreign or domestic, great or small, there is a recurring temptation to feel that some spectacular and costly action could become the miraculous solution to all current difficulties. A huge increase in newer elements of our defense; development of unrealistic programs to cure every ill in agriculture; a dramatic expansion in basic and applied research—these and many other possibilities, each possibly promising in itself, may be suggested as the only way to the road we wish to travel.

But each proposal must be weighed in the light of a broader consideration: the need to maintain balance in and among national programs—balance between the private and the public economy, balance between cost and hoped for advantage—balance between the clearly necessary and the comfortably desirable; balance between our essential requirements as a nation and the duties imposed by the nation upon the individual; balance between actions of the moment and the national welfare of the future. Good judgment seeks balance and progress; lack of it eventually finds imbalance and frustration.

The record of many decades stands as proof that our people and their government have, in the main, understood these truths and have responded to them well, in the face of stress and threat. But threats, new in kind or degree, constantly arise. I mention two only.

A vital element in keeping the peace is our military establishment. Our arms must be mighty, ready for instant action, so that no potential aggressor may be tempted to risk his own destruction.

Our military organization today bears little relation to that known by any of my predecessors in peacetime, or indeed by the fighting men of World War II or Korea.

Until the latest of our world conflicts, the United States had no armaments industry. American makers of plowshares could, with time and as required, make swords as well. But now we can no longer risk emergency improvisation of national defense; we have been compelled to create a permanent armaments industry of vast proportions. Added to this, three and a half million men and women are directly engaged in the defense establishment. We annually spend on military security more than the net income of all United States corporations.

This conjunction of an immense military establishment and a large arms industry is new in the American experience. The total influence—economic, political, even spiritual—is felt in every city, every State house, every office of the Federal government. We recognize the imperative need for this development. Yet we must not fail to comprehend its grave implications. Our toil, resources and livelihood are all involved; so is the very structure of our society.

In the councils of government, we must guard against the acquisition of unwarranted influence, whether sought or unsought, by the military-industrial complex. The potential for the disastrous rise of misplaced power exists and will persist.

We must never let the weight of this combination endanger our liberties or democratic processes. We should take nothing for granted. Only an alert and knowledgeable citizenry can compel the proper meshing of the huge industrial and military machinery of defense with our peaceful methods and goals, so that security and liberty may prosper together.

Akin to, and largely responsible for the sweeping changes in our industrial-military posture, has been the technological revolution during recent decades.

In this revolution, research has become central; it also becomes more formalized, complex, and costly. A steadily increasing share is conducted for, by, or at the direction, of the Federal government.

Today, the solitary inventor tinkering in his shop, has been overshadowed by task forces of scientists in laboratories and testing fields. In the same fashion, the free university, historically the fountainhead of free ideas and scientific discovery, has experienced a revolution in the conduct of research. Partly because of the huge costs involved, a government contract becomes virtually a substitute for intellectual curiosity. For every old blackboard there are now hundreds of new electronic computers.

The prospect of domination of the nation's scholars by Federal employment, project allocations, and the power of money is ever present—and is gravely to be regarded.

Yet, in holding scientific research and discovery in respect, as we should, we must also be alert to the equal and opposite danger that public policy could itself become the captive of a scientific-technological elite.

It is the task of statesmanship to mold, to balance, and to integrate these and other forces, new and old, within the principles of our democratic system—ever aiming toward the supreme goals of our free society.

Characteristics of the
Military-Industrial Complex

JOHN KENNETH GALBRAITH

It is an organization or a complex of organizations and not a conspiracy. Although Americans are probably the world's least competent conspirators—partly because no other country so handsomely rewards in cash and notoriety the man who blows the whistle on those with whom he is conspiring—we have a strong instinct for so explaining that of which we disapprove. In the conspiratorial view, the military power is a collation of generals and conniving industrialists. The goal is mutual enrichment; they arrange elaborately to feather each other's nest. The industrialists are the *deus ex machina;* their agents make their way around Washington arranging the pay-offs. If money is too dangerous, then alcohol, compatible women, more prosaic forms of entertainment, or the promise of future jobs to generals and admirals will serve.

There is such enrichment and some graft. Insiders do well. H. L. Nieburg has told the fascinating story of how in 1954 two modestly paid aerospace scientists, Dr. Simon Ramo and Dr. Dean E. Wooldridge, attached themselves influentially to the Air Force as consultants and in four fine years (with no known dishonesty) ran a shoestring of $6,750 apiece into a multi-million dollar fortune and a position of major industrial prominence.[1] (In 1967 their firm held defense contracts totalling

From *How to Control the Military* by John Kenneth Galbraith, copyright © 1969 by John Kenneth Galbraith. Reprinted by permission of Doubleday & Company, Inc., and NCLC Publishing Society Ltd.

[1] *In the Name of Science* (Chicago: Quadrangle Press, 1966). This is a book of first-rate importance which the author was so unwise as to

$121,000,000.) Senator William Proxmire, a man whom many in the Defense industries have come to compare unfavorably to typhus, has recently come up with a fascinating contractual arrangement between the Air Force and Lockheed for the new C-5A jet transport. It makes the profits of the company greater the greater the costs in filling the first part of the order—with interesting incentive effects. A recent Department of Defense study reached the depressing conclusion that firms with the poorest performance in designing highly technical electronic systems—and the failure rate was appalling—have regularly received the highest profits. In 1960, 691 retired generals, admirals, naval captains, and colonels were employed by the ten largest defense contractors—186 by General Dynamics alone. A recent study made at the behest of Senator Proxmire found 2,072 employed in major defense firms with an especially heavy concentration in the specialized defense firms.[2] It would be idle to suppose that presently serving officers—those for example on assignment to defense plants—never have their real income improved by the wealthy contractors with whom they are working, forswear all favors, entertain themselves and sleep austerely alone. Nor are those public servants who show zeal in searching out undue profits or graft reliably rewarded by a grateful public. Mr. A. E. Fitzgerald, the Pentagon management expert who became disturbed over the C-5A contract with Lockheed and communicated his distaste and its causes to the Proxmire Committee, had his recently acquired civil service status removed and was the subject of a fascinating memorandum (which found its way to Proxmire) outlining the sanctions appropriate to his excess of zeal. Pentagon officials explained that Mr. Fitzgerald had been given his civil service tenure as the result of a computer error (the first of its kind) and the memorandum on appropriate punishment was a benign gesture of purely scholarly intent designed, it seemed, to specify those punishments against which such a sound public servant should be protected.

Nonetheless, the notion of a conspiracy to enrich and corrupt

---

publish some three years before concern for the problems he discusses became general. But perhaps he made it so.

[2] General Dynamics 113, Lockheed 210, Boeing 169, McDonnell Douglas 141, North American Rockwell 104, Ling-Temco-Vought, Inc. 69. All of these firms are heavily specialized to military business and General Dynamics, Lockheed, McDonnell Douglas and North American Rockwell almost completely so.

is gravely damaging to an understanding of the military power. It causes men to look for solutions in issuing regulations, enforcing laws, or sending people to jail. It also, as a practical matter, exaggerates the role of the defense industries in the military power—since they are the people who [would] make the most money, they are assumed to be the ones who, in the manner of the classical capitalist, pull the strings. The armed services are assumed to be in some measure their puppets. The reality is far less dramatic and far more difficult of solution. The reality is a complex of organizations pursuing their sometimes diverse but generally common goals. The participants in these organizations are mostly honest men whose public and private behavior would withstand public scrutiny as well as most. They live on their military pay or their salaries as engineers, scientists, or managers, or their pay and profits as executives, and would not dream of offering or accepting a bribe.

The organizations that comprise the military power are the four Armed Services, and especially their procurement branches. And the military power encompasses the specialized defense contractors—General Dynamics, McDonnell Douglas, Lockheed or the defense films of the agglomerates—of Ling-Temco-Vought or Litton Industries. (About half of all defense contracts are with the firms that do relatively little other business.) And it embraces the defense divisions of primarily civilian firms such as General Electric or AT&T. It draws moral and valuable political support from the unions. Men serve these organizations in many, if not most, instances because they believe in what they are doing—because they have committed themselves to the bureaucratic truth. To find and scourge a few malefactors is to ignore this far more important commitment.

The military power is not confined to the Services and their contractors—what has come to be called the military-industrial complex. Associate membership is held by the intelligence agencies which assess Soviet (or Chinese) actions or intentions. These provide, more often by selection and bureaucratic belief than by any outright dishonesty, the justification for what the Services would like to have and what their contractors would like to supply. Associated also are Foreign Service Officers who provide a civilian or diplomatic gloss to the foreign policy positions which serve the military need. The country desks at the State Department, a greatly experienced former official and ambassador has observed, are often "in the hip pocket of the Pentagon—

lock, stock and barrel, ideologically owned by the Pentagon."[3]

Also a part of the military power are the university scientists and those in such defense-oriented organizations as RAND, the Institute for Defense Analysis, and Hudson Institute who think professionally about weapons and weapons systems and the strategy of their use. And last, but by no means least, there is the organized voice of the military in the Congress, most notably on the Armed Services Committees of the Senate and House of Representatives. These are the organizations which comprise the military power.

The men who comprise these organizations call each other on the phone, meet at committee hearings, serve together on teams or task forces, work in neighboring offices in Washington or San Diego. They naturally make their decisions in accordance with their view of the world—the view of the bureaucracy of which they are a part. The problem is not conspiracy or corruption but unchecked rule. And being unchecked, this rule reflects not the national need but the bureaucratic need—not what is best for the United States but what the Air Force, Army, Navy, General Dynamics, North American Rockwell, Grumman Aircraft, State Department representatives, intelligence offices and Mendel Rivers and Richard Russell believe to be best.

In recent years Air Force generals, perhaps the most compulsively literate warriors since Caesar, have made their views of the world scene a part of the American folklore. These in all cases serve admirably the goals of the Service and the military power in general. Similarly with the other participants.

Not long ago, Bernard Nossiter, the brilliant economic reporter of the *Washington Post*, made the rounds of some of the major defense contractors to get their views of the post-Vietnam prospect. All, without exception, saw profitable tension and conflict. Edward J. Lefevre, the vice-president in charge of General Dynamics' Washington office, said "One must believe in the long term threat." James J. Ling, the head of Ling-Temco-Vought, reported that "Defense spending has to increase in our

[3] Ralph Dungan, formerly White House aide to Presidents Kennedy and Johnson and former Ambassador to Chile. Quoted in George Thayer, *The War Business* (New York: Simon and Schuster, Inc., 1969), *passim*. The appearance of the State Department as a full-scale participant in the military power may have been the hopefully temporary achievement of Secretary Rusk. Apart from a high respect for military acumen and need, he in some degree regarded diplomacy as a subordinate to military purpose. In time, such attitudes penetrate deeply into organization.

area because there has been a failure to initiate—if we are not going to be overtaken by the Soviets." Samuel F. Downer, one of Mr. Ling's vice-presidents, was more outspoken. "We're going to increase defense budgets as long as those bastards in Russia are ahead of us." A study of the Electronics Industries Association also dug up by Mr. Nossiter (to whom I shall return in a moment) discounted the danger of arms control, decided that the "likelihood of limited war will increase" and concluded that "for the electronic firms, the outlook is good in spite [sic] of [the end of hostilities in] Vietnam."

From the foregoing beliefs, in turn, comes the decision on weapons and weapons systems and military policy generally. No one can tell where the action originates—whether the Services or the contractors initiate decisions on weapons—nor can the two be sharply distinguished. Much of the plant of the specialized defense contractors is owned by the government. Most of their working capital is supplied by the government through progress payments—payments made in advance of completion of the contract. The government specifies what the firm can and cannot charge to the government. The Armed Services Procurement Regulation states that "Although the government does not expect to participate *in every management* decision, it may reserve the right to review the contractors' management efforts. . . ." (Italics added.)[4]

In this kind of association some proposals will come across the table from the military. Some will come back from the captive contractors. Nossiter asked leading contractors, as well as people at the Pentagon, about this. Here are some of the answers:

From John W. Bessire, General Manager for Pricing, General Dynamics, Fort Worth:

We try to foresee the requirements the military is going to have three years off. We work with their requirements people and therefore get new business.

From Richard E. Adams, Director of Advanced Projects, Fort Worth Division of General Dynamics, who thought the source was the military:

---

[4] Murray L. Weidenbaum. "Arms and the American Economy: A Domestic Convergence Hypothesis." *American Economic Review*. Papers and Proceedings, 1968, p. 434.

Things are too systematized at the Pentagon for us to invent weapons systems and sell them on a need.

On the influence of the military, he added:

We know where the power is [on Capitol Hill and among Executive Departments]. There's going to be a lot of defense business and we're going to get our share of it.

From John R. Moore, President of Aerospace and Systems Group of North American Rockwell:

A new system usually starts with a couple of military and industry people getting together to discuss common problems.

After noting that most of his business came from requirements "established by the Defense Department and NASA," he concluded:

But it isn't a case of industry here and the Government here. They are interacting continuously at the engineering level.

And finally from a high civilian in the Pentagon:

Pressures to spend more. . . . In part they come from the industry selling new weapons ideas and in part from the military here. Each military guy has his own piece, tactical, antisubmarine, strategic. Each guy gets where he is by pushing his particular thing.

He added:

Don't forget, too, part of it is based on the perception of needs by people in Congress.

If the origin of the actions on arms is unclear, the consequence is not. In the language of labor relations, it is a sweetheart deal between those who sell to the government and those who buy. Once competitive bidding created an adversary relationship between buyer and seller and with numerous sellers, a special relationship with any one provoked cries of favoritism. But modern weapons are bought overwhelmingly by negotiation and in most cases from a single source of supply. (In the fiscal year ending in 1968, General Accounting Office figures show that 57.9 per cent of the $43 billion in defense contracts awarded in that year was by negotiation with a single source of supply. Of the remainder 30.6 per cent was awarded by negotiation where alternative sources of supply had an opportunity to participate and only 11.5 per cent was open to advertised competitive bidding.)[5] Under these circumstances, the tendency to any adversary relationship between the Services and the suppliers disappears. Indeed, where there are only one or two sources of supply for a weapons system, the Services will be as much interested in sustaining these firms as the firms are in being sustained.

Among those who spoke about the sources of ideas on weapons needs, no one was moved to suggest that public opinion played any role. The President, as the elected official responsible for foreign policy, was not mentioned. The Congress came in only as an afterthought. And had the Pentagon official who mentioned the Congress been pressed, he would have agreed that its "perception of needs" almost always results from prompting by either the military or the defense industries. It was thus, for example, that the need for a new generation of manned bombers was perceived (and provided for) by Congress though repeatedly vetoed as unnecessary by Presidents Kennedy and Johnson. But mostly the role of the Congress has been overwhelmingly aquiescent and passive.

> . . . an established tradition . . . holds that a bill to spend billions of dollars for the machinery of war must be rushed through the House and Senate in a matter of hours, while a treaty to advance the cause of peace, or a program to help the underdeveloped nations . . . guarantee the rights of all our citizens, or . . . to advance the interests of the poor must be scrutinized and debated and amended and thrashed over for weeks and perhaps months.[6]

We see here a truly remarkable reversal of the American political and economic system as outlined by the fathers and still portrayed to the young. That view supposes that ultimate authority —ultimate sovereignty—lies with the people. And this authority is assumed to be comprehensive. Within the ambit of the state the citizen expresses his will through the men—the President and members of the Congress—whom he elects. In the private sector he accomplishes the same thing by his purchases in the market.

---

[5] Testimony by Elmer B. Staats, Comptroller General, before the Proxmire Committee, November 11, 1968.

[6] Senator Gaylord Nelson, U. S. Senate, February 1964. Quoted by Julius Duscha, *Arms, Money and Politics* (New York: Ives, Washburn, 1965), p. 2.

These instruct supplying firms—General Motors, General Electric, Standard Oil of New Jersey—as to what they shall produce and sell.

Here, however, we find the Armed Services, or the corporations that supply them, making the decisions and instructing the Congress and the public. The public accepts whatever is so decided and pays the bill. This is an age when the young are also being instructed, rightly though with vast solemnity, to respect constitutional process and seek change within the framework of the established political order. And here we find the assumed guardians of that order, men with no slight appreciation of their righteousness and respectability, calmly turning it upside down themselves.

Nixon and the Arms Race: The Bomber Boondoggle

I. F. STONE

I

The No. 1 question for the new Nixon Administration is what it will do about the arms race. If it opts for higher military spending, the consequence will be intensified social conflict. If the new President's policies in office follow his campaign pledges, the decision has already been made. Nixon has begun by promising to perpetuate one of McNamara's greatest errors and to undo his greatest accomplishment. The error is that miscarriage of an airplane, the TFX, now known as the F-111, which has already cost the country several billion dollars. His accomplishment was to make the country realize that at a certain point in the awful arithmetic of nuclear power, superiority in weapons became meaningless.

In his Security Gap speech over CBS on October 25, Nixon said one of his major aims would be to "correct its [the Pentagon's] over-centralization" in order to give greater weight in decision-making to the military as against the top civilians. "I intend to root out the 'whiz kid' approach which for years," Nixon said, "has led our policies and programs down the wrong roads." But he is following McNamara down his most costly wrong road, just when the military have been proven right and the top civilians wrong, and indeed—as we shall see—on the one issue where the "whiz kids" sided with the military against McNamara. On the other hand, Nixon has set out, in the search for nuclear superiority, to follow the military down a dead-end

Reprinted with permission from *The New York Review of Books*. Copyright © 1969, The New York Review.

path where the military are demonstrably wrong and the "whiz kids" are demonstrably right. To examine these two divergent courses is to see the trouble which lies ahead, on many different levels, for the new Administration and the country.

Let us begin with the TFX and with the speech Nixon made on November 2 at Fort Worth, Texas. Fort Worth is where General Dynamics builds the TFX or F-111, the plane that was the focus of the longest and bitterest controversy of McNamara's years in the Pentagon. "The F-111 in a Nixon Administration," the candidate said at Fort Worth that day, "will be made into one of the foundations of our air supremacy." This pledge, which received too little attention, may prove to be the biggest blooper of the campaign, and the beginning—if Nixon tries to keep that pledge—of the biggest fight between the Nixon Administration and the very forces he might have counted on for a honeymoon, the Senate conservatives who specialize in military policy and who were most critical of McNamara in the TFX affair.

This Nixon pledge at Fort Worth will repay patient examination. It is startling that a man as cautious as Nixon should have made so unqualified a pledge to a plane which has become a tragic joke.

Last May, when the Senate Appropriations subcommittee on the Department of Defense was holding hearings on the budget for the fiscal year 1969, the chairman, Senator Russell of Georgia, booby-trapped the Air Force Chief of Staff, General McConnell, with what appeared to be an innocent question on this plane, the F-111:

SENATOR RUSSELL: Would it be a very serious matter if one of these planes were recovered by any potential enemy in a reasonably good condition?

GENERAL MCCONNELL: Yes, we have quite a few things in it that we would not want the enemy to get.

SENATOR RUSSELL: That is mainly electronic devices.

GENERAL MCCONNELL: That is true of practically all the aircraft we have.

SENATOR RUSSELL: Of course the Russians got a B-29 when they were one of our allies. They fabricated a great many of them as nearly comparable to the B-29's as they could. I was hoping if they got a F-111 they would fabricate some of them as near ours as they could and see if they had as much trouble as we did. It would put their Air Force out of business.[1]

[1] Senate Appropriations Committee Hearings on the 1969 Defense Department budget, Part I, Department of the Air Force, p. 103. Released September 19, 1968.

Neither General McConnell nor his civilian superior Air Force Secretary Harold Brown dared to say one word in reply to Senator Russell's cruel jibe.

Russell's sardonic view of the F-111 is shared on both sides of the aisle in the Senate. On October 3, Senator Curtis of Kansas, a senior Republican, a member of the Aeronautical and Space Sciences Committee, delivered a devastating attack on the F-111 in the Senate, in which he said McNamara's "obstinacy" in producing the F-111, "will be a major problem that the new Administration must face." Just one month later Nixon began to face it by pledging himself at Fort Worth to make this plane "one of the foundations of our air supremacy."

Either Nixon and his staff do not read the newspapers, much less the *Congressional Record* and the hearings, or Nixon like McNamara is determined to override military judgment and keep the billions flowing into General Dynamics for this jinxed plane. The difference is that when McNamara overrode the military, it was difficult for outsiders to judge so complex a technological controversy, especially when so many of the facts were still classified. Newspapermen like myself, who start with a strong bias against the military, assumed that McNamara was probably right. But 1968 is the year when the F-111 finally went into combat; the results have led many people inside and outside Congress to look at the old controversy with a fresh eye.

Nixon's reckless pledge was the only bright spot for the F-111 in the year 1968. The latest, 1969, edition of *Jane's Aircraft*[2] says succinctly,

The 474th Tactical Fighter Wing at Nellis [Air Force Base, Nevada] was the first to be equipped with the F-111As [the Air Force version of the F-111]. Six aircraft from Nellis arrived at the Takhli base in Thailand on 17 March 1968 and made their first operational sorties over Vietnam on 25 March. Two were lost in the next five days.

The Foreword, which went to press later, says "Three of the first 8 F-111A's dispatched to Vietnam were lost in a matter of weeks and the type was grounded shortly afterwards." No mention was made of these losses by Secretary of the Air Force Brown when he read his prepared statement to the Senate appropriations defense subcommittee in executive session last May 6.

[2] *Jane's All the World's Aircraft, 1968–69*, ed. by John W. R. Taylor, (New York: McGraw-Hill). p. 279.

On the contrary he said the F-111 "is proving, in its tests and operational units, to be an outstanding aircraft." By then three of the original six had been lost, as may be seen from the following colloquy, where the reader will notice Secretary Brown's squeamish reluctance to use the word "lost."

SENATOR RUSSELL: How many of these have we sent over to Southeast Asia?
SECRETARY BROWN: We sent six and have sent two replacements.
SENATOR RUSSELL: You have lost three, so you have five?
SECRETARY BROWN: There are five there now.
SENATOR RUSSELL: Do you have any information on these three that were lost? Do you know whether any of them fell into the hands of the North Vietnamese to be sent to Moscow along with all the secret equipment of the Pueblo?
GENERAL MCCONNELL: [Air Force Chief of Staff]: No, sir.[3]

In his Senate speech of October 3, Senator Curtis disclosed, "Thus far, 11 F-111 aircraft have crashed with a number of fatalities." He revealed that the wings were broken off one plane during a "static ground test" just six weeks before the first six planes were deployed to Southeast Asia, and that the week before his Senate speech another F-111A had crashed during a training flight owing to "a fatigue failure in the wing carry-through structure."

If rightists treated Nixon and the Defense Department the way he treated the State Department in the days when he was a practicing witch-hunter, a proposal to make such a plane, with such a record, a foundation stone of American air supremacy would have been adduced as proof positive that the Pentagon had been infiltrated with Red and pinko saboteurs.

Last January the British Royal Air Force cancelled its order for fifty F-111K's. In March Congress ordered work stopped on the F-111B's, the version for the US Navy. On October 7, Senator Symington followed Senator Curtis with a speech suggesting that production of the F-111's for the Air Force also be stopped: He said "the series of crashes in the past five months" makes it doubtful that it will ever prove to be "a truly reliable airplane" and declared that its future should "receive highest priority upon convening of the new Congress."

The strangest discovery which turns up in studying Nixon's pledge at Fort Worth is that he and his staff were either unaware

[3] Senate 1969 Defense Appropriations Hearings, *op. cit.*, pp. 102–103.

of, or ignored, his own famous "position papers." The one on "Research and Development: Our Neglected Weapon,"[4] which was made public in May, 1968, says of the F-111:

> The effort to transform the TFX (F-111) into an all-purpose all-service aircraft has created serious problems. Against military advice, the F-111 was selected as a superior, yet economical, weapons system. . . . The aircraft were to cost approximately $2.4 million each. Now they are priced at more than $6 million each. . . . In view of the recent decision that the F111B, the Navy version, is unacceptable, and a substitute aircraft be initiated, the final cost of the program will increase enormously coupled with years of delay. The program has resulted in the Air Force having a new aircraft that does not meet the original requirements. . . . The F111B has been found unacceptable and the F111 Bomber version does not meet Air Force requirements for an advanced bomber in the 1970 time frame.

Nixon devoted one of his main campaign speeches to "the research gap." The Fort Worth speech showed his own research gap. Did he and his staff fail to read their position papers? Another of these papers, "Decisions on National Security: Patchwork or Policy?" is also in conflict with his Fort Worth speech. That paper says "a notable example" of how the top civilians overrode military judgment in the McNamara years was the original award of the contract for the F-111. "The contractor unaminously recommended by both the military analysts and the Weapons Evaluation Systems Group," it says, "was rejected." The rejected bidder was Boeing. The contractor McNamara chose was General Dynamics. Nixon at Fort Worth affirmed the same choice.

II

We are not dealing here with a minor item. General Dynamics is the country's biggest weapons producer. A Defense Department press release of November 18 on the nation's top ten defense contractors showed General Dynamics as No. 1. In the fiscal year ending last June 30, it received $2.2 billion in arms contracts, or 5.8 per cent of the total awarded in those twelve months. More than 80 per cent of the firm's business comes from the government. The TFX represented the biggest single plum

---

[4] All these position papers have been reprinted in a one-volume compilation, *Choice for America: Republican Answers to the Challenge of Now*, published July, 1968, by the Republican National Committee, 1625 Eye St. N.W., Washington 20006.

in military procurement. The original contract was for 1,700 planes at a total cost of $5.8 billion, or about $3 million per plane. These figures have since skyrocketed. This year, before the Navy contract was canceled, the Pentagon admitted the cost of the Navy version would be $8 million apiece and of the Air Force version $6.5 million. As usual these, too, were understatements. Senator Curtis disclosed that the contractor's cost information reports put the average cost of the Navy plane at $9.5 million and that internal budgeting projections at the Pentagon put the Air Force plane at $9.1 million each. The original contract would have run up in the neighborhood of $15 billion.

Even with the cutbacks, more than $6 billion has already been spent and at least between $3 and $4 billion more "will be added in succeeding years," Senator Curtis said, "if present Defense Department plans are carried to completion." If Nixon keeps his word, they *will* be completed, perhaps expanded. But if he tries to do so, he will almost certainly find himself embattled with the Air Force buffs in Congress. For Curtis, Symington, Russell, and McClellan speak for a group of Senators who feel that the Air Force has been starved and stunted while all this money has been wasted on the TFX. We are in the presence of a wide-open split not only between the proponents of General Dynamics and Boeing respectively but within the Air Force and the whole military-industrial complex.

History is repeating itself, and it is the history of subordinating military efficiency to moneyed and political pressures. The only difference is that Nixon will find it harder than did McNamara to hide the realities, now that the F-111 has finally begun to fly—and fall. When the Kennedy Administration took over, General Dynamics was drifting close to receivership. It lost $27 million in 1960 and $143 million in 1961. *Fortune* magazine in January and February of 1962 published a fascinating two-part study by Richard Austin Smith of its misjudgments and its business losses. Smith said its losses on its civilian plane business had been so disastrous that its working capital had dropped below the minimum required by its agreement with its bankers and that if the bankers had not reduced the minimum this "technically could have started the company down the road to receivership." Smith wrote that the output of the General Dynamics plant at Fort Worth in 1962 would be half what it was in 1961. *Fortune* said in its strangulated prose that General Dynamics would have to shut down its facilities "unless it gets contract for joint Navy-Air Force fighter." This was the TFX.

The TFX contract saved General Dynamics in 1962. The cancelation of the F-111 could ruin it in 1969. The effect of canceling the Navy version of the plan was already reflected in a third quarter deficit, as of September 30, 1968, amounting to $1.51 a share compared with a net profit of $1.13 a share in the third quarter of 1967. *Moody's News* showed General Dynamics had to write off $39.6 million in contracts in 1968 as against only $12 million in 1967. Its net after taxes for the first nine months of 1968, after allowing for sales of assets which made the accounts look better than they otherwise would have, was only $9 million as compared with $36 million for the same period the previous year.

Standard & Poor's Outlook, October 7, 1968, said the stock of General Dynamics was "a speculation in the success of this F-111 program" and that "the most important price determinant over the near term will be developments in this trouble-plagued F-111 program." *The Value Line* October 18 said, "Since our July review the ever sensitive stock market has sold these shares down to a two-year low." It said that if the problems of the F-111 were not soon resolved, it was "vulnerable to further procurement cutbacks." This was the bleak outlook two weeks before Nixon's speech at Fort Worth. McNamara saved General Dynamics in 1962. Nixon promised on November 2 to save it again.

III

McNamara's error on the TFX, which Nixon is now taking over, is worth close study because it shows the diminishing relationship between military procurement and genuine considerations of defense. It demonstrates the growing extent to which procurement is determined by military-bureaucratic and industrial considerations. The prime determinants were to save the largest company in the military-industrial complex financially and to appease the bomber generals, who simply will not admit that their expensive toys have grown obsolete. Billions which could do so much for poverty are squandered to maintain these favorite Pentagon clients on the military relief rolls in the lush style to which they have become accustomed.

General Dynamics, behind its glamorous front, is almost as much a creature of the government as the Air Force. In 1967 some 83 per cent of its sales were to the government. *Moody's* observes of the huge Fort Worth establishment, where Nixon gave so much solace to this peculiar form of free and private enterprise, that the "plant, including most machinery and equipment, is leased from the US government." The chief asset of General Dynamics seems to be its ability to wangle contracts out of the Pentagon.

The error in the TFX affair occurred on three levels, which have had varying degrees of attention, in inverse ratio to their importance. McNamara was wrong—so events seem to have proven—in giving the TFX contract to General Dynamics instead of Boeing, in insisting that the same basic plane be adopted for the diverse needs of the Air Force and Navy, and in surrendering to the pressure of the Air Force for a new bomber and the Navy for a new missile weapons system to meet a non-existent Soviet bomber threat just so they could go on with their expensive bomber game.

The first, the least important, got the most attention in earlier years since it promised Republican and conservative Democratic critics of the Kennedy and Johnson Administrations a scandal. But the shock of the Kennedy assassination cut short the McClellan committee investigation. A key figure was Roswell Gilpatric, a corporation lawyer who has done two tours of duty at the Pentagon, the first as Under Secretary of the Air Force in 1951-53 and again as Deputy Secretary of Defense in 1961-64, returning on each occasion to the famous Wall Street law firm of Cravath, Swaine and Moore with which he has been associated since 1931. Through Gilpatric's efforts the firm became counsel for General Dynamics in the late fifties and Gilpatric has combined his law work with activity in foreign and military policy in the Council on Foreign Relations and as a member of the Rockefeller Brothers Special Study project, which called for a sharp increase in military expenditures in January, 1958. In 1960 he was named as adviser on national security affairs by Kennedy during his campaign for the Presidency and after the election became Deputy Secretary of Defense, No. 2 man to McNamara at the Pentagon. There he played a major role in awarding the TFX contract.

General Dynamics has always been adept at having friends at court. It chose for its president in the fifties a former Secretary of the Army, Frank Pace. The $400-million losses of its Convair division during his incumbency make one wonder whether his chief qualification for the job was that he knew his way around Washington. Similarly it did not hurt General Dynamics to have its ex-counsel as No. 2 man in the Pentagon while it was fighting for the contract which could alone save it from receivership. Nor was General Dynamics hurt by the fact that Fred Korth, whom the Kennedy Administration had for some unfathomable reason made Secretary of the Navy, was a Fort Worth, Texas, banker, a past president of the Continental Bank which had loaned money to General Dynamics, "and that Korth had kept an active, though not a financial, interest in the activities of this bank"[5] while in public office.

Korth told the McClellan committee "that because of his peculiar position he had deliberately refrained from taking a directing hand in this decision [within the Navy] until the last possible moment."[6] But it was "the last possible moment" which counted. Three times the Pentagon's Source Selection Board found that Boeing's bid was better and cheaper than that of General Dynamics and three times the bids were sent back for fresh submissions by the two bidders and fresh reviews. On the fourth round, the military still held that Boeing was better but found at last that the General Dynamics bid was also acceptable.

It was at this last moment that the award was made to General Dynamics. The only document the McClellan committee investigators were able to find in the Pentagon in favor of that award, according to their testimony, was a five-page memorandum signed by McNamara, Korth, and Eugene Zuckert, then Secretary of the Air Force, but not—interestingly enough—by Gilpatric. Senator Curtis charged in his Senate speech, October 3, that some months after the contract was announced in November, 1962, "a team of experts was assembled in the Pentagon to review the designs. . . . The experts were directed to find strong points for General Dynamics and weak points for Boeing so the decision could be defended in Senate hearings."

During the McClellan committee hearings in 1963, Senator Ervin of North Carolina focused on another angle to this contract when he said to McNamara, "I would like to ask you whether or not there was any connection whatever between your selection of General Dynamics, and the fact that the Vice President of the United States happens to be a resident of the state in which that company has one of its principal, if not its principal office." The reference of course was to Lyndon Johnson, to Texas, and to Fort Worth. McNamara answered, "Absolutely not."[7] In the dissolute atmosphere of Washington there were few to believe such political virginity possible. When General Accounting Office investigators asked McNamara how he came to

[5] Robert J. Art, *The TFX Decision* (Boston: Little, Brown, 1968), p. 4.
[6] *Ibid.*, p. 5.
[7] *Ibid.*

override military judgment, "The Secretary said that, after finding the Air Force estimates inadequate for judging the cost implications of the two proposals [i.e., General Dynamics' and
Boeing's], he had made rough judgments of the kind he had made
for many years with the Ford Motor Company." The most
charitable comment is that the TFX, then, proved to be the Edsel
of his Pentagon years.

Under normal circumstances one would have expected all this
to be aired in the 1968 campaign. But the military-industrial complex plays both sides of the political fence, and the defense contractors are an easy source of campaign funds. Nixon not only
kept silent but pledged himself to the very same plane. The same
cynical charges made behind the scenes about the original TFX
contract will no doubt be made again about Nixon's reaffirma-
tion of it. The first point in favor of General Dynamics was and
is its financial weakness. Boeing, with a better record for engineering and on costs, is in good shape; half its business is commercial, a testimony to its reputation. Why let the weaker company
go down the drain? The TFX affair illustrates the survival of the
unfittest in the military corporate jungle.

The second point in favor of General Dynamics was and remains political. General Dynamics is in Texas, a swing State with
twenty-four electoral votes, and its biggest subcontractor on the
F-111, Grumman, is in New York with forty-five electoral votes.
Boeing would have produced the plane in Kansas with eight
votes, which go Republican anyway, and in the State of Washington with nine. Nixon's November 2 pledge shows that any
major new plane must show it can fly successfully through the
electoral college. Its aerodynamics must be designed for a maximum number of votes. Nixon's pre-election speech at Fort
Worth recalls two other comparable appearances there, one *opera
buffa*, one tragic. The former occurred on December 11, 1962, a
month after General Dynamics won the TFX contract, when
Johnson made a triumphant visit to the plant at Fort Worth and
was greeted by union members waving banners which said "LBJ
Saved The Day" and "We're Here to Say Thanks to LBJ."[8] The
other was the morning of November 22, 1963, a few hours before he was assassinated, when President Kennedy addressed a
rally in Fort Worth and paid tribute to the TFX as "the best
fighter system in the world."[9] For Johnson and Kennedy, as for

[8] *Fort Worth Star-Telegram*, December 12, 1962, quoted in McClellan
Committee hearings on the TFX, Part X, p. 2658.
[9] *Public Papers of the Presidents: John F. Kennedy 1963*, p. 887.

Nixon, in the TFX contract electioneering and defense were inextricably mingled.

A key word in the TFX controversy was "commonalty." McNamara wanted a plane which could be used by the Air Force and the Navy in common. With the cancellation of the contract for the Navy's version of the F-111, the battle for commonalty between the two services was lost. But Nixon's pledge on the F-111 shows that commonalty still exists in defense politics. For Republican as well as Democratic administrations, what is best for General Dynamics is best for the country.

IV

This mention of "commonalty" brings us to the other two misjudgments involved in the TFX decision. One was to try to build one plane for many diverse Air Force and Navy missions. The other was to counter a Soviet bomber threat which does not now exist and is unlikely ever to come into being. With these misjudgments[10] we come to technological details which must become part of public knowledge if we are to understand the expensive and nightmarish nonsense in which the arms race has engulfed us.

President-elect Nixon, as we have seen, pledged himself to "root out 'the whiz kid' approach" to national defense. As it happens the "whiz kids" were as opposed to the TFX as generals and admirals to the idea of trying to build a common plane for both services. "Pressure within the Defense Department for a single sophisticated multimission aircraft [using the new swing-wing design] came from the Office of Defense Research and Engineering which was headed in the early 1960's by Harold Brown, the present Secretary of the Air Force," *Congressional Quarterly* reported last February 16. "Although the concept was opposed by the young systems analysts that Defense Secretary McNamara had brought with him to the Pentagon, they were not then in a position to conduct a running battle with Brown. At the time the Office of Systems Analysis was subordinate to the Pentagon comptroller, which was one level below Brown." Nixon to the contrary, this mistake might not have been made if the "whiz kids" had had more influence.

McNamara had been trying to cut down duplication in supplies among the three services, a source of enormous waste, and

[10] I venture to speak so dogmatically not only because of what has happened this year to the F-111, but because among men at the Pentagon devoted to McNamara I have found no one who does not feel the TFX was a mistake.

he accomplished substantial savings in this field. His critics in Congress say privately that to an automobile man, accustomed to mounting various kinds of cars on much the same chassis, the idea of using the same "chassis" in military planes must have seemed a natural. Indeed to an outsider there seems to be little reason why the same plane should not be used by the various services for the same type of mission. Why—for example—can't the Air Force and the Navy use the same dogfighter?

The trouble in the case of the TFX or F-111 is that the Air Force and the Navy had such diverse missions to be performed by the common plane on which McNamara insisted. It is being built for a tactical fighter, a long-range strategic bomber, a reconnaissance plane, and—until the Navy contract was canceled—a new weapons system, a plane carrying a new type of missile.

The Navy wanted the plane to be light enough for a carrier but big enough to carry a special missile—the Phoenix—and a big load of radar equipment. Its naval mission would be to loiter hour after hour over the fleet to protect it from a nuclear supersonic bomber attack; the radar would enable the plane to detect an incoming plane and hit it with the missile far enough away so that the fleet would be safe from nuclear blast and radiation. The Air Force wanted the plane to be able to fulfill a very different mission. It was to be able to fly at supersonic speed under the radar defenses around the Soviet Union and then, after unloading its nuclear bombs on target, make altitude swiftly enough to elude not only enemy ack-ack or fighter planes but the effects of the nuclear blast it had set off. To fit one plane to two such diverse purposes would seem to require the ingenuity of a Rube Goldberg. This particular mistake has been thoroughly debated, since it serves intra-service animosity. There's nothing the Navy hates worse than losing a battle to the Air Force.

A second level of misjudgment, the most basic of all, has hardly been discussed at all, at least in public. Here one is led to question the good sense of both the Air Force and the Navy. The Navy is still as full of bomber admirals as the Air Force is of bomber generals. They started the bomber gap nonsense in the fifties and still suffer from the obsessions which the arms lobby exploits so skillfully. "In the early 1950's we were told the Russians were going to build thousands of supersonic bombers," Senator Symington commented ruefully last May during the Senate hearings on the 1969 defense budget. "They did not build any long-range bombers of that type."[11] Symington was himself once the captive and

[11] 1969 Senate Defense Appropriations Hearings, Part V, p. 2664.

spokesman of those inflated fears, as he was several years later of the "missile gap" campaign which he later helped to expose as fraudulent.

In the hearings last April on "The Status of US Strategic Power," which reflected the views and fears of those who favor a bigger arms budget, Chairman Stennis said of the present Soviet bomber fleet, "I have never looked upon these bombers as a serious threat to the US unless we just let our guard down completely. They are the same old bombers, the Bear and the Bison." These are the subsonic bombers whose appearance in Moscow in the fifties set off the bomber gap scare. The Russians just aren't spending money on long-range supersonic nuclear bombers when the same delivery job can be done so much more cheaply and quickly by missiles.

When Stennis's Preparedness Subcommittee of Senate Armed Services filed its report October 4 on the US Tactical Air Power Program, it said "The F-111B [i.e., the Navy version of the F-111 armed with the Phoenix missile—IFS] was designed primarily for fleet air defense against a Soviet supersonic bomber. But that threat is either limited or does not exist." Yet the Navy, having got rid of the F-111B, is planning its new VFX-1 to carry a Phoenix missile for use against the same non-existent supersonic Soviet bomber attack. The Navy insisted in the fiscal 1969 hearings that the Phoenix-armed plane "is the only system that provides the Navy with an acceptable level of Fleet Air Defense for the 1970-80 era, particularly for any missile threat against the fleet."[12]

This assumes that the Soviets will play the game our way and build the supersonic nuclear bombers the Phoenix is designed to counter. In chess, when one sees the other side concentrating his forces in one sector, one attacks in another. But our Joint Chiefs of Staff do not seem to play chess. *Congressional Quarterly*, which has good sources in the Pentagon, reported last May 3 that many Navy aviators were hostile to both the F-111B and its successor, the VFX-1 project, for a Phoenix-armed plane. It quoted a Pentagon source as saying the whole program was based on a false premise. It said Soviet doctrine envisioned the use of fighters, submarines, and missile-launching patrol boats instead of nuclear supersonic bombers for attacks on carriers and battleships. Obviously an attack would come where the other side can see we are least prepared. The Phoenix is likely to prove not only a waste

[12] *Ibid.*, Part IV, p. 1426.

of funds but an impediment to genuine defense by concentrating on a threat which does not exist now and is not likely to exist later.

V

The main Air Force mission for the F-111 is a reflection of the same bomber delusions, but on a larger scale. To see this in perspective one must step back and observe that we now have three major ways of destroying the Soviet Union. One is the ICBM, the intercontinental ballistic missile. The second is the submarine-launched nuclear missile, the Polaris. The third is the intercontinental bomber force of the Strategic Air Command. Any one of these three forces can itself deliver much more than the 400 megatons which McNamara estimates would destroy three-fourths of the Soviet Union's industrial capacity and 64 million people, or one-third its population.

Of the three mega-murder machines, the only one which can be stopped is the bomber fleet. It's an expensive luxury, a toy on which the bomber generals dote, and which the aircraft industry is only too happy to supply. High-flying bombers cannot get through the Soviet's radar and SAM (surface-to-air) missile defenses. So the F-111 is designed to duck low under Soviet radar defenses, drop nuclear bombs, and make a high fast getaway, all at supersonic speeds. The basic argument against the F-111 is that if we ever want to hit major targets in the Soviet Union, we would do so with missiles which can reach their targets in thirty minutes with fifteen-minute warning time instead of planes whose flight and warning time would be measured in hours. If we tried to use bombers first, they would only warn the enemy and provide plenty of time for retaliatory missile strikes against our cities. If these bombers were to be used for a second strike *after* a Russian attack on us, the bombers (if any were left) would arrive hours after the missiles, and there would be little if anything left to destroy anyway. The intercontinental bomber is a surplus and obsolete deterrent but $1 1/3 billions is allocated to the F-111 in the fiscal 1969 budget, much of it for these bombers.

But this is not the end of this expensive nonsense. The military always assumes that the enemy will do what we do, that anything *we* produce *they* will produce. This is sometimes but not always true. The geographical and strategic situation of the Soviet Union is not the same as that of the United States; this dictates differences in weapons systems. In addition—no small consideration—the country which is poorer and has fewer resources to waste will be more careful in its expenditures. But we always estimate that the enemy will spend as prodigally as we do. This is how the bomber and missile gap scares originated. So we are spending billions to "keep ahead" of Soviet bombers and bomber defenses. We are also assuming that the Soviets will be as silly as we are and also build a fleet of F-111's to "get under" our radar defenses. So Congress has already embarked on another multi-billion-dollar program of building new radar "fences" and new types of interceptor planes to deal with these hypothetical Soviet F-111's.

To make all this plausible, the Air Force does its best to hide from the Congress the true facts about the Soviet air force. Twice during the past year Senator Symington, who feels that the billions spent on this bomber are diverting funds which could more sensibly be spent on new fighter planes, has asked Pentagon witnesses for the numbers of the various Soviet bombers. "Do you believe," he asked Dr. John S. Foster, Jr., director of Defense Research and Development, "that the Soviet Union poses a serious bomber threat to the United States today?" The answer was "Yes, Senator Symington, I do." Symington replied incredulously, "The Soviets have not built a bomber for years, except the Blinder—and the latter's performance is not as good as the B-58 which we abandoned. In spite of that we now have to spend billions of dollars defending against bombers also."

He then asked Dr. Foster to supply the Appropriations Committee with the numbers of each type of Soviet bomber. The numbers were deleted by the censor.[13] But if one turns to McNamara's final statement in the same hearings[14] he gives the number of Soviet intercontinental bombers as 155 as compared with our 697. These Soviet bombers are mostly the old subsonic Bear and Bison bombers, neither of which could possibly duck under US radar defenses in the way the F-111 is supposed to duck under the Soviet Union's.

Even the report on *The Status of US Strategic Power* filed last September 27 by the Senate's Preparedness Subcommittee under Senator Stennis, which argues for larger arms expenditures, says, "There is no evidence that the Soviets are proceeding with the development of a new heavy bomber and, should they elect to develop one, it is probable we would see indications of the program 3 to 4 years before the aircraft becomes operational."

To counter this, the Air Force sophists have come up with a

[13] See p. 2362, 1969 Defense Department Budget Hearings, Part IV.
[14] *Ibid.*, Part V, p. 2718.

new argument. When Senator Symington asked Dr. Foster, as head of Pentagon research and development, why they were planning new types of bomber defense against non-existent types of Soviet planes, Dr. Foster replied, "discouragement of Soviet aspirations to develop a more advanced bomber."[15] But why spend billions to discourage the Soviets from building a bomber they show no signs of building anyway?

Another favorite reason often used by the Air Force may be found in Air Force Chief of Staff General McConnell's presentation to the Stennis hearings on strategic power last April. "A bomber force," the General said, "causes the Soviets to continue to develop bomber defenses rather than concentrating their expenditures just on missile defenses."[16] *So we waste money to make them waste money.* Though we are richer, this may be worse for us than them, because our planes are far more elaborate and expensive.

Since the Air Force thus admits that there is no sign as yet of a new supersonic Soviet bomber able to penetrate our existing defenses, why does it go on talking of a Soviet bomber "threat"? As usual, it turns out that this simple word has an unexpected meaning in the special language developed at the Pentagon. This prize item of military semantics may be found in the testimony of Air Force Secretary Brown to these same Stennis committee hearings. Dr. Brown was explaining to the committee that if Soviet anti-aircraft defenses were improved and we had to build in additional "penetration aids" to get past more efficient radar devices, we would have to build bigger bombs than we now have. "Otherwise," he said, "we will find ourselves carrying many penetration aids and comparatively few weapons." Dr. Brown went on to say there was "general agreement" at the Pentagon that such an advanced US bomber "probably will be needed at some time in the future" but just when would depend on "how fast and far the Soviet threat is likely to evolve." Then he explained, "By threat here we are principally talking about Soviet defenses against bombers."[17]

The threat, in other words, is not that they might be able successfully to attack us with their bombers but that they might build up their anti-bomber defenses to the point where we might not be able to attack them successfully with *our* bombers! It

[15] *Ibid.*, p. 2719.
[16] "Status of US Strategic Power," Preparedness Investigating Subcommittee of the Senate Committee on Armed Services. 90th Congress, 2nd Session, April 30, 1968, Part II, p. 169.
[17] *Ibid.*, p. 179.

would be only a short step from this to defining aggression as
the building of defenses to discourage an enemy attack.

The reductio ad absurdum is in a passage I found in the fiscal
1969 defense budget hearings before the House Appropriations
Committee. Mahon of Texas, the able chairman of the defense
subcommittee, was questioning Air Force officials about the Soviet bomber menace. Here is the colloquy which spills the whole
and final truth about this costly nightmare:

MR. MAHON: Officials of the Department of Defense have not indi-
    cated to this committee that they think the Soviets will go very
    strong on the manned bomber. They will rely principally on the
    ICBM. Is that right?
GENERAL MCCONNELL: [Air Force Chief of Staff]: That is the con-
    sensus.
MR. MAHON: The Air Force has a little different view?
GENERAL MCCONNELL: [Deleted by censor].
MR. MAHON: [Deleted by censor].
GENERAL MCCONNELL: [Deleted by censor].
MR. MAHON: How long have the Soviets had, Secretary [of the Air
    Force] Brown, to develop a follow-on[18] bomber?
SECRETARY BROWN: They have had ten years.
MR. MAHON: Have you seen any evidence?
SECRETARY BROWN: I see no evidence of it, Mr. Chairman. The Air
    Force view is at least as much a view that "they ought to have one"
    as it is "they will have one."[19]

Billions in contracts for new bombers and new bomber defense
are threatened should the Russians stubbornly persist in not building a new bomber force. In extremity perhaps Congress might
be persuaded to add the Soviet Union to our foreign aid clients
and give them an advanced bomber force to keep the US aircraft business strong and prosperous. Or General Dynamics and
the other big companies in the military-industrial complex might
pass the hat among themselves and buy Moscow a new bomber.
Should those old obsolete subsonic Bears and Bisons stop flying
altogether, it would be a catastrophe for Fort Worth, a form of
economic aggression in reverse. Ours—the rich man's strategy—
is to make the Russians waste their resources by wasting ours.
Theirs—the poor man's strategy—might be to strike a mortal
blow at the arms business here by cutting their own expenditures
to the minimum the balance of terror requires.

[18] Air Force lingo for a new bomber.
[19] House Appropriations Committee Hearings on the Fiscal 1969 Defense Budget, Executive Session, February 26, 1968, Part I. p. 751.

Military-Industrial Complexities

CHARLES WOLF, JR.

The Setting

I recently watched a television rerun of the movie, "Dr. Strange-love," and had a strong feeling that its caricatured portrayals of the military establishment and the defense intellectuals may fall on much more receptive eyes and ears now than they did when the movie was first released in 1964. What accounts for this change?

The simplest explanation, and certainly a good part of the truth, lies in the immense cost and small yield associated with Vietnam, as well as other episodes that have raised questions about the professional competence of the military—for example, the F-111B, nuclear carriers, and the transport of nerve gas across the country for disposal "somewhere" in the Atlantic Ocean. However, these are not the matters I want to dwell on now. What I'd like to ask instead is, what are the views people hold of the so-called military-industrial complex (MIC)? What allegations about the MIC now disturb people who would not have been disturbed, or would have been less disturbed, five years ago? (After all, the original Eisenhower phrase was enunciated in January 1961, although it acquired vogue only recently.) How much is truth and how much fantasy in these allegations?

Reprinted by permission of the RAND Corporation.

Any views expressed in this paper are those of the author. They should not be interpreted as reflecting the views of The RAND Corporation or the official opinion or policy of any of its governmental or private research sponsors.

I suppose the views that most people have about the military-industrial complex can be bracketed between those of Dean Acheson and David Shoup. Acheson's view is that the problem really doesn't exist, or is at most "marginal." General Shoup's view is that "the new American militarism" has an insidiously controlling grip at virtually all levels of our society, including local community affairs in which, he alleges, the performance-orientation of retired military officers gives them a decisive influence.

My own view, very briefly, is that the standard assertions about the so-called military-industrial complex do indeed point to a real problem; that the problem is neither accurately nor usefully conveyed by the sinister implications of General Shoup (one of his errors is to greatly overestimate the influence and unanimity of the military); that the MIC is much more heterogeneous and divided than is conventionally believed; that, contrary to the view commonly held, budgetary controls have been developed and applied in the defense sector much more than in other public sector activities that also involve enormous resource allocations; and that these "other industrial complexes" (or OICs as I shall call them) should be examined no less carefully than the MIC. This, in fact, could be one of the more useful byproducts of the current clamor about MICs.

In other words, there are many more complexities surrounding this matter than are usually acknowledged. These complexities are worth exploring, and that is what the rest of these comments will try to do.

Defense Resources, National "Needs" and the MIC

Let me summarize the main points I propose to make. First, I want to suggest a way of posing the problem of the military-industrial complex that is more precise and more useful than the way the issue is usually put. Second, I want to discuss this approach in terms of a model that can account for the widely divergent views of people like General Shoup and Dean Acheson. Third, I want to examine briefly the characteristics of the MIC that explain why different people attribute different values to some of the variables in the model. Then, finally, I want to consider the extent to which these characteristics are peculiar to the MIC, or also are to be found in the OICs.

To begin, then, let me suggest that a useful way of posing the problem of the military-industrial complex is to ask this question: "How much more defense do we buy than we 'need'?" To avoid misunderstanding at the outset, let me make two comments about the question. The first is that the word "need" has quotation marks around it; I might have used instead the words "can afford." I will make clear later what I mean by using either term. The second comment is that the question is not intended to offer a Hobson's choice, in the sense of "have you stopped beating your wife?" I am prepared to accept as an answer zero or negative, as well as positive, numbers.

Now let me turn to the simplified model that I mentioned as my second point. The answer to the question of the extent to which we buy defense above our "needs" depends on estimates concerning three variables. Put another way, the answer depends on whether one thinks that the national decision-making process tends to mis-estimate one or more of these variables. Each of the three is important; all of them are difficult to pin down.

The first variable concerns the *threat*, and whether the way the decision process actually works tends to bias the threat estimates. (Incidentally, one might maintain this view without imputing collusion or conspiracy to the military-industrial complex.) If one believes that the threat tends to be overestimated, the answer to my initial question is biased upward. With this belief, one is bound to argue that if the cardinal assumption presently underlying U.S. planning for general-purpose forces is to prepare for 2-plus simultaneous major contingencies, in fact a better assumption should be 1-plus simultaneous contingencies,[1] or something similar, instead.[2]

Lying behind this notion of the proper threat estimate are a number of basic premises and complex reasoning chains. For example, there is the premise one adopts about the interdependencies between the estimate itself, the decisions we make based on

[1] Ed. note: Since the time Wolf wrote this, the Administration has adopted the lower figure as a planning assumption.

[2] The *composition* of threat estimates is, of course, as important as their total size. For instance, the strategic threat may be overestimated while the conventional threat is, at the same time, underestimated. The result is not one good estimate, but two bad ones. Mis-estimates can take different forms—often by the same estimator. Thus, the U.S. military *both* overestimated and underestimated the Viet Cong: including tanks and anti-tank weaponry in the equipment of U.S. divisions in Vietnam reflected an error of the first type; the heavy casualties repeatedly incurred by U.S. troops on large-unit actions, due to booby traps and land mines, was a consequence of the second type of error.

the estimate, and the actions of others, both allies and adversaries. (Are these actions wholly or only partially compensating, or are they largely independent of our own actions? And over what time period does one or the other answer apply? Is the interaction stabilizing, or destabilizing?) What estimate is proper also depends on how willing one is to bear the risks of underestimating rather than overestimating.

In other words, the more one views the Soviet Union or the Chinese as implacably hostile (or simply disposed to exploit any opportunity for advantage against us or our allies), the higher one tends to assess the threat and the number of simultaneous contingencies we should be prepared for, and hence the greater the defense that we need. On the other hand, the more one views potential adversaries as behaving in compensatory ways—that is, responding to whatever we do in ways that will offset what we do—and the more one feels disposed to bear risks, the less the amount of defense that we need.

A second variable is the *social opportunity costs* associated with other public (as well as private) resource claims; that is, the benefits that are foregone in the other uses to which military resources would be put if they were not expended on defense. To the extent that people believe that military activities take resources away from other national purposes (especially those at home), and to the extent that they assess the other domestic needs as more compelling at the margin than national security needs, to this extent people feel that we buy more defense than we need, or can afford. In passing, let me make one point about the opportunity costs of foregone domestic programs. In principle, these costs depend on the *output* resulting from using resources for other purposes. When someone says that resources should, from the standpoint of national goals, be devoted to poverty rather than defense, they are implicitly saying something about the *consequences* of devoting more resources to the poverty problem. All too frequently, however, one stops with the foregone inputs, and avoids the critical question of what the output would be. The point is an important one that I won't stop to develop.

The third set of variables concerns the *efficiency of defense production*. In this case, we take as given the need or demand for military activities, derivable from the preceding variables. We then ask whether there are aspects of the MIC that tend to raise the cost of meeting that demand (in addition to the underestimate of opportunity costs)? That is, are there characteristics of the MIC that inflate the costs of producing defense services—

for example, in the weapons acquisition process, in the way we man and operate bases, perhaps in the way we tend to fight unconventional wars in a conventional manner, in the inertial momentum within the Services to maintain or expand budgets and procurement, and so on?

In other words, the first variable concerns whether, and to what extent, the Services, the Congress, defense industry, and the defense research community tend to inflate *demand* (in relation to other national needs); while the third variable is concerned with the effect of the MIC in inflating the cost of meeting any given demand. Underestimates of social opportunity costs can affect both demand and supply.

Characteristics of the MIC

Let me next turn to those characteristics of the MIC which people have in mind when they contend that some of these variables tend to be mis-estimated, and that consequently we tend to buy more defense than we need or can afford. They are the characteristics that give people more doubts about our military establishment than perhaps they have ever had before. Moreover, they are presumed to be either unique to the MIC, or to differ in substantial degree from those associated with OICs. What are these characteristics and how do they affect the variables of the model?

1. *Secrecy* is one such characteristic. Unavailability of information impedes independent judgment of both the gravity and uncertainty of the threat. The demand for defense is exaggerated, it is argued, because those with access to secret information are part of the military-industrial complex and so are biased on the side of higher threat estimates. On the supply side, the view is that unavailability of classified information protects inefficiency in the production and operation of forces and systems, and prevents careful comparison of the returns from defense with those from other public sector activities.

2. *The complexity of weapons systems* makes it additionally difficult for the outsider to judge whether a system is being produced or employed efficiently, or whether a proposed system is needed at all. More generally, questions relating to strategy and deployment, as well as to development and procurement of weapons systems themselves, are so complex, according to this argument, that public judgment of performance may be extremely difficult, if not impossible.

3. Supported by secrecy and complexity is the supposed *absence of countervailing forces* to oppose or control the MIC. The forces competent to judge, and to influence, the magnitude and composition of defense expenditures tend to be largely within the MIC itself. As a result, not only do threats get overestimated and production costs inflated, but the opportunity costs of non-defense uses of resources get inadequately represented as competing claimants for defense resources.

4. Related to the absence or weakness of countervailing forces is the contention that the MIC is riddled with *conflicts of interest*. Thus, so the argument runs, the military provides the rewards for defense industry and the so-called defense intellectuals, who then exercise pressure for larger defense budgets, in collaboration (though not necessarily collusion) with the Armed Services Committees in the Congress. Those who exercise a disproportionately large influence in determining demand are in (or at a later time acquire) a position also to benefit from higher costs in meeting that demand. Both demand and supply can be biased upward as a result.

5. The appeal which can be made to *patriotism* and *national tradition* is another characteristic that putatively strengthens the MIC's hand in overestimating threats, inflating production costs, and underestimating social opportunity costs. Consider the familiar cliché that we can "afford" whatever national security expenditures we "need," as a case in point; and the well-known axioms that "nothing is too good for our fighting men," that human life is of infinite value, and that the best weaponry is justifiable regardless of cost. All of these considerations, supported by nationalism and sustained by tradition, may also protect inefficiencies and inflate costs.

6. The *scale of defense spending* is a sixth relevant characteristic. Since the magnitudes already involved are so huge (nearly 9% of GNP), additions to them may be more easily obscured. And when major additions are made to defense expenditures in wartime, the urgency of the circumstances and the pace at which the additions occur are often so pressing and the amounts so large that, once again, circumspection and independent review go by the board. As examples, one might point to the $13 billion increase in the defense budget between 1965 and 1966 and the increases between 1965 and fiscal 1970 of $30 billion, largely though not exclusively as a result of Vietnam.

7. *Institutional rigidity* is advanced as a final perverse characteristic of the military that contributes to excessive defense ex-

penditures. The "go-by-the-manual" syndrome tends to impede innovation and adaptation. Again, Vietnam is a clear and recent example. The consequence for inefficiencies, and for an increased cost of providing given defense services, can be substantial.

I do not intend to make a detailed evaluation of the seven characteristics and of their implications for the answers to my initial question: How much more defense do we buy than we need? But let me suggest a few personal reactions.

While there is truth in some of the points, others seem to me to be distorted and misleading. Consider the question of secrecy. Anyone who invests a modest amount of time in reviewing the Secretary of Defense's annual posture statements has a great deal of readily accessible information on which to base independent judgments about strategy and weapons systems for meeting national security purposes. To some extent, security is, and should be, an impediment to full disclosure. There are certain aspects that must be protected. But the extent to which this restricts discussion is very exaggerated. Much of the relevant information on threats and systems, and on the uncertainties surrounding them, is available (as suggested by the recent public debate on the SS-9, the uncertainties connected with its warhead delivery characteristics, and so on). Nonetheless, I would agree that more information should be made available to raise the level of public understanding and discussion.[3] I also believe that the communications media, as well as other institutions, can do a far better job of presenting the available information than they have in the past. Still, in order to participate as an intelligent "consumer" in the continuing debate on defense expenditures that is already, fortunately, with us, a citizen does have to invest in a non-negligible amount of learning; an amount, however, which is perhaps not much greater than that required to be knowledgeable about the World Series or the stock market, but probably well in excess of that necessary to have a strong position on the MIC.

As to contentions about the *absence* of countervailing forces and the *prevalence* of conflicts of interest, these, too, seem to me grossly exaggerated. In fact, there are numerous and strong countervalences within the MIC. One minor example is that quite a number of individuals, who, to outsiders, would be identified as MIC members in good standing (including some present and past members of the Armed Services as well as The

---

[3] Incidentally, it is worth pointing out that secrecy can lead to underestimates, as well as overestimates, of threats. Consider the United Kingdom before World War II, or the United States before Pearl Harbor.

RAND Corporation, who have served in the Pentagon and the Budget Bureau), have been active in holding expenditures down, cutting out or deferring systems and procurement, and helping to structure better decision-making processes for using constrained resources. Indeed, it is indisputable that systems analysis, planning-programming-and-budgeting systems (PPB), and other means of analyzing costs in relation to effectiveness, have been much more extensively applied in the military sector than in any other public activity. Admittedly this record has experienced a setback by the Vietnam effort of the last four years, though it has not—in my judgment—been changed in any fundamental respect.

The MIC and OIC Compared

Finally, let me briefly compare the MIC with other industrial complexes, in terms of several of these characteristics. The basic point I want to make is that most of them are not unique to the MIC. They apply equally, or with greater force, to other complexes, especially health care and education—the two cases from which I will draw most of my examples.

As to *scale*, it's worth noting that the federal budget for the Department of Health, Education, and Welfare is over $60 billion in the current fiscal year. (Over $20 billion is for health and education.) If one adds state and local expenditures in health and education (another $40 billion), the total amount exceeds the defense budget. The health care industry alone (public and private, including hospital, physician, and other medical services) runs to annual outlays of about $50 billion, of which more than 30 per cent is public expenditure. The education industry entails annual outlays of about $60 billion, three-quarters of which is public expenditure. In their extensive interactions with the public sector at all levels—federal, state, and municipal—both of these complex industries are highly organized, politicized, and influential. While their efforts are not as centralized at the federal level (particularly in the case of education) as are those of the MIC, this difference entails disadvantages, as well as advantages, from the standpoint of public awareness and control.

Consider next the point about *institutional rigidity* in the military tending to inflate costs through inefficiency. By way of comparison, the educational system has always operated so as to prevent or impede differentiation of teachers' salaries according to market value. Thus, the costs of getting better mathematics and science teachers in high school are enormously inflated, because salary levels that would enable the schools to compete for these skills have to be extended to teachers of physical education, home economics, and history as well. More particularly, this costly institutional rigidity results from the inertia of school administrators, as well as the political power of teachers' unions.

Or consider the effect of institutional inertia on the introduction of new technology. Here the education industry is at the opposite pole from the military services: technological innovations (such as computer-assisted instruction, or automated record-keeping and information retrieval systems) have been painfully slow in developing, in sharp contrast to the military services, which sometimes latch onto the newest technology, almost regardless of its effectiveness. In both cases the effect is increased costs. Moreover, this institutional malpractice cannot be extenuated in education by one of the serious impediments to efficiency in the military: the fact that fully reliable testing procedures for new systems can only be provided in wartime.

Now consider the notion I discussed in connection with the MIC, that "nothing is too good for our men," and that life has infinite value. In the health industry, conventional wisdom tends to justify increased costs in much the same way that inefficiencies are protected in defense matters. The same umbrella over inefficiency that has been provided by appeals to patriotism in national security matters is furnished in health and education by appeal to national pride. Both fields are such sacred cows, with the purposes they serve so highly valued, that even raising the question of efficiency may be regarded as crass and unfeeling. As a barrier to innovation in health care, the institutional rigidity of the American Medical Association is no less a force to be reckoned with (for example, in its opposition to large-scale expansion of group practice, prepaid comprehensive medical care programs like the Kaiser Foundation, or the substitution of para-medical for medical personnel), than is the professional military in its insistence that war be played by the (last) book, almost irrespective of changed circumstances, as in Vietnam.

When one looks for *countervailing forces*, it is hard to find them in health care or in education. Opponents of the AMA and the teachers' unions, with the knowledge and organization to argue effectively for cost-reductions, and for institutional and technological innovation, are rare and short-lived—in Congress or among the public generally.

When it comes to analytical countervalences, such as PPB and systems analysis, there has been nothing in health care and education approaching their application to the defense sector. Without discounting the technical difficulties involved in such new applications (and without exaggerating the effects already obtained in defense), political pressures in opposition to the application of these techniques for relating costs to effectiveness have been decisively stronger in these fields than in the military. I am not for a moment ignoring the difficulties connected with the measurement of effectiveness (as well as costs) in both of these industries. My point is just that non-analytic obstacles to applying improved techniques of budget control and resource management have been and are much more severe in health and education than in defense.

Concerning *conflict-of-interest* problems within the MIC (for example, in connection with the 2,000 retired military officers who are employed in executive positions in defense industry), one should note the existence of a similar problem in the health-care industry. For example, the National Institutes of Health have often been hard pressed to find panel members to decide on research allocations in a particular field who would not themselves be in a position to benefit, or to have their institutions, students or colleagues benefit, from such allocations. Paneling does in fact often come close to conflicts of interest, with attempts made to relieve the problem by such unsatisfactory devices as having a panel member leave the room when a grant for his institution is considered, or using foreign panel members.

Concluding Remarks

The main points can be summarized briefly:

1. Stripped of the heated and often obscure words that surround the subject, the problem of the MIC can be approached usefully by asking whether and to what extent we buy more defense than we "need";

2. If we break down this question into manageable parts, we can then look at the various factors that influence the demand for, and the costs of, defense services;

3. We can next consider the extent to which certain charac-

teristics of the military-industrial complex make for mis-estimates in these areas; they sometimes do.

4. When we look even superficially at these characteristics, we find that relationships between the military, the Congress, defense industry, and the research community can indeed bias resource allocations, but that this defect is not unique to the MIC. For example, most of the characteristics apply at least as strongly in the health and education industries, with similarly perverse effects on the use of public resources.

One of the numerous complexities about the MIC is that it is surely not the sole offender, nor probably the most egregious.

Making Defense
Defensible

Evaluating and controlling military expenditures have become central concerns of American political life. High levels of defense spending are often laid to a quasi-conspiratorial "military-industrial complex," and the consequences of militarization are alleged to be economic waste, neglect of social priorities, and distortion of the political system. Yet discussion of a "military-industrial complex" is a symptom rather than a diagnosis. Very little solid information exists, and in any case there is no reason to think that the causes or consequences of all kinds of military spending are the same. If we are to control military spending so as to avoid excesses, yet to defend as much armed forces procurement as is necessary for our security, we must consider the matter with careful concern for objectivity, discrimination, and evidence. Some recent research on these matters has been completed, and the results do illuminate certain aspects of the problem. I shall summarize that research here, without all the difficult methodological and data discussion needed to support my statements. For details I refer readers to my new book, *What Price Vigilance? The Burdens of National Defense* [Yale U. P., 1970].

Military expenditures in the United States are now high by American standards. For the last twenty-five years they have regularly taken a greater share of the nation's produce than at any time in its history, other than in periods of all-out war. Since the Korean War the military budget has always been above 7 per cent of the country's G.N.P., with at least two and a half million men under arms. We may regard this as a normal state

Reprinted by permission of the author and the *Virginia Quarterly Review*.

of affairs, but it is not. Before 1939 the peacetime military budget was rarely more than 1 per cent of G.N.P., and in the late 1920's and 1930's the armed forces included only about a quarter of a million men. Our country had a tradition of close scrutiny of military budgets and suspicion of a peacetime army that is very different from the latitude given the armed forces during the cold war. The military effort also is high by international standards. In both defense expenditures as a proportion of G.N.P. and military manpower as a percentage of working-age males, the United States ranks, with Russia, among the most "militarized" of the world's nations. No American under fifty can recall a time in his adult life when our armed forces were small.

Yet during the past two and a half decades there has been, until recently, extremely little questioning of, let alone opposition to, the maintenance of a large military force by the United States. In a rich and expanding economy the burdens seemed tolerable, even demanded by the international situation. Presidential candidates campaigned against missile gaps; Congressmen almost never cut proposed military budgets, and indeed often increased them; in opinion surveys a large majority of the populace consistently expressed the view that the defense budget was either about right or too low.

The standard explanations are obvious enough: cold war, an arms race forced upon us by the Russians, and the need to defend weaker nations of the free world. Yet in our toleration of large armed forces as at worst a necessary evil we lost sight of some salient facts. One of the most intriguing is a standard pattern of wartime expansion and only partial postwar contraction of the military. Over the past century, the proportion of the budget devoted to military expenditures has never, after any war, returned to the prewar level. The figures on absolute numbers of military personnel are especially revealing. The Spanish-American War, World War I, World War II, and the Korean War each produced a virtual and permanent doubling of the armed forces over the size characteristic of the preceding years. It is not enough to invoke the image of American global responsibilities after each war. While that explanation surely has some truth, Parkinson's Law also comes to mind. So too does an image of a political system where each war weakened the restraints on the activities of military men and their civilian allies.

We are in an arms race with the Soviet Union, in the sense that many kinds of military procurements by one side demand some response by the other. But the race can be carried on at high or low levels of expenditure. A willingness to accept parity, or even inferiority, results in a much more limited set of inter-actions than does an insistence on predominance. So too does a readiness to accept a fairly wide margin of error in intelligence estimates in place of a rule always, when in doubt, to err on the side of exaggerating rather than underestimating the other side's capabilities and aggressiveness. Thus even the arms race explana-tion requires attention to the prevalent images and expectations of domestic politics. For instance, it is widely assumed that former President Johnson's 1968 decision to proceed with his Sentinel ABM system was to protect himself from right-wing political critics who were already unhappy about lack of prog-ress in Vietnam—not out of any great sense of need for the system to protect the national security. During the 1969 debate on ABM the critics argued that if the system were once begun, even on a small scale, it would set off Russian counter-measures that in turn would demand further American expenditures, and so on in an upward spiral. By that logic, the arms race would force both us and the Russians into basically unwanted procure-ments—but only because of an initial erroneous and avoidable step by the United States. Hence American domestic politics would greatly influence whether the arms race proceeded at a sprint or a creep.

Without minimizing the arms race pressures, and without ignoring the blindness of Russian domestic politics, we must look more closely at the confluence of interests among elements of the military, the civilian defense bureaucracy, Congress, and industry. The armed services play bureaucratic politics in com-peting with one another for resources. During the 1950's the Navy sought a strategic war capability, first in aircraft carriers and later in missile-carrying submarines, to avoid being sub-merged by the Air Force. Likewise, Army personnel sought an anti-missile system, and within the Air Force advocates of manned bombers fought to keep the Air Force from being grounded, for strategic war purposes, in unglamorous missile silos deep below the western plains. Many industrial firms have become heavily dependent on Defense Department orders. Their production methods are geared to the manufacture of a few units of hardware, each very expensive and requiring very high per-formance reliability. A Poseidon missile or submarine is most unlike the typical output of civilian-oriented industry, not only in its purposes but in its mode of production. Expense often is much less important than performance; the deliberate decision not to worry much about cost and to employ very high-quality components is quite different from the mass production of automobiles that made Detroit famous. The development of modern weapons carries great uncertainties and risks to the firm, requiring special contractual arrangements as compensation. For all these reasons, defense contractors are often unenthusiastic about converting to civilian production, and make great efforts to keep their defense business by coming up with new weapons.

Finally, Congressmen too develop interests in maintaining the flow of defense contracts to their constituents, and in retaining military bases in their districts. The consequence is an alliance among men from very different points in public and private life, each of whom supports military procurement programs in the classic tradition of American politics concerning public expenditure. Businessmen support Congressmen's electoral campaigns; Congressmen roll logs for one another; and military and civilians in the bureaucracy seek and exchange favors with legislators and industrialists.

This is *not* to imply there is great waste in military procurement programs, or that political activities and favor-swapping in the military realm are dishonest or illegal. I would guess that the level of probity is at least as high as in the realm of purely civilian public expenditures. Nor is it surprising or censurable that the Armed Services and their suppliers should undertake political activities. Virtually all firms which sell to the government establish similar relationships, in other countries as well as in the United States. That the military should take steps to protect itself in the bureaucratic and political arena is entirely to be expected, as is the willingness of civilian enterprises to assist.

What *is* disconcerting, however, is the size of the American military establishment, and thus the enormous impact unavoidably made whenever generals, admirals, Congressmen, and businessmen combine to promote multi-billion dollar expenditures. The Defense Department's annual budget is larger than the total G.N.P. of all but six or seven of the world's countries. Its size is particularly disconcerting in light of the demonstrated staying power of the military establishment; that is, its ability to retain, after war, much of its wartime expansion. We cannot help but ask whether our armed forces are bigger than they need to be. If so, then what are the costs to the rest of the social and economic system? Among the often alleged offenses of defense are these:

   1. There is a symbiotic relationship between spending and

politics; for instance, Congressmen who support military expenditures benefit disproportionately from them in their constituencies. More important, this relationship has wider effects on the political system as military spending provides political support for legislators with "hard-line" positions across a spectrum of military and foreign policy issues, and some domestic matters as well.

2. The United States has failed, perhaps less for a lack of effort on its own part than from the "selfishness" of its allies, to use its system of military alliances as a means of reducing the American defense burden.

3. Military spending tends to come largely at the expense not of private consumption, but of investment and public expenditures for social needs such as health and education, thus endangering the long-run welfare of the country.

Here is some of the evidence on those questions.

II

The power of the purse has for centuries been the primary legislative instrument for restraining an extravagant or self-serving executive. In the United States, Congress must authorize and fund all Defense Department expenditures, yet its success, or even interest, in cutting military budgets has been unimpressive. The Defense budget is rarely scrutinized to evaluate many individual items; for every debate on ABM or manned bombers, hundreds of major programs are passed as proposed by the executive.

If items really were examined on their *individual* merits, we should see shifting patterns of alignment among Congressmen on defense issues. Some legislators would approve of bombers and others prefer missiles; still others would support needs of the Navy, or the Army, against any Air Force requests. But while each service and major weapons program does have its legislative champions, for the great majority of lawmakers the military effort is seen as a whole. A close study of the Senate shows that in the 90th Congress (1967–68) the alignments on virtually all Defense appropriation and authorization measures were very much alike, appearing as aspects of a more general attitude toward defense spending. Senators who voted to limit military research and development also voted, almost without exception, against the ABM in the preliminary skirmish over that system. Similarly, those who favored allocating $280,000 to a Charleston, South Carolina, Air Force base also virtually always favored the ABM.

One possible explanation for this behavior is logrolling; one Senator gets funds for the military base in his state while another, in exchange for his support, gets missile-manufacturing contracts for the aerospace firm in his constituency. Surely this happens. Another explanation, however, is that Senators have general convictions about the merits or perils of defense spending. Each may have a different cut-off point above which he would not approve more expenditures, but on either side of that point he implicitly ranks controversial spending measures in an order of desirability that agrees generally with the rankings of other legislators. The roots of these general convictions may lie in ideology, patriotism, intellectual evaluation, or partisan advantage.

In light of this second explanation, another and not entirely expected result is important: Senators' alignments on defense expenditure measures are very closely related to their alignments on a much wider spectrum of issues regarding defense and East-West relations. In the 90th Congress this broad spectrum included votes on the Vietnam War, money for the Arms Control and Disarmament Agency, various reforms in the Draft, aid to communist countries, and conditions for ratifying the Consular Convention with the Soviet Union. These matters, unlike many defense appropriations measures, have little to do with direct economic gains for anyone's constituents; they are not subject to logrolling in the same way as are military expenditures. Thus the logrolling explanation, while doubtless partly correct, is incomplete. More general convictions are operating. The positions of Senators are fairly clear to anyone who has followed legislative debates in the past couple of years. The extreme conservatives or hawks are composed almost exclusively of Republicans and southern Democrats; the liberals or doves are mostly northern Democrats, though Senators Fulbright, Yarborough, and Hatfield are prominent.

This alignment, it must be noted, is not the same as those that appear for gun control, Space Agency appropriations, or foreign military assistance. These other issues show lineups of Senators that only moderately resemble the major defense and foreign policy alignment. Among the notable exceptions are Senator Dodd, most hawkish of northern Democrats, who has worked for moderate gun control legislation, and Senators Yarborough and Edward Kennedy who, though doves, pretty consistently championed NASA activities. A coalition of doves and fiscal conservatives has set itself against heavy arms shipments to underdeveloped countries. Thus the image of the "military-industrial complex" uniformly promoting weapons and aerospace expenditures is oversimplified. Rather, some procurement programs are outside the normal concerns of the preparedness advocates, who nonetheless give consistently "conservative" treatment to a variety of related but not strictly defense issues of foreign policy.

A time-perspective extending back to the first years of the Kennedy Administration adds the following information: There is substantial continuity over time on the general cluster of defense and East-West relations matters. Senators who were proponents of heavy military spending and a hard line in the 90th Congress behaved much the same way six years earlier. But in the 87th Congress the defense expenditure issue was largely latent. Few military authorization or appropriation measures came to roll-call votes; if they did, the overwhelming majority of the Senate always favored them. Only more recently have military expenditures become controversial issues on which a large number of legislators were ready to take a critical stance. It may be no coincidence that in December, 1968, for the first time since the beginning of the cold war, the Gallup poll found a majority who thought the nation was spending too much for defense. Current partisan positions on defense have become reversed since the 1950's. When the Eisenhower Administration was trying to hold down the defense budget, many Democratic Congressmen found "preparedness" a good vote-getting issue, and the Democrats as a group were more pro-defense than were Republicans. This was as true of northern Democrats as of their southern colleagues.

"Hawkishness" and "dovishness" are related to the distribution of some kinds of military spending around the country. Regardless of a Senator's party affiliation or whether he comes from a northern or a southern state, the greater the impact of Department of Defense spending on his state's labor force, the greater is the likelihood that he adopts a hard-line or hawkish stance in Congress. For example, six of the twenty Senators from the ten states which derived the largest proportion of their total payroll from direct Department of Defense employment (in descending order of defense dependence: Alaska, Hawaii, Virginia, Utah, Georgia, New Mexico, South Carolina, Oklahoma, Colorado, Kentucky) were among the most hawkish one-fifth of the Senate. These same states produced only two members of the most dovish fifth of the Senate.

Certainly these two doves—Senator Moss of Utah and the very dovish former Senator Gruening from the very defense-dependent state of Alaska—prove that there can be exceptions to the general rule. Furthermore, it is impossible to establish any clear causal relationship even for those cases where the principle does hold. It is not obvious whether defense-dependence produces among voters a hard-line foreign policy attitude that is reflected by their legislative representatives, or whether hard-line Senators seek and find rewards in the form of defense installations for their districts. Probably some of both occur. In any case, it is rare to find an outspoken critic of recent American foreign policy from a state where the military employment impact is high. Even the most prominent instance, Senator Gruening, proved not to be such an exception. He was one of only three incumbent Democratic Senators not to be re-elected in 1968, perhaps because he had been more independent than his constituents would tolerate. Defense expenditures for military installations go to support and reinforce, if not actually to promote, a set of hawkish and strongly anti-communist postures in American political life. This support may well be inadvertent rather than deliberate, but it does exist. In turn, the Pentagon is supported, and its expenditures promoted, by those voters and political figures.

More than just military spending levels is at stake. Many of the defense-related issues on which the doves or liberals were defeated in the 90th Congress concerned highly controversial matters, especially regarding military expenditures. There they were opposed by a broad coalition of conservatives and moderates. But many of the votes which were just won by liberals, or on which they were narrowly defeated, were not at all extreme, at least by this liberal's view: in 1967–68 the Consular Convention with the Soviet Union; a 3 per cent reduction in military procurement; a $20 million authorization for the Arms Control and Disarmament Agency; withholding funds for the ABM until its cost and practicality were known; reform of Selective Service procedures. These were mild measures, offering minor restrictions on the military establishment or very tentative steps toward better East-West relations. The same applies to some of the 87th Congress issues; for example, support for the United Nations Congo operation, and authority for the Arms Control and Disarmament Agency to do research on disarmament! Some such steps and more, reciprocated by the communists to be sure, will have to be taken if the cold war is ever to end.

On the other hand, it is just as important to know that there seems to be no similar relation between hawkishness and a state's proportionate income from Defense Department contract awards. This is contrary to some of the most common ideas about American politics, and demands notice just as does the above finding. Some very slight association between foreign policy position and contract dependence exists, but its slightness is more striking than the fact of its existence. A variety of possible explanations can be offered. Perhaps because they are relatively enduring, military bases contributing direct employment to the state's economy exert a political influence on Capitol Hill that here-today, gone-tomorrow government contracts cannot. Direct hire by the Defense Department may more strongly mold the attitudes of workers, both military and civilian, than does employment for a firm which in turn sells its products to the Pentagon. Other possible explanations concern the likelihood that defense weapons and equipment contractors, unlike local suppliers of military bases, try to exert political influence on key Senators from other states as well as their own. And there is some question about the reliability of the publicly available data on the distribution of defense contracts—more accurate data might show a relationship that now eludes us.

Nevertheless, the difference between the political effect of direct employment and spending on contracts is clear. If there is a "military-industrial complex," the industrial part, composed of the big manufacturing establishments, does not itself reinforce the hawkish or uncompromisingly anti-communist forces in this country in any strong, simple, or direct way. That is not to say that military spending on particular weapons systems is not promoted by industry. Certainly Senators with defense industries at home do look out for them. California, Colorado, and Washington represent three of the centers of the aerospace industry; on twenty specifically aerospace questions in the 90th Congress their Senators show exactly one vote (out of 120 possible) against the aerospace industry. But the political effect of that spending is not the same as that of money spent to maintain a large army of many men, with bases scattered freely around the country. Perhaps this is one argument, to be weighed against others, for abandoning Selective Service in favor of a smaller, even if heavily automated, volunteer army.

III

United States military and political spokesmen have long complained that their allies provide less than a fair-share contribu-

tion to the joint defense of the West. This lament has focused
primarily on the NATO allies where, despite their long-accom-
plished economic recovery, the European states spend very
much less of their national income for defense than does the
United States. In most cases, in fact, the Europeans' defense share
of G.N.P. is half or less than America's. It appears that our allies
are shirking their burdens by relying excessively on an American
nuclear deterrent to which they do not contribute. Senator Mans-
field and other Congressional leaders have recently been especially strong in their insistence that Europeans pick up a larger
share of the common costs if the United States is to maintain its
current force strength in Europe.

But the difficulty is not specific to NATO, nor even to American alliances. For America it stems from a fundamental con-
tradiction between two aims of postwar alliance policy. The
United States sponsored NATO to achieve two goals. One, and
probably the primary, was to protect the weak states by extending over them the umbrella of America's nuclear deterrent. The
other was to augment American military strength with that of
the European allies, and ultimately to reduce the burden of our
commitments by creating strong local military capabilities in
the path of any Soviet advance. Yet to the degree the former
succeeds the latter is endangered. So long as the alliance organization is voluntary and the big power cannot coerce the smaller
ones to build their armies, the smaller states are likely to regard
the big country's armed forces as a substitute for their own.
They will feel able to relax their own efforts because they have
obtained great-power protection, especially if the external threat
of attack is not considered very grave. Their effort will be less
the greater is their confidence in the big power's guarantee.
Moreover, the greater the size disparity between small powers
and a big one, the less military effort the smaller ones make as
a proportion of their income. This last rule varies where a
small power is especially exposed to an external threat (for
instance, Turkey) or where its military forces are used for
some purpose other than defense against the common enemy
(for example, Portugal with its colonial difficulties). Nevertheless, the general principal holds, that the smaller the nation
relative to its big-power guarantor, the fewer sacrifices it will
make to build a military force.

The same general pattern is in evidence in SEATO, CENTO,
and the Rio Pact. Even in Eastern Europe, the Soviet Union
has recently encountered the same dilemma. The Warsaw Pact

is certainly no voluntary organization in the sense that members can enter or leave it at will, but in recent years at least the member states do seem to have developed considerable ability to determine for themselves what their levels of military effort will be. In the 1950's the Soviets were able to extract a fairly uniform military share of G.N.P. from each of them, but from the middle 1960's onward the East Europeans' proportionate contributions took on much the same shape as those of the NATO allies. All of them devote a much smaller share of G.N.P. to military ends than does the Soviet Union, and the defense proportion of G.N.P. varies closely with the size of the country. In 1967 Poland and Czechoslovakia, the second and fourth largest nations in the Warsaw Pact, had the largest military-to-G.N.P. ratios behind Russia; and Bulgaria and Hungary, the smallest members, had the lowest defense ratios. East Germany, the third largest state, was only about average, since for obvious reasons the Russians have not encouraged the Ulbricht régime to build too large an army. Thus the Soviets, like the Americans, find that they have taken on alliance responsibilities and commitments, but without the accretion to their own military strength that they initially expected or were able to extract in the Stalinist days. Now they still can keep Rumania, for example, from leaving the Pact, but cannot coerce Bucharest into making much of a military effort.

This phenomenon, where the small in a sense "exploit" the great by bearing less than what the great might consider a "fair share" of a common burden, is widely recognized by economists as an aspect of the theory of collective goods. For our purposes, however, the point is not that there is a label for the phenomenon, but that there is so much strong evidence for this relationship in international military pacts. Actually, of all the important multilateral alliances in the world the only one where this relationship does not hold at all is in the Arab League—an instance where there is very little common effort and where the Egyptians, as the largest power, are still so weak as to be manifestly unable to extend any sort of deterrent umbrella over the other members.

The phenomenon tells us enough about what one can reasonably expect from various kinds of alliances to offer much guidance to Americans. In forming or keeping an alliance with other states and providing them with deterrence, a great power must expect that its allies will spend less on defense than they would do in the absence of the protective alliance. If the American goal is to bring other nations more effectively under its deterrent shield, then the United States should so judge the alliance's success. While it may still make every reasonable effort to persuade allies to do more for themselves, it would be short-sighted to slip into acrimony. Nor, from disgust, should it do anything to weaken its protective guarantee so long as it still places great value on preserving the independence and security of its allies. Perhaps paradoxically, it should actually be a bit worried when an ally persists in very heavy military expenditures of its own, as that may be a signal that the ally really does not have full confidence in the guarantee. American policy makers must realize that efforts to reduce American defense spending by shifting major burdens to our current allies are most unlikely to succeed. Rather, each alliance must be evaluated in terms of the benefits it brings to us relative to the cost incurred by accepting a commitment to protect others. If the latter is too high, we will probably be able to cut our defense expenditures more by dropping the alliance than by trying to extract greater effort from the smaller state while the alliance is still in effect.

IV

There is a widespread myth in America that defense spending, even if higher than strictly necessary for national security, is not really a waste because the alternative use for resources would be equally frivolous civilian spending. That is, if the money were not going for weapons it would be turned back to the taxpayers for personal consumption, not used in the public sector for education, pollution control, urban development, or public health programs. If that were true, then the real price of defense would only be in the loss of some luxuries for middle- and upper-class America, and we might well prefer always to err on the side of too much defense spending rather than too little. Certainly congressional behavior with the 1969 tax reform and tax reduction bill did little to ease the impression that among legislators tax cuts had higher priority than social needs.

The truth, however, differs substantially from the myth. When we look at patterns of spending over the past thirty years rather than just the most striking acts of recent congressional behavior, it is clear that public spending for domestic needs is in large part the real alternative to military expenditures. In periods of rising defense needs in the United States, the resources to provide military goods have had to be extracted from various parts of the civilian economy. The mirror-image of an increase in defense spending tells us what happens when military expenditures are reduced. Typically, the alternative uses for a defense dollar have been as follows: 42 cents from personal consumption, 29 cents from fixed capital formation (investment), 10 cents from exports, 5 cents from Federal Government civilian programs, and 13 cents from state and local governments' activities. Of course the transfer was not always direct or entirely the result of conscious choice, and was effected by a mixture of means. On the defense upswing, for instance, there might be overt controls (as on prices and resource allocation during World War II and the Korean War), taxes, or elements of laissez-faire distribution from the pressures of inflation induced by government deficit spending. But by looking at what went down when defense went up, or vice versa, we get a pretty good idea of what sectors of the civilian system did in fact pay the bill or, on the downswings, reap the benefits.

Private consumption has indeed been the largest alternative use of defense money, at 42 cents to the dollar. Personal consumption, however, always represents the largest segment of the economy anyway, usually almost two-thirds of the G.N.P. except in times of all-out war. Fixed investment is normally only about a fifth of that amount. Thus the absolute dollar shares are very deceptive if one wants to know what parts of the civilian economy bear *proportionately* heavy costs from defense. For that we must take a model of the "average" American economy for the past thirty years and ask from where, on the basis of what actually did happen in a number of military ups and downs, would a hypothetical $25 billion defense increase come. On that picture, private consumption would have been reduced by an amount equal to about 4 per cent of itself—but fixed investment would have declined by 14 per cent of its original level. Expenditures of the Federal Government and state and local governments also would have suffered heavily, going down by 16 per cent and almost 11 per cent respectively.

Therefore investment and government civil spending are major casualties of high levels of defense expenditures. So too is the balance of payments. The Vietnam War has imposed direct foreign exchange costs to maintain troops in Southeast Asia. It has also imposed indirect costs, heavier ones. Exports have been hampered by the high level of demand, which diverts many products away from foreign markets. From the other side of the coin, imports have been boosted to meet internal demand and because the inflation has made some foreign goods cheaper

than those produced here. By my calculations, which are if anything conservative by comparison with those of many economists, the direct and indirect effects of the war account for very
roughly three-quarters of the American balance of payments
deficit in 1967.

The trade-off between defense spending and particular kinds
of public expenditures over the past thirty years can also be
identified. Typically the proportionate change in spending for
public education has been approximately the same as that for
fixed capital formation, and for health and hospitals only slightly
less—still about three times the relative effect on private consumption. In both cases federal spending has been proportionately harder hit than has that of state and local agencies, as
is not surprising since it is the federal budget that must immediately make room for an increased defense share.

Over the long run, the effects of this defense trade-off cannot
help but be very great. The implication of past patterns is that
if a cut could be achieved in the military budget, both fixed
capital formation and social investments in health and education
would benefit significantly. Or the reverse, the inability to cut
defense spending deprives the nation of many of the long-term
underpinnings of national strength. The economy's future resources and power base are damaged much more severely than
is current indulgence. According to some rough estimates, the
marginal productivity of capital in the United States is between
20 and 25 per cent; that is, an additional dollar of investment
in any single year will produce 20 to 25 cents of additional production in perpetuity. Hence an extra dollar for defense in any
one year has, on the average, reduced investment by 29 cents,
and therefore the level of output in the economy has been permanently diminished by on the order of 6 or 7 cents per year.
Similarly, one authority has estimated that what was done to
strengthen education earlier in this century accounted for nearly
half of the United States per capita income growth between 1929
and 1957. Again, the implication is that where needs to build a
better-educated citizenry have been left unmet, the long-term
prosperity of the economy suffers seriously.

It is true that public spending on education has been given
high priority in the past two decades, as it is true that public
expenditures for health also have increased as a proportion of
the national income. The absolute dollar figures or shares of
G.N.P. are nevertheless very deceptive, because they hide the
fact that the price level of health and educational services has

risen much faster than the general price level of the economy. If expenditures are corrected for the especially rapid inflation in these areas, the relative gain for education becomes rather modest. And health costs have been the fastest-rising item in the American cost of living index, as anyone who has recently paid a hospital bill knows. Making the necessary price corrections there shows that the real share of public health expenditures in the national income actually *fell* very slightly between 1950 and the end of the 1960's. Some of this may be attributable to defense needs.

Certainly, there are important benefits, even in the civilian sector, from defense spending. The various spin-offs, and in some cases actual defense stimulation of certain kinds of public civil spending (for example, education after Sputnik) must not be ignored. Yet a careful evaluation points unavoidably to the conclusion that defense spending, with spin-offs, is hardly the most efficient way to achieve civilian benefits. Medical research still is more likely to produce medical breakthroughs than is weapons research, though occasionally the latter does help. Defense spending does hamper civil needs, and ultimately will leave us with a poorer, more ignorant, and less healthy population than if the military spending had not been thought necessary.

Past trade-offs between defense and civilian needs indicate what some of the opportunity costs of military spending have been; what has, intentionally or not, been given up. Some of the losses have been in consumer frivolities; many have been more damaging if not so immediately painful. Perhaps many or most of them were unavoidable, to meet pressing defense demands that, if not supplied, would have damaged the long-run welfare of the country in other ways. But some of the costs were inadvertent, the result of choices whose implications were not fully understood. Thus even when the defense expenditures were entirely justifiable in terms of most Americans' interests, the costs were not necessarily distributed in a way consonant with those interests. Where the defense spending was not necessary, the damage to the rest of the society is doubly regrettable.

Past opportunity costs provide no perfect guide to what the costs will be for future military spending. Both the political system and the economy change, and the costs may be distributed differently. Other countries' experience has not been quite the same as America's. In Britain the greatest trade-offs have been between defense and government spending for the welfare state; the 50 per cent decline in Canada's defense share of G.N.P. since the early 1950's has been devoted overwhelmingly to public education; in France the overall defense trend has also been down despite the *force de frappe*, and that drop has made possible a fully equal increase in fixed capital formation.

At the same time, we must recognize that there are many features of great stability and resistance in the political system. The pressures that have in the past directed the costs of defense so heavily toward investment and government civilian programs, rather than toward private consumption, are likely to retain most of their influence. The American political system is composed of a different balance of pressures than is that of Canada, Britain, or France, and the values of Americans are not precisely the same as those of our allies. Any decision to maintain or increase military spending, therefore, probably will have effects not so very different from those in the past unless a very great effort is made to do things differently. It may well be easier to vary the level of military spending than to change drastically the distribution of trade-offs. If so, especially careful evaluation of military demands is essential, in terms of their probable actual if not always intended consequences.

V

In summary, the burden of military expenditures in the United States is great, since 1950 far heavier than ever before during peacetime. In large part the burden has been thrust onto America by the demands of international politics, but domestic pressures also play a role. If defense spending is higher than necessary for national security, there are heavy costs to the domestic political and social systems. One obvious set of costs is the neglect of socially beneficial programs. New programs, even to meet desperate social needs, are harder to fund than are old ones. In the long run a nation's strength depends on continuing its investments; present arms can be bought at the expense of future strength—even military strength.

An equally pernicious and less well-known cost arises in distortion of the political system. The pattern of congressional voting on Defense Department appropriations is very similar to that of voting on a wide variety of issues related more generally to defense, arms control, and East-West relations. The alignments are related to the economic importance of defense payrolls and employment in legislators' constituencies. The larger the Defense Department share of employment in his state, the more "conservative" a Senator is likely to be. Maintenance of a large defense establishment helps to sustain those forces in American political life with a viewpoint stressing excessive "preparedness," a hard-line foreign policy, and over-reliance on military power in dealings with other nations. Without surrender, ultimate control of the arms race requires mitigation of those attitudes. The size of the military is not just a matter of a little waste, unfortunate but tolerable.

The United States probably does not need to fear a coup by its soldiers, on the order of *Seven Days in May*, the French army's attempt in 1958, or the politics of Latin America. In established political systems military coups require a tradition of military involvement in politics that is utterly lacking in the United States. Few Americans expect their soldiers to take direct political action, and the army itself is well imbued with the norms of civilian primacy. Though the basic ideology of most military men is rather conservative, it is rarely fascist and seldom leads to overt acts of political insubordination. Military men essentially view themselves as legitimate in politics only for the purpose of maintaining their role as defenders of the nation from external danger. The General Walkers are striking because of their rarity. Maintaining good relations with Congressmen and the civilian executive is one thing, direct politicking in the public arena, let alone revolt, is quite another. Protecting the national security also is narrowly conceived—America's military officers do not see themselves as needed to modernize the country, to bring political order, or to eliminate civil corruption, as often do their counterparts in the emerging nations.

Maybe severe and repeated military defeat could widen military officers' conceptions of their role in protecting national security. A pattern of what seemed civilian incompetence in the direction of conflict could make soldiers feel that the country's interest required them to become more active politically. I suppose this risk is to some degree inherent in Vietnam withdrawal efforts, but it would probably take more than one such defeat to change the climate seriously. So long as the normal political order is reasonably efficacious, and holds the confidence of most citizens, military men will not be greatly tempted to reach for wider power. A further breakdown in the political system might make the reins of power more inviting, but despite America's agony that danger does not yet seem close.

The real and present problem with the armed forces in American politics is how to control spending for armaments, and how to limit the spill-over from alignments on defense expenditures into other issues of domestic and foreign policy. We should worry not about a sudden takeover of power by our soldiers, but about how to prevent slow accretions in the scope of military influence in the "normal" political system. Here we must concern ourselves as much with the military's civilian allies, who use arms spending for their own purposes, as with our soldiers and sailors.

We also need to limit arms spending because of the dangers of an arms race. So far, the arms race has not been rapidly run. While the absolute expenditure levels have risen, neither the United States nor the Soviet Union now devotes a larger share of its national resources to arms than it did in the mid-1950's. Were it not for Vietnam, the United States would show a clear decline in its defense share since the early 1960's. Also, the technology of the last decade has been kind to us, Russians and Americans alike—more kind than most of us realize in the face of awful weapons of death and pain. The kindness has been in the strength given to the defender. In a world of balance of terror, both superpowers have been able to build secure deterrents, making the initiation of nuclear war unattractive. The invulnerability of our deterrents, however, may not be a permanent gift. Technology is not autonomous; the hasty, ill-considered, or foolish procurement of new weapons could rapidly erode the invulnerability of one side or both. ABM systems, MIRV's, orbital bombs, and myriad other possibilities could destroy the contemporary balance that preserves the power which would reply to an attack but not initiate one. This is the greatest risk of the arms race: that we, and the Soviets, will do whatever is technologically feasible without properly considering its military and political implications. Like climbing mountains, trying to build new weapons just to see if it can be done has its attractions.

At the same time, we must not forget that a failure of deterrence can also come from a *neglect* of our weapons, both current and projected. Until there is an essential change in the international system, a failure to buy a needed new weapon could have effects as calamitous as a run-away arms race. For this reason too, money wasted on the wrong wars or the wrong weapons threatens our security, because after the waste we might then not have the resources for what we needed. Waste can provoke a wide reaction against all defense. For these reasons too, sound evaluation is required to make defense spending defensible. Not even the most ardent advocate of preparedness can favor a system that blinds rational choice, retains old programs beyond their usefulness, and selects new ones according to the accidents of political influence.

If we are to establish and maintain enlightened democratic control over defense expenditures, it is crucial that we understand both their causes and consequences. If we think that heavy military burdens are thrust upon us *solely* by the forces of international conflict, we shall never be able to evaluate properly the new military requests that will be made of American taxpayers. Nor if we fail to understand the consequences of such expenditures will we have the incentive to limit them.

PART III

The Military
and
Foreign Policy

The Military Impact on Foreign Policy

STEPHEN E. AMBROSE

One of the basic beliefs of American liberalism is that professional military men are right-wing, anxious to extend America's overseas bases, quick to urge the use of force to settle problems, eager to increase the size of the armed forces, and above all powerful enough to enforce their views on the government. Americans are prone to worry about the dangers of the military to a free society and a secure world. In the recent past, the supposed power of the military has been used to provide an explanation for the failures of American overseas intervention, most notably in the cases of the Bay of Pigs and Vietnam. According to this interpretation[1] it was the bad advice the Joint Chiefs of Staff gave President John Kennedy, plus the momentum the military and the CIA had been able to generate for the clandestine operation, that led to the Bay of Pigs disaster. Kennedy's two principal biographers also imply that the Joint Chiefs forced the President into Vietnam through a combination of bad advice and actions already taken.

But the idea that Kennedy was forced into the Bay of Pigs or Vietnam against his will, although it has an obvious appeal to the men who helped him to power and who have since been embarrassed by the outcome of these tragic adventures, is so fanciful as to be absurd. Everything in Kennedy's record, everything in the history and structure of the men and groups that supported him, pointed directly and inevitably to the Bay of

[1] Put forward most directly by Arthur Schlesinger, Jr., *A Thousand Days: John F. Kennedy in the White House* (Boston: Houghton Mifflin, 1965), and Theodore Sorensen, *Kennedy* (New York: Harper and Row, 1965).

Pigs and Vietnam. The same is true of the enormous expansion
in armaments that Kennedy inaugurated. Democrats may take
comfort in believing that these disasters occurred because of the
power of the military, John Kenneth Galbraith may argue that
we can end the arms race and American overseas adventures by
re-establishing civilian control of the military and nationalizing
the armament industry,[2] but we should all know better.

The trouble is that, for the most part, we seem not to. While
there is much talk about the role of the military, there is a disturbing lack of solid literature on the subject. History as a field
has been most guilty of the neglect, with political science not
much better. Only a few sociologists have taken up the challenge
in a systematic fashion, and even they tend to ignore the crucial
subject of the military role in decision-making.

What, in fact, is the position of the military in the making of
American foreign policy? Gabriel Kolko argues[3] that it is composed of lackeys, mindless bureaucrats (albeit highly visible ones)
who do what they are told and should not be taken into account
by those engaged in finding out who rules America. However,
Kolko's position, like that of other military critics, tends to be
an over-simplification. The American military does contribute
to, although it by no means controls, American foreign policy
decisions. It does play a role in the formulation of national decisions on domestic issues, especially those that involve funding.
Delineating the impact of the military on foreign policy and
domestic issues, however, in a diverse society in which various
factions hold varying degrees of power, is obviously a complex
task.

A first point to note in an assessment of the role of the military
is that the Armed Services are not an entity with a single world
view, but rather a loose association of groups which, while
agreeing on certain basic necessities, nevertheless is full of internal contradictions. These contradictions go far beyond simple
struggles over a larger share of the budget. After World War II
the Air Force, for example, was anxious to put all defense funds
into big bombers and atomic weapons and seemed willing to
abandon the Army and Navy altogether, placing exclusive reliance for the national defense on the Air Force's ability to deliver
the bomb. The admirals, meanwhile, argued vehemently that

[2] *How to Control the Military* (Garden City, New York: Doubleday,
1969).
[3] *The Roots of American Foreign Policy: An Analysis of Power and
Purpose* (New York: Beacon, 1969).

nuclear war was immoral. In those days it was accepted as axiomatic that the fleet had no role in a nuclear war and, as no limited wars were expected, that meant there was no longer any need for a navy. So the admirals tried, to the best of their ability, to get the United States to abolish nuclear weapons, on the ground that to use them would be immoral. Since the development of Polaris, the Navy has changed its position. On a more practical level, the Army—charged with the occupation of Germany, Japan, and other conquered territory—argued that America could hardly expect to influence events overseas if the only force available to the United States were nuclear weapons. What good, the generals asked, would atomic bombs do in controlling a civil uprising in Latin America or elsewhere?

It must be emphasized that these differences, even though they seemed to revolve around narrow parochial issues, actually involved basic questions about the relations between America and the rest of the world. The Air Force program accepted as a given the notion of a monolithic communism directed from the Kremlin and assumed that atomic bombs could stop Russian expansion. In the view of the Army and Navy, trouble could erupt anywhere, from a variety of causes, at a whole series of different levels. The challenge to stability was less Russian, more the world-wide revolt against political and economic colonialism. If the United States wished to control, or even influence, events outside North America and West Europe, it would need ground troops to do so. None of the services won the struggle, either in the sense of getting all of what it wanted or in persuading the politicians to adopt its point of view about the nature of the challenge. In fact, as will be seen, the politicians forced the military to adopt *their* view of the world and to gear military build-ups to the challenges perceived by the politicians. That the Services fought between themselves enhanced, rather than weakened, civilian control of the military and made it easier, not more difficult, for the White House and the State Department to make the fundamental decisions about American foreign policy.

There is an even deeper division within (not between) the Services on foreign policy, one that reflects a division among the policy makers themselves. In its simplest form, the division is a question of Europe-first vs. Asia-first. In 1941 Army Chief of Staff George Marshall convinced President Roosevelt that America should go on the offensive in Europe while accepting a defensive role in the Pacific. Marshall's reasons were manifold (distance, economic importance, cultural ties, the presence of allies in Europe with whom Americans could work, etc.) but what stood out was Marshall's judgment that Europe was more important to America than Asia. General Douglas MacArthur, commander in the Southwest Pacific Theater, disagreed. He felt the future lay with Asia. Marshall and his followers (most notably Omar Bradley and Dwight Eisenhower) prevailed, but only because Presidents Roosevelt and Truman agreed with them. By the late 1960's, there were numerous signs that the MacArthur approach would triumph. The point is, disagreement within the military makes civilian domination of foreign policy possible—indeed, inevitable. The President, within limits, can always find professional military support for whatever decision he makes.

A second point about the military is that its power is derivative. The brass neither own nor control the means of production, not even the industries that feed the arms race. They do have a near-monopoly of the means of violence, which has theoretical dangers but few if any practical ones. The very diffuseness and the traditions of the Armed Services have insured—and continue to insure—against any military coups in the United States. The Armed Services do possess huge tracts of valuable land and own other real property, but they cannot use it to generate their own income. Admirals do not own the aircraft carriers they command and they cannot use them as they see fit. The brass must rely on America's civilian rulers for a steady manpower supply (denied to them throughout most of American history) as well as for all materièl. If the top brass expect and receive unambiguous personal obsequiousness from their subordinates in uniform, they are even more obsequious themselves in their dealings with the key members of Congress.

In theory, any administration could cut the Department of Defense budget back to 1939 levels, although obviously in practice such a move could only follow a calling off of the cold war (that is, a fundamental switch in foreign policy), which is hardly likely. Still, severe cuts are possible, if the President wishes to fight the cold war in Eisenhower rather than Kennedy-Johnson style. It should be recalled that the Republican-dominated Congress of 1949 got the Defense budget down to $13 billion, and throughout his Presidency Eisenhower kept the Defense expenditures about 40 per cent below what the Democrats—not to mention the Services—wanted. If the Administration ever adopted a less interventionist foreign policy, there is relatively little the military could do to prevent a reduction in its size and influence.

As long as America remains hostile to the Soviet Union and China and staunchly opposed to the emergence of radicalism in the world, however—as it almost surely will—the military will play a role, albeit circumscribed, in the decision-making process. How various elements of the military have acted in the past can provide something of a guide as to what to expect from them in the future. Before taking up a series of cold war case studies, however, a word about the military's general stance is in order. Samuel Huntington, America's leading conservative political scientist and champion of the military life, argues that the true professional soldier is inclined, by the nature of his profession, to caution.[4] According to Huntington, the soldier recognizes the need for civilian supremacy in an ordered society and therefore stays out of politics. Because the soldier's ultimate responsibility is the security of his nation, and because few events endanger that security more than the hazards of war, the true military man fears and attempts to avoid war. The civilian politician, on the other hand, is apt to be expansive and adventurous, and thus the real warmonger. Hitler's drive to war, and the way the German generals tried to hold him back, is Huntington's favorite example of the cautious soldier and the reckless politician.

There are some insights in Huntington's analysis, but not many. To say that the cautious soldier who avoids war and stays out of politics is the true professional, while those who welcome conflict and try to make foreign policy are really jingoists masquerading in uniform, is simply to define away the problem. Huntington's concern is to defend the military, not understand it. Some generals do fear and abhor war—others welcome it. Some avoid overt political activity—others embrace it. Those soldiers who are apolitical, incidentally, are simply for the *status quo*, which they will support with force if necessary. Huntington's ideal type bears little resemblance to reality.

General Lucius Clay, U.S. Army, is a good cold war case study of Huntington's ideal type in action, as opposed to theory. Clay also illustrates the impact certain key soldiers can have on foreign policy, if only as an indispensable agent. After World

---

[4] *The Soldier and the State: The Theory and Politics of Civil-Military Relations* (Cambridge: The Belknap Press of Harvard University Press, 1957).

War II, Clay headed the American occupation of Germany. He came to the job with the reputation of a brilliant administrator who had no politics to hamper his work. But he was actually violently anti-communist, a fact well known to the Secretary of War who pushed him for the position. The general thought all ideas about punishing the Nazis were dangerous nonsense; he was also suspicious of native German socialists (and the British Labor Party as well) and determined to prevent the creation of a socialist state on the ruins of Nazi Germany. The correct policy, Clay felt, was to revive capitalism in Germany and bring it into a new anti-Soviet alliance, in order to create a new *cordon sanitaire*. Thus from early 1946 onward he encouraged the Germans to rebuild their heavy industry, refused to send the reparations to the Russians the Americans had promised to deliver from western Germany, and ignored denazification.

For the cold warriors in America, Clay's actions were welcome, since Germany was the key to a policy of containing the Russians. Indeed, the general could not have undertaken to rebuild Germany without the support of the Truman Administration. German industrial and manpower resources and geographical position made her essential to an anti-Soviet Western Europe. Clay saw this truth, if not first, then at least very early in the game; he worked closely with John J. McCloy in the War Department and Dean Acheson in State. It was not so easy, however, to sell the policy to the French, or even the American public, especially in 1946 as evidence of Nazi atrocities continued to be discovered and publicized. A further complicating factor was the shoddy performance of American troops in Germany.

The issue, which was nothing less than the role of Germany in the cold war and was therefore basic, began to come to a head in November, 1946, when Senate investigator George Meader reported on conditions in the U.S. zone of Germany. Meader charged that there was widespread misconduct on the part of the Army personnel. The demands for luxurious accommodations by Army officers had created a desperate housing situation and high-ranking officers were deeply involved in black-market operations. More serious than the personal corruption was Clay's policy. Meader declared that denazification was a glaring failure because neither Clay nor anyone else pushed it. Clay had also allowed the Germans to raise their industrial production beyond the limits envisioned in the Potsdam agreements on Germany and had done nothing to break up the cartel system. Clay, in short, had made the Germans into allies at a time when most Americans still regarded them as enemies who needed to be punished and re-educated. What Meader did not recognize was that Clay was merely an agent, carrying out policies deemed essential by the civilians like McCloy and Acheson, not to mention the President.

The Truman Administration, according to the *New York Times* of December 2, 1946, subjected the Senate War Investigating Committee to "tremendous pressure . . . to suppress the report and drop the inquiry." The newspaper also reported that Clay threatened to resign if the investigation was pressed. The Secretary of War, Robert Patterson, meanwhile sent the editor of the *Saturday Evening Post*, Forrest Davis, to Germany to make a report on what was happening there. Davis had the full cooperation of the Army and was a guest at Clay's headquarters. After three weeks he sent a ten page report to Senator Robert Taft, the leading Republican, emphasizing that "our record in the military government of Germany is magnificent" and urging Taft to oppose any investigation. Davis' main function was to convince the Republicans not to make political capital out of Germany by convincing them that the budding alliance with the Germans was absolutely necessary. He praised Clay for avoiding "vindictiveness in his attitude or policies" toward the former Nazis and quoted with approval a comment Clay had made at dinner one evening: "In the event of another war, the Germans probably would be the only continental peoples upon whom we could rely."

Looking to the immediate future, Davis was greatly impressed by Clay's thoughts on the importance of the Western sectors in Berlin. Davis pointed out that "Berlin affords us an unique observation post into Soviet Europe" and advocated the continuation of the active intelligence operation there. He wanted the Voice of America programs increased, for Berlin was not only a listening post but also "an enormously useful outpost of our civilization." This defined rather neatly the role Clay and his superiors had assigned to Berlin, a role it would play with increasing success over the next two decades. On the broader question of Germany as a whole, Davis agreed with Clay's advocacy of abandoning all efforts at reunification, still the official policy of both the American and Soviet governments, and instead accepted as a fact the division of Germany into two parts. The next step would be to integrate West Germany into an anti-Soviet alliance.

On January 29, 1947, Taft received Davis' report. After some hesitation, he agreed to call off the investigation. The Administration had won. Later that year, Clay introduced a currency reform in the Western zones of Germany, designed to unify West Germany, facilitate trade between Germany and America, and keep the Russians permanently out of the Ruhr. The Russians argued that since the West no longer intended to reunify Germany, it had no business staying in Berlin, as it was obvious Berlin would never again be the capital of a united Germany. Clay, however, wanted both a divided Germany and a West Berlin integrated into West Germany, and he introduced the new currency into the divided city. The Russians responded by blockading the city—as Clay knew in advance they would. Clay wanted to let his troops shoot their way through the blockade, but Truman—who always kept a tight control on Clay's action—was more cautious and overruled him. The President decided to supply the city by air. So Clay did not get everything he wanted, but still he could not complain, for within four years the West German Republic had come into existence, built along the social and economic lines Clay wanted, and West Germany had joined NATO and started its rearmament.

The important point about Clay is that he could not have achieved his goals without active support in Washington. He was clearly something more than a bureaucrat carrying out settled policy, as Kolko would have it, something less than the apolitical cautious professional Huntington admires.

MacArthur, head of the occupation in Japan, played a similar role and followed broadly parallel policies. But in the end the liberals, who supported and worked with Clay, broke with MacArthur. The issue, supposedly, was one of civilian control of the military, and beyond that of the proper conduct of the Korean War. MacArthur became the liberals' public enemy number one, the bogeyman to be used whenever the military got out of line, the supreme example of the general run amok. But for all the bleating about MacArthur proving the need for tight civilian control of the military, the real issue was one of an isolated soldier (MacArthur had *no* support whatsoever in the Pentagon) meddling in foreign policy. The MacArthur case illustrates how quickly the Administration can crush a soldier who steps out of line no matter how deep and wide his public support, and throw him into the ash can of history.

The issue arose in September, 1950, when MacArthur's troops drove the North Koreans from South Korea, thus achieving the stated aims of the American intervention in the war. MacArthur, however, continued to march north. He did so on explicit orders from the Joint Chiefs, who in turn had been told to move into North Korea by Secretary of State Acheson and the President. The Administration wanted to destroy the North Korean army and reunify the country under South Korean President Syngman Rhee. MacArthur's successes in the field had gone to the Administrations head, and Acheson and Truman decided to undertake an adventure. They would go beyond containment of communism to the liberation of communist satellites. The policy originated in Washington, specifically in the State Department and the White House, not at MacArthur's headquarters—although to be sure MacArthur was an enthusiastic supporter of the switch in policy.

All eyes now turned to China and Russia. How would they react to the loss of North Korea and the presence of American troops on their borders? Truman and Acheson had assumed they would not interfere. With the full concurrence of the State and Defense Departments, the President and the Secretary made the decision to liberate North Korea and accept the risks involved. But the Chinese did not cooperate. They attacked and sent MacArthur's forces streaming southward. Truman later implied, and millions believed, that MacArthur had gone ahead on his own, that it was the general in the field, not the government at home, who had changed the political objective of the war in the middle of the conflict and brought about the rout. Such was never the case.

Even before the Chinese entered the war, MacArthur had wanted to bomb north of the Yalu River, for he was not at all sure he could unify Korea without striking at the Chinese bases. After Chinese entry, MacArthur wanted to employ Nationalist Chinese troops, blockade China, and use atomic weapons. Truman insisted on keeping limits on the area and scope of military operations, partly because he feared a Russian as well as Chinese entry into the war, more because he wanted to concentrate America's resources on building NATO and rearming Germany. The difference between the general and the President, in other words, was one of means, not ends. All the Joint

Chiefs agreed with Truman, and MacArthur never gave the slightest indication that he was prepared to disobey orders.

Supposedly, Truman's relief of MacArthur restored sanity to American foreign policy, averting the danger of all-out war in the Far East. There is a modicum of truth in this widely accepted interpretation, but the implication—that the Truman-Acheson administration was prudent in dealing with the Korean War, while the military consisted of saber-rattling fanatics—is obviously false.

MacArthur did want to widen the war, but he stood alone and, when he stressed the point, Truman fired him. The reason was less one of adventurism vs. caution than a difference in geographical emphasis. MacArthur continued to believe that the future lay in Asia and wanted to make the main effort there; Truman, Acheson, and the Joint Chiefs (supported by the Secretary of Defense, George Marshall) remained convinced that Europe was the primary theater. They feared that the effort required to destroy China—even if nuclear weapons were used—would leave Western Europe defenseless, and they would not consider paying such a price. MacArthur misjudged his personal strength, but it was always clear that he did not have the remotest chance of turning the American policy of Europe-first around.

In fact, the Korean War emphasized the American commitment to Europe, as NSC 68 showed. On January 30, 1950, Truman had authorized the State and Defense Departments "to make an overall review and re-assessment of American foreign and defense policy in the light of the loss of China, the Soviet mastery of atomic energy and the prospect of the fusion bomb." Through February, March, and early April, the State-Defense committee met. By April 12 it had a report ready, which Truman sent to the National Security Council. It came back as an NSC paper, number 68; it was one of the key historic documents of the cold war. NSC 68, Senator Henry Jackson declared, was "the first comprehensive statement of a national strategy."

NSC 68 began by listing the four alternatives of American policy as: 1) continuation of the present course of action without strengthening American capabilities or reducing American commitments; 2) preventative war; 3) withdrawal to the Western Hemisphere, a Fortress America policy; and 4) the development of free-world military capabilities. In the light of the Russian bomb, the communist victory in China, and Senator Joseph McCarthy's charges that the Democrats were soft on communism, the first was not considered a viable alternative; the second was probably beyond American capacities and in any case would have meant the sacrifice of Western Europe to the Red Army; the third had no appeal whatsoever to the leading figures in the Administration. The fourth alternative was the only logical choice.

As one of the principal State Department authors stated, NSC 68 advocated "an immediate and large-scale build-up in our military and general strength and that of our allies with the intention of righting the power balance and in the hope that through means other than all-out war we could induce a change in the nature of the Soviet system." The statement became the basis for American foreign policy over the next twenty years.

NSC 68 was realistic in assessing what it would cost America to prevent any change in the non-communist world, and it was at this point that the relative militancy and influence of the soldiers and the politicians became clear. The three relatively low-ranking military representatives[5] on the State-Defense committee that drew up the program had come to the meetings believing the most money that could be gotten from Congress was around $17 billion a year. They quickly learned that the State representatives were thinking in much bigger terms. The State Department officials estimated that defense expenditures of $35 billion a year would be required immediately, while eventually the program would require $50 billion per year.

The soldiers were shocked. They could not convince themselves that the American public would support a permanent standing army, a Defense Department budget of 20 per cent of the gross national product, an armament industry of the size the program envisioned, a peacetime draft, or even a policy of permanent hostility to China and Russia. Truman, Acheson, and the Democrats showed the soldiers they were wrong. By 1951 the draft had been reintroduced and the Defense budget was up to $50 billion. Truman had sent six U.S. divisions to Europe at a time when manpower was short in Korea and started an extensive program of European rearmament. The important point is that it was the Truman Administration, not the military, who dreamed up the program and pushed it through, and it was the NSC 68 program that made the military-industrial complex, as well as armed American intervention all over the world, possible.

[5] Major General Truman Landon of the Air Force, Major General Ray Maddocks of the Army, and Rear Admiral Thomas Robbins.

The real role of the military in the half-decade after World War II was to serve as ornaments for the politicians, not as decision makers. Truman got Generals Omar Bradley and George Marshall into his camp and displayed them in support of his policies at every opportunity, but the Republicans eventually came up with the biggest catch of all, the most popular and visible of all the brass, Dwight Eisenhower. He became the first professional soldier to serve as President since Grant. But Eisenhower was almost as much a captive hero as Bradley and Marshall. As President, he was far more responsive to the wishes of the great corporations than he was to the military. With only the most minor of exceptions, his chief advisors and Cabinet members came from the corporate world.

The main thrust of the Eisenhower Administration was to balance the budget and hold down or reduce taxes. The President realized that the only way to accomplish these ends was to reduce military expenditures (or at least hold them level while the G.N.P. went up), which he proceeded to do with gusto. Democrats charged that the Republicans were allowing their Neanderthal fiscal views to endanger national security, and the Army—which took the brunt of the fiscal cuts—was so furious that its Chief of Staff, Maxwell Taylor, resigned to publish a blistering criticism of Eisenhower's defense policy. But the President ignored the critics, kept the Defense Department budget at around $40 billion for all eight years of his administration, and—despite Mr. Dulles' bluster—carried on a relatively inactive foreign policy. Lebanon was Eisenhower's only important intervention. He found it not at all difficult to ignore the generals and admirals clamoring for more money for their services.

It was only with the coming to power of John Kennedy and Robert McNamara that the military got all that it asked for, and then some. Three examples illustrate the difference between the Eisenhower and Kennedy Administrations, as well as serving to show the relative impact of the military on decision-making. The first is Berlin, the second Vietnam, and the last the creation of an ICBM force.

When in late 1958 Soviet Premier Khrushchev threatened to write a peace treaty with East Germany and turn control of access to Berlin over to the East Germans, Eisenhower was under intense pressure from the Democrats and the military to increase America's Armed Services dramatically as a prelude to taking a hard line with Khrushchev over Berlin. But in March, 1959, as

Khrushchev's deadline approached, and the Pentagon prepared plans for mobilization, Eisenhower told Congress that he did not need additional money for missiles or conventional warfare forces to deal with the crisis. At a press conference on March 11, with considerable emotion, he dismissed demands that he stop reducing the size of the Army. He wanted to know what in heaven's name the United States would do with more ground forces in Europe. Thumping the table, he declared, "We are certainly not going to fight a ground war in Europe," and pointed out the elementary truth that a few more men or even a few more divisions in Europe would have no effect on the military balance there. He thought the greatest danger in the Berlin crisis was that the Russians would frighten the United States into an arms race that would bankrupt the country.

Two years later Kennedy faced a similar crisis. He received the same military advice Eisenhower had received, but he took it. Kennedy put a $3.2 billion additional military budget through Congress, tripled the draft calls, extended enlistments, and mobilized 158,000 Reserves and National Guardsmen. Altogether he increased the size of the Armed Forces by 300,000 men, sending 40,000 of them to Europe and making six "priority divisions" in the Reserves ready for quick mobilization.

On an earlier occasion, Eisenhower had rejected a similar opportunity to initiate a bold new foreign policy. In the spring of 1954, as the French position at Dien Bien Phu steadily got worse, he was under intense pressure to save the Western outpost in Southeast Asia. Vice President Richard M. Nixon said, on April 16, that "if to avoid further Communist expansion in Asia and Indochina, we must take the risk now by putting our boys in, I think the Executive has to take the politically unpopular decision and do it." Secretary of State John Foster Dulles heartily agreed. Air Force Chief of Staff Nathan Twining wanted to drop three small atomic bombs on the Vietminh around Dien Bien Phu "and clean those Commies out of there and the band could play the Marseillaise and the French would come marching out . . . in fine shape." The Chairman of the Joint Chiefs, Admiral Arthur Radford, said he had aircraft carriers in the area and was anxious to intervene. Only Army Chief of Staff Matthew Ridgway was opposed; he feared that America would get tied down in an endless war on the Asian mainland.

Eisenhower agreed with Ridgway, both then and later in the year. After the Geneva Accords were signed in July, Dulles and Radford and Twining, along with others at the Pentagon,

worked out an invasion scheme calling for a landing at Haiphong
and a march to Hanoi, which American troops would then liberate. Again, Ridgway opposed; again, Eisenhower refused to
act. The President was thankful for Ridgway's support, but it
probably was not crucial. There was no way the military could
have forced Eisenhower into Vietnam against his will, even had
the generals and admirals been united, and Eisenhower never came
close to using atomic bombs on Asians for the second time in
a generation or intervening without allies—especially the British—
in a far corner of the world.

Kennedy, when faced with a similar crisis in Vietnam, also
had divided advice from the military. Eisenhower had agreed to
send 600 military advisers and small quantities of military equipment to South Vietnam (with the caveat that it would be cut
off unless there were democratic reform within the country),
but the aid proved to be insufficient and, when Kennedy took
office, South Vietnam was on the verge of collapse. The President turned to Walt Rostow, McGeorge Bundy, Dean Rusk,
McNamara, Taylor, Lyndon Johnson, and others for advice.
Taylor was the only professional soldier in the group. All made
trips to South Vietnam; all enthusiastically recommended greatly
increased American aid. Many active duty soldiers were skeptical, but the interventionists carried the day, and by late 1963
Kennedy had 16,000 Americans involved in South Vietnam.

In the cases of Berlin and Vietnam, each President could pick
and choose from divided military advice. That Kennedy was
active, even belligerent, while Eisenhower was peaceful, even
passive, reflected their own styles and the interest groups they
responded to, not the influence of the military. Eisenhower did
not use military force to oppose Castro, while Kennedy inter-
vened in Cuba twice, but neither acted solely, or even mainly,
on military advice.

This should not be taken to indicate that Eisenhower was a
man of peace, Kennedy a warmonger. Eisenhower might very
well have stepped up American involvement in Vietnam had he
been President in the early sixties, just as he might have given
the go-ahead to the Bay of Pigs invasion of Cuba (which was
planned while he was in the White House). But even had he
done so, it would not have been as a result of military domination of the civilian head of government, but rather as a result
of his own and his civilian advisers' view of the world.

On the question of ICBMs, it is difficult to find any significant
military pressure to increase the number of missiles. In general,

the Army preferred putting any additional defense funds into its own ground strength build-up; the Navy wanted to use extra money to build aircraft carriers, other surface ships, and Polaris submarines; the Air Force argued that its bomber force ought to be modernized. Eisenhower refused to do any of these things on a scale remotely satisfactory to the three Services, but he also refused to increase the ICBM force, despite the so-called missile gap. Throughout his second term, Eisenhower kept the number of ICBMs steady at around 200. Kennedy and McNamara multiplied the missile force by a factor of five (to 1,000 plus); those who wish to understand why they launched the greatest arms race in the history of mankind must begin their search outside the Armed Services, for the pressure for the build-up did not come from the Army, Navy, or Air Force. Simultaneously with the missile program, Kennedy did bolster the three Services, and the military obviously benefited from the arms race. Like all bureaucracies, the Services were happy to grow and could find rationalizations to justify the growth, but they did not initiate the program. Kennedy and McNamara were the drivers; the generals and admirals joyfully went along for the ride.

The Johnson and Nixon years showed the same pattern. Once again, the President could choose from conflicting military advice, or even ignore the military if he wished (Johnson picked the bombing targets in Vietnam during his lunch hour on Tuesday, often with no professional soldiers present). Again, some military advisers wanted to expand operations into Cambodia, Laos, and North Vietnam, while others argued that the United States should get out of Southeast Asia altogether and use the money saved to re-build the Armed Services, elements of which had reached a crisis situation with regard to equipment after six long years of war (by 1970, the average age of the Navy's destroyers was 25 years, at a time when the Russians were launching brand new vessels, with the most advanced modern weapons, almost weekly). The foreign policy differences that divided the nation also divided the Services. Many professional soldiers were unhappy with the American concentration on Southeast Asia, to the neglect of Europe, while some admirals were furious as they helplessly watched the Soviets build up their naval strength in the Mediterranean.

Yet despite overwhelming evidence to the contrary, the American public continued to believe that the military dominated foreign policy. When in May, 1970, Nixon decided to invade

Cambodia, the immediate response of television and newspaper commentators was that after a battle between the diplomats and the generals, the generals had won. The evidence, however, was hardly as conclusive as the statements. Certainly some high ranking military men had urged the President to invade, just as they tried to push Johnson in that direction for five years. But others opposed. Nixon invaded Cambodia not because military influence had increased since Johnson's days in the White House, but because Nixon saw the political situation differently than Johnson had.

All of which points to the rather vapid conclusion that the military is nowhere near as powerful as the liberals fear, not as unimportant as Kolko argues, and certainly not cast in the mold Huntington creates. The top military leaders are only a minor part of the governing establishment, by no means the driving force. The great need is to understand the military and its role more exactly, primarily because this will aid in illuminating the men who really rule, and how they do it.

The Joint Chiefs of Staff and Defense Policy Formulation

Many prominent writers on military affairs are gravely disturbed about "the excessive influence of civilians" in the field of defense policy-making. The following statements are illustrative.

. . . the Secretary [Secretary of Defense McNamara] has penetrated deep into fields once reserved for the military. He has barked shins throughout the country's polity and economy. A stream of complaints has flowed from the Armed Services and their friends and clients. Carl Vinson, the powerful chairman of the House Armed Services Committee, has semipublicly "warned" the Secretary against abridging the independence of the Services and their Secretaries. Virtually the whole press has joined in criticizing McNamara for what the *Washington Post* has called "The Closed Door Policy of the Defense Department." Blue suits and brown alike have charged that, as the *Army, Navy, and Air Force Journal* put it, "the professional military leadership of the nation is being short-circuited in the current decisionmaking process at the Pentagon."[1]

In structural terms, the military establishment may be one of the tripods of a "power elite," but in sociological fact the military officers feel dispossessed. . . . Since the end of World War II, the military has been involved in a number of battles to defend its elite position, beginning in 1945 with the young physicists and nuclear scientists, down to the present action against the "technipols" (the military's derisive term for technicians and political theorists whom Secretary McNamara has brought into the Department of Defense).[2]

Reprinted by permission from *Air University Review*, May-June 1966, pp. 40-45; July-August, 1966, pp. 11-20.
[1] Joseph Kraft, "McNamara and His Enemies," *Harper's Magazine*, August, 1961, p. 41.
[2] Daniel Bell, "The Dispossessed—1962," *Columbia University Forum*, 5 (Fall 1962), p. 6.

In common with many other military men, active and retired, I am profoundly apprehensive of the pipe-smoking, tree-full-of-owls type of so-called professional defense intellectuals who have been brought into this Nation's Capital. I don't believe a lot of these over-confident, sometimes arrogant young professors, mathematicians and other theorists have sufficient worldliness or motivation to stand up to the kind of enemy we face. . . . It seems to me the old strengths still apply. In my opinion the two that count for most in the nuclear space age, regardless of academic cerebrations, are national determination and military forces designed to achieve victory, not tailored to obtain compromise. Professional military training teaches the philosophy of victory whereas politics is based on compromise.[3]

Do civilians have inordinate power in the strategy-making field? If they do, is it because of the energetic personality and management philosophy of our [former] Secretary of Defense?

It is a thesis of this article that a variety of civilian groups have begun to play and—barring a large-scale war situation—will continue to play a major role in the determination of strategy and military policy. Moreover, Secretary McNamara did not create the phenomenon of civilian influence. At most, the Secretary's energetic implementation of an activist management philosophy has accelerated an existing trend—and exacerbated the debate over its desirability and consequences. . . .

There are . . . many . . . reasons why defense policy formulation is no longer just the military's bailiwick. I will briefly discuss some of them without belaboring the obvious. Most, if not all, the reasons discussed are permanent rather than transitory characteristics. I make this statement because some observers, though astute enough to understand why the civilian has "invaded" the strategy domain, seem to believe the present civilian "occupation" may be temporary.

One reason why there is now a furor over civilian dominance of strategy-making is that a comparison with the immediate past presents a remarkable contrast. As I have already indicated, World War II military leaders had an unusual amount of influence in policy formulation. When events in the postwar era made it clear that the United States could not again shirk international responsibilities, government agencies were unable to find sufficient numbers of competent civilians to man important national security posts. As a result, "military officers were ap-

[3] General Thomas D. White, "Strategy and the Defense Intellectuals," *Saturday Evening Post*, 236 (May 4, 1963), pp. 10-12.

pointed to key State Department offices, ambassadorial posts and positions in other foreign affairs agencies." Thus, throughout the late forties, military men occupied many of the prominent positions in both the foreign and defense branches of the national security policy structure.

It was inevitable that administrations would change this situation as circumstances permitted. Under Presidents Eisenhower and Kennedy the overall participation of military officers in civil office declined until very few professional military officers [had] been appointed to top civil governmental positions during the 1961–65 Kennedy and Johnson Administrations. Even in the defense policy area itself, each political party had, by the early sixties, built up a reservoir of men knowledgeable and experienced in military affairs to man top positions in the Department of Defense. The present *modus operandi* undoubtedly is more logical and relevant to the American political system than the practice followed in the immediate postwar era.

Therefore, the clamor against civilian strategists is in part due to fond memories of a yesteryear unusual in the degree of military occupancy of important national security positions. A far more significant factor, however, is that civilian influence *has* been introduced into heretofore sacrosanct military arenas.

As Professor S. P. Huntington says, three groups of civilians have "invaded" the strategy domain. The first group is composed of the "defense intellectuals."

Most of the significant writings on strategy produced after World War II were produced by civilians. . . . Experts such as Brodie, Kaufman, Kissinger, Wohlstetter, Schelling, and Kahn took the lead in articulating theories of stabilized deterrence, limited war, tactical nuclear war, arms control and civil defense. . . . Traditionally, the professional military officer is supposed to be contemptuous of the ignorance of civilians on military problems and strategy. One striking aspect of the McNamara Pentagon, however, has been the allegation that the civilian "whiz kids" are unduly contemptuous of the military officers for *their* backwardness and ignorance.

The second civilian group is comprised of the natural scientists. In the [defense policy] debates of the late 1950's and the early 1960's concerning technology, space activities, nuclear testing, arms control, disarmament and even weapons development, the role of the scientists was as important or more important than that of the soldiers.

The Department of Defense civil servants make up a final civilian group which, quite unostentatiously, has gained power and influence. Military men normally rotate through top staff positions. Many top civil servants have been with DOD since 1947. Their experience, knowledge, contacts, and power permit them to restrict and control many defense policy matters.

These three groups are, I think, permanent occupiers of the strategy domain. Given the complexity of modern strategic planning, the cost of new weapon systems, and—most important—the absolutely crucial requirement that defense policy contribute maximally to national security, then the defense intellectual, the natural scientists, and the DOD civil servant are welcome additions to the strategy team.

Another important cause of the decline of the military's input into defense policy-making is the changing nature of the political process through which strategic decisions are made. The role of Congress in determining the military budget, force levels, weapons, and uses of the Armed Forces has been practically pre-empted by the executive branch. Reflection seems to indicate that this development was inevitable and is irrevocable. Congress is not organized to formulate the strategic decisions at the heart of force-structure determination. Still, diminution of congressional influence in military affairs has removed one of the military strategists' power sources. Congress may heed plaintive cries of service advocates and appropriate additional military funds—but almost without exception the President has effectively "vetoed" the legislative action by impounding the funds.

Many of the traditional, heretofore mundane, problems of military affairs are no longer handled exclusively by military professionals. Here is another area of civilian invasion of the defense policy field. For instance, choices of modern weapon systems involve extremely long lead times in planning, testing, procurement, and production. With choices now involving billions of dollars, civilian participation has become routine, especially since "unnecessary" monies spent on defense may increase the national debt, intensify the balance of payments problem, decrease amounts spent on foreign aid, poverty programs, etc. Moreover, with political primacy demanding interrelated defense and foreign policies, civilians naturally are concerned with what types of weapon systems are being planned, produced, and made operational.

Finally, because of cost and other factors such as the increasing rate of technological obsolescence, only a few weapon systems now become operational. The ideal pattern seems to be a single, long-lasting weapon system for each combat function. For example, DOD wants the Navy and the Air Force to use the same aircraft throughout the 1970's to fill their tactical fighter needs.

It is evident that civilians are entering the weapon systems decision-making process quite forcefully. The argument that "we must have this particular weapon system as soon as possible"—a contention which, if accepted, maximizes military control of weapon system decisions—will carry much less weight than it has in the past. Civilian DOD leaders feel that there *is* time to make a fully staffed study before making decisions on weapon system selection and management problems—and that their participation in these decisions is not only possible but essential. Consequently, if civilians are going to participate in decisions on weapon systems, they are normally going to be involved in the strategic analysis which usually precedes the production of armaments. Ordinarily, one asks what defense policy one wishes to adopt *before* asking what kinds of technically and financially possible weapon systems are desirable.

Changes in defense organization have greatly accentuated the trend toward civilian dominance of the strategy-making process. Much water has gone over the organizational dam since the National Security Act of 1947 created the office of Secretary of Defense and vaguely instructed the Secretary "to preside" over the National Military Establishment. Through various organizational acts, the Department of Defense has been given increasing power and control over the separate services and the military professionals. Unified and specified (i.e., operational) commands have been created. Today these are directly responsible to the President and the Secretary of Defense. In regard to forces assigned to unified and specified commands, military departments are accountable only for their training, support, and administration. Functional offices at the Assistant Secretary of Defense level have been expanded in both numbers and powers. For instance, since the office of the Director of Research and Engineering was created in 1958, the Director has supervised *all* military research and development. Defense-wide agencies have been established to unite common supply and service functions and to reduce service duplication.

These defense organizational trends have unmistakably led to increased centralization and functionalism and to decreased authority of the military professionals in strategy areas. As one commentator observed:

As a result of the expansion of the unified command concept, the authority of the Service Chief as an individual has been supplanted by the corporate authority of the Joint Chiefs, while the authority of the Chiefs of Staff has been reduced through the creation of the elaborate superstructure for defense policy-making in Washington.

Moreover, Secretary of Defense McNamara and his predecessors have acted fully within legislatively permitted limits, though perhaps Congress did not intend for Defense Secretaries to *utilize* their powers as actively as they have.

Crisis Now

My own involvement with Vietnam began in 1954. I was then
Chief of Plans of the Army, serving under Matthew B. Ridgway,
the Chief of Staff. I knew Ridgway and had served with him in
the past. He is a man of incisive intelligence and great moral
courage—in brief, a good man to work for.

At that time in 1954 the French were involved in the defense
of Dien Bien Phu. They had chosen to defend this isolated
fortified area in an effort to provoke the Vietminh into a major
battle in which the communist troops could be destroyed. But
it was clear by then that the battle was not going as the French
planned; and they were making tremendous demands on the
United States for war material. Vietnam was already becoming
a swamp-ridden jungle Moloch with an insatiable appetite for
aircraft, arms, ammunition and other military supplies.

The Joint Chiefs of Staff had been doubtful about the Dien
Bien Phu strategy from the beginning. Our military adviser in
Saigon, Major General Thomas Trapnell, had never thought
well of the scheme. I myself had felt that genuine French con-
cessions to make Vietnam independent were far more important
in the situation than mere fire power.

As the situation at Dien Bien Phu worsened, the French in
desperation asked us for carrier strikes against the communists
attacking the fortified area. Admiral Arthur W. Radford, a
strong advocate of carrier air power, then chairman of the Joint
Chiefs of Staff, was in favor of such a U.S. military action. So
were Chief of Staff of the Air Force Nathan F. Twining and
Chief of Naval Operations Robert B. Carney. There was even

Reprinted by permission of Random House, Inc., and The Sterling Lord
Agency, Inc., from pp. 40–48, *Crisis Now*, by James Gavin. Copyright 1968
by James M. Gavin and Arthur T. Hadley.

talk of using one or two nuclear weapons. Secretary of State
John Foster Dulles sounded out our allies on their reaction to
such a U.S. air attack. Fortunately General Ridgway refused to
bend in his opposition to this "quickie" solution. He believed
that the air attacks would be indecisive and further that they
would lead to American ground troops being involved in Indochina. We in the Army felt that to fight on the ground in Indochina alongside the French was a war America did not want.

Though under tremendous pressure to conform, Ridgway
refused to endorse the majority view. Instead he carried his disagreement over the air strike, or "split" as it is known in Penta-
gonese, up to the President. I am convinced that Ridgway's
determined opposition plus that of our allies was crucial in
aborting this early effort to involve us in Vietnam. I well remember my feeling of relief when President Eisenhower's decision
went against the strike. A feeling that was regrettably brief.

The situation at Dien Bien Phu worsened and on May 7th it
fell. The next day the French sat down in Geneva at the conference table with delegates from Vietnam, the Vietminh regime
and six other countries and submitted armistice proposals. Sur-
prisingly quickly, or so it seemed to us in the Pentagon, an
agreement was reached to end the then Vietnamese war. The
Geneva agreements and Final Declaration of July 1954 provided
for Vietnam to be partitioned along the seventeenth parallel
into North and South Vietnam, with nationwide elections to
determine the nature of reunification to be held in July, 1956.
An international control commission was also established to
supervise the implementation of the agreements.

To understand what happened next, it is important to understand the attitude of the Pentagon back in 1954 because this
atmosphere led to the initial decisions that brought us to our
present position in Vietnam today. And this attitude is still all
too prevalent in our military thinking. Indeed it has deep roots
elsewhere.

In 1954 the recent Korean War decisively influenced Pentagon
thinking. For the Air Force, Korea had been a disillusioning and
frustrating experience. Air Force leaders had assumed that air
superiority, air surveillance and air attacks would smash the
North Korean drive and demolish the North Korean military
establishment. They had trumpeted this point of view both to
the public and to the President. When the bombing failed to
halt the North Korean war effort they developed the myth of
the Yalu sanctuary. If only they could bomb Red Chinese

Manchuria, which lay beyond the Yalu River, they said, everything would turn out all right. Thus the Air Force was able to avoid, at least in public, confronting the evidence that in Korea both strategically and tactically air power had failed. Unfortunately, from their frustration sprang a readiness to answer any challenge to American power with threats of total nuclear war.

To the Army, Korea had been embittering and costly. Of the 147,000 casualties most had been in the ground forces. Despite the Army's wealth of combat experience from World War II, its abundance of logistical support, and its modern fighting equipment, major units had been surprised and routed by Chinese forces. The Army felt that ground forces had done the major share of the fighting, that more wars like the Korean War were a possibility, that the Army's accomplishments should be recognized, and that it should receive the funds to train and equip itself for such contests in the future. Instead the Army was beginning to feel the pressure of the "new look" cutbacks that followed the promulgation of the doctrine of massive retaliation; its funds and troop strengths were slashed while the forces for strategic nuclear bombing were built up.

But above and beyond this, everyone in the Pentagon—including, let me add, myself—tended to see the world in terms of good guys and bad guys. Moreover I met no one who doubted who the good guys were. (It was a simple vision of the world, which held much truth in the period when we faced the byzantine greed of Stalinism.) And we had many supporters outside the Pentagon. Speaking of the Geneva Accords in August of 1954, Francis Cardinal Spellman of New York stated:

> If Geneva and what was agreed upon there means anything at all, it means . . . taps for the buried hopes of freedom in Southeast Asia. . . . Now the devilish techniques of brainwashing, forced confessions and rigged trials have a new locale for their exercise. . . . Communism has a world plan and it has been following a carefully set-up timetable for the achievement of that plan. . . .

We had excuses for our belief. Still, we should have been wiser.

Instead we assumed that Peking was a mere pawn of Moscow, that thwarted by NATO and the Marshall Plan for taking over Europe, Stalin was now on the march in Asia. The communist world was assumed to be an integrated, monolithic bloc. Only a few of us were beginning to distinguish between the nationalistic communism of Tito and the Stalinism of Russia; I can recall the hours of thought I devoted to the question before recommending the Army's support of military aid to Tito. And for even fewer of us did that clearer vision extend as far as the Vietnamese brand of communism under Ho Chi Minh. The belief that communism itself was changing and that there were types of nationalistic communism with which the United States could quite safely co-exist would have been regarded as close to heresy.

It was in this atmosphere that we closely followed the negotiations at Geneva. We had the feeling that the French had not only failed in combat, but that now they were about to let down the team. Despite our lavish support of their efforts to reestablish themselves in Indochina, they were now acting in their own self-interest, rather than in the interest of the free world as a whole. Through intelligence sources we learned about what later became known as the Sainteny Commission, named for its chairman, whose purpose was to negotiate directly with the Ho Chi Minh government to assure the safety of French investments in communist-held territory.

Parenthetically, I had occasion some years later, in December 1965, to discuss at lunch the Sainteny Commission with General de Gaulle. General Paul Ely, who had been the French commander in Vietnam in late 1954, was also present. I asked General de Gaulle how the commission got along with Ho Chi Minh; he assured me that they had worked well toegther. When I asked him whether he thought a similar *modus vivendi* could be made with whatever type of government appeared in Saigon in the event North and South Vietnam settled their differences, he said without hesitation that he was confident this could be done. It is important to remember these remarks when evaluating French pronouncements on Vietnam and to be aware that France was concerned about protecting a rather large economic investment.

But to return to 1954, the attitude of the Pentagon staff when the Geneva Accords were finally reached was that the French had unwisely folded. Now it was obviously up to us to assume the full burden of combat against communism in that area. Secretary of State John Foster Dulles and the Central Intelligence Agency agreed with the Pentagon. At that time Secretary Dulles was building, as a good lawyer might, a paper wall of treaties to contain communism. Germany joined NATO, then came SEATO (Southeast Asia Treaty Organization), and then

CENTO (Central Treaty Organization). In this atmosphere the Joint Chiefs began with the highest priority to study a proposal to send combat troops into the Red River delta of North Vietnam.

As Chief of Plans of the Army Staff I was responsible for recommending what attitude the Army should take toward this proposal to put American ground troops into North Vietnam. I began by bringing together the best Asian experts. We decided that to be honest with ourselves we had to face the fact that if we entered North Vietnam we were going to war, not with Ho Chi Minh, but with Red China. Red China would be providing most of the arms, vehicles, ammunition, and other sinews of war because of what she would feel was a threat to her national self-interest. Once again, let me reiterate that this did not mean that either I or the Army staff wanted or urged war with Red China. In the weeks and months to come we were to argue forcefully and frequently against such a war. Rational consideration of the alternatives should not be mistaken for advocacy.

Having assumed Red China as the enemy, we had to further assume that the entry of an expeditionary force into the Hanoi area would bring a reaction from the Chinese, exactly as they had reacted when we crossed the 38th Parallel in Korea. If this happened we would find ourselves confronting Chinese field armies that vastly outnumbered our own forces. And we would not have the narrow peninsula in which they could be contained as in Korea. We were also in agreement that we had to prepare for the reopening of the Korean front by the Chinese if we committed ourselves heavily to Vietnam. Then followed the agonizing decision as to whether we should wait to be attacked in Korea, or whether we should take the initiative in reopening that front.

Remembering our experience in World War II and Korea, the Army staff anticipated a bloody and costly war that would engage a tremendous portion of our manpower and national wealth. This cost could be met only at the expense of our other global commitments and by the diversion of resources from the well-being of our domestic society. In all probability we would have to resort to tax increases, wage controls and rationing.

As to Vietnam itself, we put the size of the necessary expeditionary force at eight combat divisions, supported by thirty-five engineer battalions, and all the artillery and logistical support such mammoth undertakings require. (At the time of my trip to Vietnam in November 1967 there were eight and two-thirds U.S. divisions in Vietnam.) Because of the size of the undertaking and the danger of involvement with Red China, we believed it would be necessary to call up the Army Reserves and National Guard. In short, we felt the operation should not be attempted unless the country was put on virtually a war footing.

Again, as at the time of Dien Bien Phu, the Joint Chiefs divided. Admiral Radford was emphatically in favor of landing a force in the Haiphong-Hanoi area, even if it meant risking war with Red China. In this he was fully supported by the Chief of Staff of the Air Force and the Chief of Naval Operations. In my opinion such an operation meant a great risk of war. Just southeast of Haiphong harbor is the island of Hainan, which is part of Red China. The Navy was unwilling to risk their ships in the Haiphong area without first invading and capturing the island. Admiral Radford and the Chiefs of the Navy and Air Force felt that, faced with our overwhelming power, the Red Chinese would not react to this violation of their sovereignty. General Ridgway and I had grave doubts about the validity of this reasoning.

Once more the embattled Ridgway "split." Using the staff study we had prepared in the Army he wrote directly to President Eisenhower, pointing out the hazards to the nation if we undertook such a war in Vietnam and the dubious gains. Again fortunately, the President decided not to commit U.S. forces to Southeast Asia.

PART IV

The Military
and
Socialization

The Social Effects
of Military Service

JAMES ALDEN BARBER, JR.

Almost half of all adult males in the United States are veterans of the Armed Forces. As of June 30, 1968, there were 26,273,000 living U.S. veterans. By the end of 1970 the number was estimated to be in excess of 28 million men, with the veteran population continuing to increase by more than a half million every year. The sheer number involved makes the shared experience of military service one of the most important agencies of socialization in our society. It is therefore useful to explore the effect of military service on the individual and in turn on the society.

The great majority of veterans have served only a relatively short time, usually from two to four years. Even in the case of the much smaller number of career servicemen, few spend more than twenty or twenty-five years in the service, then retire to a civilian community to pursue a second career.[1] Thus a high "flow-through" is maintained within the Armed Services, resulting in a continuous rapid turnover of personnel. The organization remains relatively stable, but the people who make up the organization are mainly transients. As one result, all of the veterans who pass through the Armed Services bring back with them to civilian society any changes which take place as a result of military service.

[1] Morris Janowitz, "Basic Education and Youth Socialization in the Armed Forces," in Roger W. Little (ed.), *A Survey of Military Institutions*, The Inter-University Seminar on Armed Forces and Society, Inc., 1969, p. 132. This article by Janowitz, a selection from which follows, is by far the most comprehensive existing review of sociological research on the effects of military service. Much of the present essay leans heavily on material assembled by Janowitz, and the debt is gratefully acknowledged.

There are two kinds of questions about the effect of military service upon individuals. One is how military service affects the way in which the individual performs his social roles when he returns to civil society. The other has to do with whether there is such a thing as the "military mind," and if so, what dangers it poses for the society. This second question is basically one of elite behavior, since the corporate behavior of military organizations is generally tightly controlled from above, and an attempt to address some of the implications of this is made elsewhere in this volume. In this section emphasis is placed on the first question. Fortunately for the purpose, sociologists have studied the question sufficiently to provide some useful data.

During the late 1940's and early 1950's a lengthy debate over the desirability of universal military training [UMT] took place in the United States. The proposal, which would have involved a period of military training and service for all adult American males, was strongly endorsed by President Truman, but although the program received wide support, it was never passed by Congress. Besides Presidential support, in 1950 UMT was recommended by a committee headed by James B. Conant, then Harvard president; was endorsed by George Marshall; unanimously proposed at a meeting of the Association of American Universities in New York City on December 4, 1950; and received labor support when Daniel J. Tobin, president of the Teamsters Union, called on the AFL on December 11 to end its 65-year opposition to UMT. Public opinion polls taken during the late forties also showed strong public support for UMT.[2]

Although the basic argument for UMT was that it was necessary for military security, an often voiced subsidiary argument was that it was of benefit both to the individual and the society. The report of a Presidential advisory commission in 1947 outlined twelve benefits that would flow from a program of universal military training. Three of these were: "6. It would present additional opportunities for inculcating spiritual and moral ideals in support of American democracy;" "10. It would help to channel qualified young men into programs of scientific and vocational training in fields important to national defense;" "11. It would bring together young Americans from all parts of the nation to share a common experience and to fulfill a common obligation to their country, thus contributing to national unity,

[2] *Report of the President's Advisory Commission on Universal Training* (Washington, D.C.: Government Printing Office, 1947), pp. 225–242.

the foundation of our security." The commission envisioned advantages to "health, education, character development, and training for citizenship," although the report goes on to state:

> We recognize that there are definite limits to the nonmilitary benefits that can be obtained, and we do not present these as in any way a justification for the adoption of a program that must be considered solely on the basis of its contribution to world peace and national security.[3]

Yet despite the disclaimer, it is clear that the unanimous report of the committee saw clear social virtues in the proposal for universal military training.

How well do these assumed virtues hold up to careful examination? The remainder of this section is devoted to examining some of the studies by sociologists on the effect of military service upon 1) education, 2) employment, and 3) social attitudes.

Education

The Military Services constitute one of the world's largest educational institutions. Because of the high rate of personnel turnover and the increasingly complex demands that the revolution in military technology places upon military personnel, the Military Services have been forced to develop a comprehensive and widespread program of education. In 1968 the American Council on Education reported having examined 8,814 formal resident service school syllabi in order to provide an evaluation of each course for possible credit at the college level, and their examination was limited to unclassified courses. Roughly one-half of these courses were recommended for credit at the undergraduate level. If classified courses are included the total number of military courses is even higher.

All of these courses are directed toward filling military requirements, and many of them are of a narrow technical orientation, without much direct correspondence to civilian occupations. Sometimes military training does serve as a primary source of training for civilian occupations, as in the case of airline pilots and electronic technicians. Technical training, however, usually requires a relatively high level of basic education as a prerequisite,

---

[3] *Ibid.*, pp. 92–93.

and tends to bypass those most in need of educational assistance. In other words, in providing technical education to individuals already possessing substantial education the services are not contributing to the solution of any social problems, but are in a sense competing with civilian sources for qualified people.

More important from a social point of view is the way in which the military handles those recruits with inadequate educational backgrounds. In some ways the military has been much more effective in handling individuals with educational deficiencies than has the public school system. In large part this is due to the task orientation of the military: the function of military education is not mainly to provide the individual with an education, but rather to provide the particular service with a man properly equipped to perform certain designated tasks. As a result the primary responsibility is thrown upon the teacher, not upon the student: it is the task of the service school to produce properly trained graduates. This is in contrast with the usual assumption in civilian life that the primary responsibility for learning lies with the student. Because of the need to train large numbers with a high percentage of success, service schools tend to assume a low level of preparation on the part of their students. In consequence the pace is rarely challenging for the well-prepared student, but is generally well-designed to insure some minimum level of preparation for the great majority of students. The rather substantial success of the military in training individuals of limited educational backgrounds is detailed in the next article.

In addition to education oriented to specific military requirements, all of the Military Services have voluntary programs designed to raise general education levels. The principal agency for this is the program of correspondence courses administered by the United States Armed Forces Institute (USAFI). USAFI offers more than 200 courses of its own, plus making available over 6,000 additional correspondence courses from the extension divisions of 46 cooperating colleges and universities. Although USAFI neither recommends nor grants credit for its courses, most high schools and state departments of education are willing to grant high school credit or issue high school diplomas or equivalency certificates on the basis of USAFI courses and test scores.

This route to a high school diploma is important because of the high proportion of servicemen who do not complete high school before entering the service. Army statistics in 1965 indicated that 28 per cent of Army enlisted men did not have high school diplomas. The USAFI program has been notably successful in providing a second educational chance for those who have not completed a civilian high school. Morris Janowitz reports that more than a quarter of enlisted men on active duty complete high school *after* entering the service.[4] Some of the reasons for this success are analyzed in the article by Janowitz which follows.

The Services also place great emphasis upon the role of education in an officer's career. Few professions place as great emphasis upon continuing education as do the military officers' corps, perhaps because the more violent aspects of the profession are practiced only at those irregular intervals when the nation is at war. Two kinds of education are emphasized: a series of graded professional schools, and the provision of opportunities for postgraduate study in specialized fields. Although there are variations among the Services, the basic pattern of professional schooling provides for four levels of schools: 1) immediately after commissioning, basic or technical schooling of a few months' duration to prepare the new officer for duties as a junior commissioned officer; 2) at about the four- to eight-year point, generally in the grade of Army captain or Navy lieutenant, a "career" course of perhaps six months in length, such as the Infantry Officer's Advanced Course at Fort Bennington, Georgia, to prepare the officer for assuming greater responsibilities, generally of a department head or command nature; 3) at the point of nine to fifteen years' service—that is, Army majors and Navy lieutenant commanders—those officers who are likely to be promoted are sent to a one-year command and staff college where they study large-scale military planning, staff procedures, and inter-service coordination; and finally 4) sometime during the sixteenth to twenty-second year of service selected officers in the grades of lieutenant colonel and colonel (Navy commander and captain) spend a year at one of the highest level military schools: National War College, the Industrial College of the Armed Forces or the Army, Naval or Air War Colleges. Not all career officers, of course, attend all four levels of school, for there is a process of weeding out along the line, but with rela-

[4] Morris Janowitz, "Basic Education and Youth Socialization in the Armed Forces," in Roger W. Little (ed.), *A Survey of Military Institutions,* The Inter-University Seminar on Armed Forces and Society, Inc., 1969, p. 138.

tively few exceptions successful completion of the appropriate level of school is a prerequisite to promotion.

In addition to professional schooling, the pattern is increasingly for officers to attend graduate school, usually sometime within their first ten years of service. About one-third of this graduate study is done at in-service graduate institutions such as the Naval Post-Graduate School at Monterey, California, and two-thirds takes place at civilian institutions.[5] Figures published by the Department of Defense indicate that by the time officers reach senior grades more than half have been to graduate school, and the announced goal is to provide an opportunity for graduate education to all qualified officers.[6]

The Armed Services place great emphasis upon continuing education, and have had relative success in raising the general educational level of their members. The implication of this would seem to be that the Armed Forces, by raising the educational level of those who spend a few years in the service, tend to incrementally raise the educational level of the society as a whole. There is another aspect to this, however. The existence of the draft operates to disrupt educational patterns, both for those who are drafted, and those who enlist under the threat of the draft. Thus presumably at least some of those whose education is raised during military service would have continued their schooling to at least the same level if they had remained civilians. It is true that the existence of the educational benefits of the G.I. Bill does encourage large numbers of veterans to continue their educations after leaving the service, but the same amount of money would finance the same amount of education whether it was tied to military service or not. The imponderable in this case is the effect the military service has upon the individual's desire for education and his ability to profit from it. Folk wisdom has it that the veteran returns more mature and serious about getting an education, but the difficulty of adequate controls has prevented any clear findings by sociologists on the point. The best assessment of the evidence is probably that the military services do enhance educational levels, particularly for careerists and for those with poor educational backgrounds before entering the service. At least some programs, however, such as gov-

[5] Department of Defense, OSD/Manpower, *Officer Education Study*, Vol. I, 1966, p. 21.

[6] *Op. cit.*, Vol. III, pp. 514–515.

ernmentally subsidized education under the G.I. Bill, do not
necessarily have to be tied to service experience.

Effects of Military Service
on Civilian Occupation

Education is, in a way, a measure of the opportunities open to
an individual. A similar measure of life chances, but in some
ways even more direct, is an individual's occupation. The cen-
trality of occupation in our culture is set forth succinctly by
Joseph Kahl:

> In the first place, a man's occupation is the source of his income,
> which in turn provides the style of life that serves as one of the
> major clues used by his neighbors in making their evaluations. But
> occupation stands for more than merely a certain level of income. It
> indicates a man's education: it suggests the type of associates he
> comes in contact with on the job; it tells something of the contribu-
> tion he makes to community welfare; it hints at the degree of his
> authority over other people.[7]

For these reasons in our culture a man's occupation is an important measure of his place in the social system, and anything which
significantly affects his occupational chances is of social importance.

What effect does military service have on an individual's
occupation? Or perhaps even more to the point, is a veteran
better or worse off in terms of occupational opportunities than
the non-veteran? The question is a difficult one to answer, for a
simple comparison of veterans and non-veterans would give an
inaccurate indication. Those who serve in the military are far
from being a pure cross section of the society. The evidence
indicates that military service is more likely to be performed by
those in the middle of the social hierarchy than by those in
either the lowest or the highest strata. Those at the bottom of
the social structure are the most likely to be rejected by the
military services on the grounds of physical, emotional or intellectual unsuitability. Those at the top of the social structure are
most likely to be able to obtain deferments. Thus the highest
proportion of veterans comes from the middle groups of the

[7] Joseph A. Kahl, *The American Class Structure* (New York: Rinehart,
1957), p. 53.

158 — The Military and Socialization

society.[8] This means that any interpretation of a comparison between veterans and non-veterans must be made with care.

If we focus upon the effect of relatively short-term military service upon later occupational chances, it is necessary to identify the ways in which this effect can take place. The most direct way, of course, is if military training provides the individual with an occupational skill which can be transferred directly to civilian life. A second way, mentioned during the discussion of the effect of military service upon education, is for the individual to equip himself for employment at a higher occupational level by raising his level of general education. A third and less obvious way is if the experience of military service improves the individual's qualifications for employment by acting on such qualities as self-esteem, self-discipline, or the ability to perform satisfactorily within a complex organization. Recruiting appeals are often directed specifically in this vein: "The Marine Corps Builds Men"; "Join the Army and be a Leader." The effect of military service can, on the other hand, prove detrimental to the veteran's occupational status if it permanently interrupts his education or if he cannot overcome the detrimental effects of a later start in his chosen occupation. The existing data make it nearly impossible to separate out the influence of each of these factors, but do permit some assessment of the general effect of military service upon occupational chances.

Several recent studies on occupation and income level of veterans reach similar conclusions: despite the disruptive effect of military service, veterans have a slight tendency to hold higher socio-economic status occupations than non-veterans of similar backgrounds, and veterans have somewhat higher incomes.[9] Almost all of this improvement, however, is concentrated among those of the lowest educational and social backgrounds.[10] For

[8] Albert D. Klassen, *Military Service in American Life Since World War II: An Overview*. Report No. 117 (Chicago: National Opinion Research Center, September 1966).
[9] Otis Dudley Duncan and Robert W. Hodge, "Education and Occupational Mobility: A Regression Analysis," *American Journal of Sociology* (May, 1964), p. 642; Irving G. Katenbrink, Jr., "Military Service and Occupational Mobility," in Roger W. Little (ed.), *Selective Service and American Society* (New York: Russell Sage Foundation, 1969).
[10] Philip Cutright, *A Pilot Study of Factors in Economic Success or Failure: Based on Selective Service and Social Security Records*, U.S. Department of Health, Education, and Welfare, Social Security Administration, Division of Research and Statistics, June 1964; Katenbrink, *op. cit.*

someone with a white, middle-class background, military service appears to make little difference so far as occupational status is concerned. But for blacks and those with poor educational preparation, military service does appear to make a substantial difference. Among these groups, the veteran is much more likely to be a foreman or skilled worker, as compared with the higher rate of laborers who appear among the non-veterans.[11] Findings are similar where income is concerned. When veterans are compared with non-veterans of similar backgrounds, earnings are similar for all but groups with the lowest levels of educations. Within that group veterans have markedly higher earnings than non-veterans.[12] The conclusion to be drawn from the available research data is that military service is of substantial benefit to the life chances of those from less privileged backgrounds, but has little impact upon those from more privileged backgrounds.

One other role played by the military services in affecting social mobility should be mentioned, although numerically it is considerably less important than that discussed above. This is the role that the military service can play in permitting social mobility for careerists. This kind of mobility takes two forms. One is that achieved by the enlisted man who works his way up to a higher status in the military than he would have been likely to have achieved in civilian life. For some this may be senior non-commissioned officer status, for others it may mean commissioning through one of the several programs which permit enlisted men to become officers. The other way is direct entry into officer programs by individuals from working-class backgrounds. Individuals from lower-class backgrounds are increasingly populating the once aristocratic officers corps. In the West Point Class of 1965, for example, 27 per cent were of working-class origin.[13] This may be compared with 2 per cent of Army officers with working-class backgrounds in 1935, and 5 per cent in 1950.[14] On this subject Morris Janowitz has commented that the present rates of recruitment of individuals of working-class

[11] Morris Janowitz, "Basic Education and Youth Socialization in the Armed Forces," in Roger W. Little (ed.), *A Survey of Military Institutions*, 1969, pp. 141–143.

[12] *Ibid.*

[13] John P. Lovell, "The Professional Socialization of the West Point Cadet," *The New Military* (New York: Russell Sage Foundation, 1964), Table 17, p. 148.

[14] Morris Janowitz, *The Professional Soldier* (New York: The Free Press, 1961), p. 90.

origin into the officers corps make "the military as open a professional group as any in the United States.[15]

There is also evidence that lower-status individuals are more likely to become military careerists than are individuals of higher status, presumably because in comparing their life chances in civilian society with those in the service the military looks relatively better than it does for someone from a higher-status background. Recent statistics on re-enlistment rates, for example, make it clear that blacks are much more likely to re-enlist than whites—which may serve more as a commentary on the lack of opportunities open to blacks in the civilian community than it does as evidence of the benefits of a service career.

In general the effect of military service upon individual occupation patterns is to improve the job chances and income of individuals from lower-class backgrounds, while having little effect on those from higher-class backgrounds. In this sense the military does appear to provide a "second chance" for at least some individuals whose life chances in the civilian society are limited. Although several years of military service delays an individual's entry into a civilian occupational field, the evidence indicates that, at least after a period of transition, veterans appear on average to have benefited occupationally from their time in the military service.[16]

Effect of Military Service on Social Attitudes

Both supporters and detractors of the Military Services argue that time spent in the Armed Forces changes social attitudes. The claims range from that of the Presidential Advisory Commission quoted earlier that a period of time devoted to military service "would present additional opportunities for inculcating spiritual and moral ideals in support of American democracy," to fears that military indoctrination results in large numbers of

[15] Morris Janowitz, "Basic Education and Youth Socialization in the Armed Forces," in Roger W. Little (ed.), *A Survey of Military Institutions*, 1969, p. 151.

[16] An example of transitional problems is the data reported during the recession of 1970, in which newly released veterans had slightly higher rates of unemployment than did non-veterans of the same age. B. Drummond Ayres, Jr., "The Vietnam Veteran," *New York Times*, Sunday, November 8, 1970, p. 32.

violent men trained to be killers.[17] Faced with these conflicting possibilities, what effect *does* a period of military service have on social attitudes?

There seems to be no question that the intent of military training includes an attempt to inculcate certain values. The military academies attempt to inculcate a complete ethical code; West Point for example, emphasizes "duty, honor, country." John Hannah, former President of Michigan State University, while serving as Assistant Secretary of Defense, defended the service academies on the grounds that:

> While there are some things they may not do as well as our good civilian institutions . . . they do one thing much better, and that is they do instill in their students . . . a loyalty to the service, a loyalty to the government, an appreciation for ethics and integrity to a degree beyond what we do at our civilian institutions.[18]

At the enlisted level basic training, or "boot camp," is aimed as much at instilling certain attitudes, responses and loyalties in the new recruit as it is at teaching him specific skills. The intent, at every level, is to produce individuals who are useful to and work well within the military, and this necessarily implies a certain amount of indoctrination.

The evidence, however, indicates that the military services are not entirely successful in their efforts. Griping about military service among enlisted men is proverbial, and more careful evidence indicates that the attitudes of enlisted men toward the military system are generally much more negative than their officers believe them to be.[19] One reason for the relative ineffectiveness of military indoctrination programs has been pointed out by Jordan, who states:

> [T]he American soldier balks at being indoctrinated. During World War II, when the average serviceman was not nearly so well-educated as his counterpart twenty-five years later, a considerable part of his sleepy resistance to official orientation efforts was traceable to

[17] Report of the President's Advisory Commission on Universal Military Training, p. 92.

[18] John Masland and Laurence Radway. *Soldiers and Scholars* (Princeton, N.J.: Princeton University Press, 1959).

[19] Samuel A. Stouffer, *et. al.*, *The American Soldier*, Vol. I, (Princeton, N.J.: Princeton University Press, 1949); Charles C. Moskos, Jr., "Racial Integration in the Armed Forces," *American Journal of Sociology*, Vol. 72 (1966), pp. 132–148.

his suspicion that he was being propagandized. . . . The soldier's wariness of the "official" line has not lessened since.[20]

Evidence is again scanty, but such careful study as is available indicates that on average the individual develops improved self-esteem and personal adjustment during basic training, but at the same time develops more negative opinions about officers and non-commissioned officers.[21] Since the latter change is presumably in a direction opposite to that intended, it is apparent that indoctrination is something less than totally effective.

There has also been an attempt by scholars to measure whether or not military training increases authoritarianism, defined as the predisposition to arbitrarily dominate others of lower status and to simultaneously submit to arbitrary higher authority. Despite the expectation of the researchers that military training would increase authoritarianism, they were unable to measure any such increase. The instrument they were using (the "F" scale) actually showed a decrease of authoritarianism among officer candidates during training—which led the researchers to conclude that perhaps their instrument was inadequate.[22] Janowitz, after examining the available evidence on the effect of military training, concludes that basic training and non-combat service for limited periods have positive effects on a portion of the recruits, particularly in developing self-esteem and social maturity.[23]

Studies of social and political attitudes of both career and non-career servicemen fail to reveal any marked deviation of attitudes of servicemen from those prevalent among civilian groups of similar social and educational background.[24] There is also some

[20] Amos A. Jordan, Jr., "Troop Information and Indoctrination," in Little (ed.), op. cit., pp. 362–363.

[21] Richard Christie, Transition from Civilian to Army Life. HumRRO Technical Report No. 13. Washington, D.C. October 1954; Eugene Uyeki, "Sociology of the Cold War Army," Paper delivered at the American Sociological Association Convention, 1966.

[22] Donald T. Campbell and Thelma H. McCormack, "Military Experiences and Attitudes Toward Authority," American Journal of Sociology, 62 (March 1957), pp. 482–490.

[23] Morris Janowitz, "Basic Education and Youth Socialization in the Armed Forces," in Little (ed.), op. cit., p. 157.

[24] James A. Barber, Jr., "Is There a Generation Gap in the Naval Officer Corps?" Naval War College Review, XXII, No. 9 (May 1970), pp. 24–40; Morris Janowitz, The Professional Soldier (New York: the Free Press, 1961); Albert D. Klassen, Military Service in American Life Since World War II: An Overview. Report No. 117, Chicago: National Opinion Research Center, September 1966; Lovell, op. cit.

evidence to indicate that the experience of serving in integrated units in the Armed Forces tends to weaken racial prejudices, although it is clear that the services have been unable to completely isolate themselves from prevailing social attitudes.[25]

There is other evidence, however, which tends to dispute some claims that have been made for the social benefits of military service—for example the contention that exposure to foreign cultures breeds tolerance and understanding. Beyond the well-known fact that servicemen serving abroad almost invariably adopt derogatory slang terms to describe any foreigners with whom they come in regular contact, there is also some scholarly evidence to the effect that foreign service is more likely to reinforce parochialism than it is to broaden understanding.[26]

The evidence indicates that military service does not usually result in any very dramatic changes in social attitudes among those who serve. On average, a certain amount of maturing does take place, but social attitudes appear to be firmly enough set by the time a man enters the military service that in most cases they are subject to only marginal changes. These findings, however, must be viewed with some caution. Almost all of the careful studies which have been done on the subject have been done on the basis of observations made during the last thirty years. This has been a period in which there has been a regular high turnover of the members of the military establishment; a continuing high flow-through of individuals who come from a civilian environment, spend two to four years in the military service, then return to a civilian environment. During this same period more officers have been drawn from ROTC units scattered on civilian campuses throughout the country and from Officer Candidate programs using mostly graduates of civilian universities than have come from the military academies. Thus there has been full and continuing contact between the military and civilian communities. If this pattern is broken and replaced with all-volunteer, long-service professional soldiers led almost exclusively by graduates of the military academies, and if the present trend toward anti-military attitudes continues, isolating

[25] Charles C. Moskos, Jr., "Minority Groups in Military Organization," in Little (ed.), *op. cit.*, p. 239.

[26] Daniel Glaser, "The Sentiments of American Soldiers Abroad Toward Europeans," *American Journal of Sociology*, Vol. 51 (1946), pp. 433–438; Charles C. Moskos, "Racial Relations in the Armed Forces," in Moskos, (ed.), *The American Enlisted Man* (New York: Russell Sage Foundation, 1969).

the serviceman from the civilian community, then it is entirely possible that military social attitudes will take on a deviance they do not now have.

Conclusion

The evidence gathered here indicates that on average a period of military service is mildly beneficial to many individuals in terms of education, occupational chances and social attitudes, although the degree of benefit falls short of the more optimistic claims. It is noteworthy that such benefits as exist work especially well for individuals from less privileged backgrounds. Moskos, for example, concludes that "black servicemen enjoy relatively better opportunities in the armed forces than in the civilian economy in every clerical, technical, and skilled field for which data permit comparison."[27] The same thing appears to be true for education, where the benefits are most apparent for those with poor educational backgrounds before beginning military service.

There is considerable doubt, however, as to whether any attempt to remedy social inadequacies is a proper role for the Armed Forces. If social benefits are only by-products generated by the Services' attempts to effectively perform their primary tasks, that is one thing, but tasking the military with specific social tasks would seem to be a dubious proposition. As Hanson Baldwin pointed out during the UMT debate:

> In any case, it is clear that the military services must not—and if they are to be efficient militarily cannot—become educational institutions, Sunday schools or health clinics. The home, the school and the church must bear this responsibility.[28]

This would not be a problem if the performance of the military services in such roles was demonstrably inferior to that of the civilian community, but the fact seems to be that in at least some cases the military can perform certain kinds of social roles more effectively than is presently being done elsewhere. Of particular interest in this regard is the educational program inaugu-

[27] Charles C. Moskos, Jr., "Minority Groups in Military Organization," in Little (ed.), *op. cit.*, pp. 236–237.
[28] Hanson W. Baldwin, "UMT—A Hot Potato," *New York Times*, Thursday, May 1, 1947.

rated under Secretary of Defense McNamara in 1966, called "Project 100,000," and designed to reach and utilize a segment of the population otherwise destined to become hard-core un-employables. The relative success of this program, and some of the reasons for it, are discussed in the following article.

Characteristics of the
Military Environment

MORRIS JANOWITZ

The final step in our analysis is to seek a clearer and more precise
identification of those particular attributes in the military environment which help to explain its impact on basic education and
socialization. First, as mentioned above, is the skill structure of
the Armed Forces. By skill structure, we do not mean merely
the particular technical and professional requirements which are
essential for the military service. We mean the logic of the
organization including the rules by which it operates in the allocation of its manpower. The military is an organization through
which each year new cohorts of young men enter. Once a
person is admitted into the institution, there is no question but
that the organization must incorporate him into a functioning
role. In this sense, despite its complex skill structure, the military is a primitive organization or a non-economic organization.
In this sense, all of its members are equal; all of its members are
soldiers in a basic sense.

There is no need for the new recruit to have any doubt as
to whether there is a place for him in the institution. This is
not to assume that all new members adjust to the system or that
the institution does not seek to reject some persons. But by comparison with most civilian institutions, and particularly by comparison with the public education system, it is an organization
based on the complete availability of opportunity plus a basic
standard of acceptance of each member.

This logic of full incorporation works precisely because there

Reprinted with permission of the author from Roger W. Little (ed.), *A
Survey of Military Institutions*, The Inter-University Seminar on Armed
Forces and Society, Inc., 1969.

is a pervasive element of reality involved. The military is a highly centralized organization in terms of strategic decision-making; and it is a highly complex organization. But in his day-to-day assignments, each soldier quickly recognizes that he has real work to perform and that he has a real capacity to assist or retard the function of his immediate group. There is a diffusion of operational responsibility throughout the institution. Even the rifleman, who is located on the bottom of a vast organization, has a sense of competence—not only because of the power of his weapon, but because in the modern military, concepts of team and group authority make him rapidly aware of his individuality. Regardless of the hierarchical features of the system, to be effective requires not merely compliance with orders, but positive participation.

Second, the military operates with a set of training procedures which assume maximum potentials for personal growth. The very notion of basic training implies that there is a set of skills which all members of the institution can and must know. Basic training is required of all members as a mechanism of assimilation. As indicated above, prior social characteristics are de-emphasized during this period, and this includes in particular social disabilities accumulated during civilian life, such as delinquency records and academic grades.

But even more pointed, the training procedures operate on the assumption that each person has the potentiality of mastering the contents of basic training, or that it is up to the system to teach each young man the essentials for success in basic training. This does not mean that there are no failures in basic training, but rather that those who manage the training develop the perspective that they can teach almost anyone.

Without the benefit of the educational psychologists, the basic training systems of the Armed Services incorporate many so-called "advanced" procedures. There is no ability grouping and all recruits are mixed together, so that the heterogeneous character of the group will create the optimum conditions for learning and group support. The training cycle is based on the equivalent of the non-graded or continuous educational development scheme. The recruit is not graded at the end of the course with a pass or fail, but at the end of each sub-section he is evaluated, given remedial help or recycled through the specific phase of his training in which he is deficient. There is extensive emphasis on instruction by the equivalent of the apprentice system in which instruction is given during the actual exercise or task.

The operation of Project 100,000 is a striking example of the operation of basic training in the military establishment. In August 1966, it was decided that an experimental program would induct 100,000 men who, according to the then existing standards, ordinarily would be screened out. Included in this group were young men with limited educational background or low educational achievement (Category Four). Project 100,000 meant that a group of "deprived" young men would be taken into the Armed Forces both because of the pressure of military manpower needs and as an experiment in basic education. If the task had been assigned to a civilian educational system, they would have likely segregated these men, devised a special curriculum and engendered in them the feeling that they are clearly inferior manpower resources. However, the Armed Forces merely included them in its regular training cycle.

As of 1967, under Project 100,000 more than 49,000 men had entered the Armed Forces under "new standards" which permitted the acceptance of men who had previously been rejected for induction or enlistment. Previously, only a small proportion of men who scored between 10 and 30 on the AFQT were accepted, and then only after they had scored above 90 on two or more aptitude tests. The revised standards permitted the acceptance of high school graduates in Category Four, without additional testing. Non-high school graduates with AFQT scores between 16 and 30 were accepted if they scored 90 or higher on at least one test; those with scores between 10 and 15 were required to pass two aptitude tests. More than a third of those who entered this program were voluntary enlistments. Their average age was 21 years. They had completed an average 10.5 grades of school. About 32 per cent had failed at least one grade of school, and 17 per cent had failed two grades. More than 29 per cent were unemployed and an additional 27 per cent earned less than $50.00 a week.

After one year, there was sufficient evidence to demonstrate the wastage of human resources that had previously occurred because of rigid entry requirements. More than 96 per cent successfully completed basic training, although the discharge rate ranged from a low of 3 per cent in the army to 9.5 per cent in the Air Force. (The defense-wide discharge rate for all other men is about 2 per cent. These rates also include medical discharges for conditions other than lack of aptitude.) Equally noteworthy was their achievement in advanced training, where the attrition rate was 12.3 per cent compared to the average Army attrition rate for all men of 8 per cent. Their success in some highly complex fields was as follows: 73 per cent in communications and intelligence and medical and dental specialties; 87 per cent in administration and clerical schools; 78 per cent in electrical and mechanical equipment repair; and 88 per cent in crafts. Over half of those in training for electronic equipment repair successfully completed their courses (55 per cent). It should be noted that these success rates were not achieved in special courses designed for the "intellectually disadvantaged," but were made under the same requirements as those established for men with higher entry attributes.

After training, not only were these men assigned to "infantry, gun crews, and allied specialties" (33 per cent), but their success in advanced training had increased their versatility so that relatively more were ultimately assigned tasks which could provide useful civilian skills: electrical and mechanical equipment repair, 20 per cent; service and supply handlers, 18 per cent; and administration and clerical, 10 per cent.

After 22 months of Project One Hundred Thousand, 125,152 men had been accepted under the new standards for recruitment, of whom about half were volunteers and the remainder were draftees. A progress report issued by the Department of Defense in September 1968 pointed out that 95 per cent of the new standards men were accepted by lowering the mental test standards, while 5 per cent were accepted for remedial treatment after induction (Office Secretary of Defense, 1968).

A comparison of these new standards men with a control group revealed them to be of the same average age (20.4 years for the new standards men and 20.2 for the control group). They were by no means predominantly black; not even a majority were black, confirming the well-known observation that deprived groups in our society are heterogeneous. In the control group 9.1 per cent were non-white, while among the new standards men the concentration of non-white was 39.6 per cent (and non-white is a broader category than Negro). The outstanding difference was in their reading ability. The control group had a median reading ability of grade 10.9, with 1.1 per cent reading below the fourth grade; the new standards men displayed a median reading ability of grade 6.1 and 14.4 per cent were reading below fourth grade.

Almost two years after the program had been launched, the preliminary results were highly successful. Nearly 96 per cent of the new standards men successfully completed basic training as compared with 98 per cent for all other men. Strong efforts were made to expose these men to skill training in a formal course. In the Army and Marine Corps, nearly all new standards men received such training while in the Air Force, about 40 per cent were given on-the-job training, and in the Navy most men also received on-the-job training. In formal skill courses the attrition rate varies from service to service, but the overall rate for these men was about 10 per cent, as compared to about 4 per cent for other men attending similar courses. Men who are dropped from training are not discharged from service, but usually re-assigned to other courses or on-the-job training more suited to their aptitudes.

As a result of such training, the new standards men could be given a wide range of assignments, and their allocation to combat and non-combat tasks was similar to the overall intake of recruits. About 62 per cent of the new standards men were assigned to non-combat type skills, while 70 per cent of the control group were assigned to non-combat type skills.

Perhaps the most sensitive measure both of the progress of new standards men and the response of the various services to these men is their rate of promotion. Of the first group of new standards men who entered the Army during October-December 1966, 84.4 per cent were E-3's and above after an average of 16½ months of service; while for the control group the percentage was 92.6 per cent. At the E-4 level and above, a wider difference emerges with 47.0 per cent of the new standards men reaching that level while the percentage was 64.3 per cent for the control group.

Disciplinary records revealed that only 2.8 per cent of the Army men of the new standards had court martial convictions after 16½ months of service. Finally, of the first group of new standards men, 90.4 per cent were still in service on March 31, 1967. This attrition from active service includes battle deaths and wounds and discharges due to physical disabilities as well as separations for unsuitability, unfitness, misconduct, hardship and other causes.

Success in basic training, which involves an opportunity for developing a sense of self-esteem and a feeling of group participation, becomes the basis in part for further education and advanced training. Of special importance are the experiences of Project Transition as representing the emerging approach of the military to technical training. As a response to the task of preparing its recruits for transition back to civilian life and as a contribution to larger societal goals, the armed forces have instituted a program of technical training for enlisted personnel who are completing their term of service and who did not have an opportunity for such technical training. Such training is of special importance for recruits from lower socio-economic backgrounds, who have entered combat units and who have developed skills which are not transferable to civilian employment.

It is important to emphasize that the skill training in Project Transition comes after the recruit develops some involvement and acceptance in the military. This is just the reverse of the civilian society where educational success is first demanded as a criterion for institutional involvement. The Israeli army, of course, is an example of a military force which strongly emphasizes its basic education function. In the Israeli Armed Forces, all citizens are eligible to serve, except a tiny group of very handicapped personnel. There are no social nor educational barriers. After mastering basic training and the rudiments of soldiering and not before, the recruits are given basic literacy education. This is also the assumption of Project Transition.

Third, the organizational climate of the military supplies an appropriate context for its basic education and socialization function, especially for recruits from the lower socio-economic background. One does not have to offer any romantic notions to point to actual realities. In contrast to the material conditions of the slum, life in the military is organized and relatively satisfactory from a material point of view.

Of particular importance are the large amounts of available food. The uniform is of special significance both because of its intrinsic quality and the fascination that develops around being conspicuously dressed. The physical activity and athletic-like character of basic training also need to be mentioned. Of equal or greater importance is the fact that the culture of the enlisted man is a direct outgrowth of civilian working-class existence. The standards of personal language, of physical contact and the style of indulgence such as "beer drinking" do not require the recruit to denounce suddenly earlier patterns of gratification.

Fourth, the basic social context is strikingly important. The recruit soon discovers that it is operated under a juridical system which, despite its particular features, offers the person from lower socio-economic groups and minority groups a greater sense of protection than he had in civilian life. His medical needs, his welfare and insurance, his personal protection are directly available and not as the result of exchange relations in which he feels he is being exploited. This is not to underestimate the resentment that develops toward authority that is always potentially present, but to emphasize the importance for the recruit of being in a stable environment. The fact that the environment is socially integrated is important both for Negroes and for the white population.

The information and control systems of the military serve to enhance the position of the recruit who enters the military from a deprived and disorganized background. The military accepts responsibility for his well-being. This implies that specific personnel are responsible for observing and monitoring the recruits' experiences and the results. The machinery is elaborate, cumbersome, and at times inefficient. But there is a peculiar sensitivity to the needs of a particular individual, especially of those who are in need of assistance. In part, this derives from the professional ethic that the officer—both commissioned and non-commissioned—has prestige among other officers to the extent that he takes care of his men. In part, it is the result of the information system which makes it possible to follow up on a particular recommendation or a particular action. The recruit is living in a residential setting and it is therefore more difficult to avoid confrontation with a human problem or to push aside personal needs. If a recruit has a medical problem, or is in need of some remedial educational assistance, the circumstances are different from civilian life where intervention often means referral to a particular agency without follow up. In the military, a report will be generated as to the final outcome.

The recruit comes to deal with, to work with, and to become the comrade of men with diverse styles and aspirations. He comes to recognize the existence of a larger world. In contrast to a social agency, or the community settlement house, the military is not based on the notion that the young man must accept himself. The military is a school for fashioning new self-conceptions, and it is a system in which informal communications serve to explore and test out these alternatives. The special character of the military means that lower-class youths can assimilate new values because during the time of military service they are on a somewhat more equal footing with the more privileged members of the larger society. It is the "underutilization" of the more middle-class groups that supplies an important ingredient for change.

The bulk of the data and observations of this chapter are drawn from the period between 1945 and the build-up of the

Armed Forces in South Vietnam. The Armed Forces during this period have mainly served as a large-scale training and logistical enterprise. The specific impacts of combat, in terms of the social, psychological and psychiatric consequences, are explored elsewhere. Moreover, limits are placed on the observations and hypotheses that are offered by the changing military environment. In particular, military operations in South Vietnam have been without popular support among specific youth and college groups, and have been strongly opposed. The result has been a negativism toward military service which—if it has had its counterpart in other historic periods, particularly the Civil War—may well produce new consequences for both those who have and who have not served. Finally, if the Armed Forces come to operate without reliance on a selective service system, there will again be profound changes in the military environment which will influence their role in basic education and socialization.

PART V

The Military
and
Race Relations

Blacks in the Army in Two World Wars

STEPHEN E. AMBROSE

As an individual the negro is docile, tractable, lighthearted, care free and good natured. If unjustly treated he is likely to become surly and stubborn, though this is usually a temporary phase. He is careless, shiftless, irresponsible and secretive. He resents censure and is best handled with praise and by ridicule. He is unmoral, untruthful and his sense of right doing is relatively inferior. . . .

On the other hand the negro is cheerful, loyal and usually uncomplaining if reasonably well fed. He has a musical nature and a marked sense of rhythm. His art is primitive. He is religious. With proper direction in mass, negroes are industrious. They are emotional and can be stirred to a high state of enthusiasm. Their emotions are unstable and their reactions uncertain.

The preceeding passage could have been written by almost any white American at almost any stage of American history. It was not intended to be racist, at least in the direct sense of providing material for further repression of blacks, but rather represented a sincere attempt by senior officers at the U.S. Army War College to assess the strengths and weaknesses of 10 per cent of the population. The officers wanted to maximize the contribution blacks could make to the Army in the event of a general mobilization for total war. They prepared the report in 1937 on the eve of war; they felt that they were being objective and realistic in summing up the lessons learned from a study of black troops in World War I, even though the report said a great deal more about predominant white attitudes than it did about the real performance of blacks in the World War and previous conflicts.

The report also succinctly illustrated why the War Department was never able to solve the black "problem."[1] Given the assumptions of most white officers, especially those at the top, it was almost inevitable that the War Department would segregate black troops, put generally incompetent white officers in charge of them (black officers served only at the most junior level), deny blacks any hope of advancement, assign them the most menial tasks, pawn off the worst and oldest equipment on black units, deliberately keep blacks out of the more sophisticated arms, such as the Signal Corps or the Air Corps, assign black units to the least desirable posts, where they received inadequate and inferior training, and in general do almost everything possible to insure that blacks would fail the test of combat. And when, despite everything, black soldiers did perform adequately—and often enough magnificently—the Army and the public simply ignored the record, so that black service and heroism in defense of the nation became another of the many forgotten pages of black history in the United States. The U.S. Army, in short, did not take the lead in promoting equality of opportunity or racial justice in America.

Yet many black Americans pinned their hopes for a better future on the Army. William E. B. DuBois, editor of *The Crisis*, official organ of the National Association for the Advancement of Colored People, who later joined the Communist Party and who hardly was an Uncle Tom, was one of these. In an editorial during World War I, DuBois wrote, "*The Crisis* says, *first* your Country, *then* your Rights!" His justification was historical. "Five thousand Negroes fought in the Revolution; the result was the emancipation of the slaves in the North and the abolition of the African slave trade. At least three thousand Negro soldiers and sailors fought in the War of 1812; the result was the enfranchisement of the Negro in many northern States and the beginning of a strong movement for general emancipation. Two hundred thousand Negroes enlisted in the Civil War, and the result was the emancipation of four million slaves, and the enfranchisement of the black man. Some ten thousand Negroes fought in the Spanish-American War, and in the twenty years ensuing since that war, despite many setbacks, we have doubled or quadrupled our accumulated wealth." If the black man would fight to defeat the Kaiser, DuBois argued, he could later present

---

[1] The Navy Department did better. After World War I it solved the problem by the simple expedient of eliminating it—i.e., no blacks at all served in the Navy. Even the mess boy jobs were allotted to Filipinos.

a bill for payment due to a grateful white America, a bill that the nation would in all conscience be obligated to pay.

DuBois was unquestionably presenting the views of the vast majority of America's blacks. His history may have been poor—what gains black Americans had made were not directly linked to service in war, and the gains were hardly as great as he indicated—but the sentiment was authentic. Blacks did take tremendous pride in their historical record as members of the Army. They knew what white America had managed to forget—that no matter how circumscribed their troops had been, no matter how limited the role they had been allowed to play, in fact black soldiers had made a significant contribution to victory in all America's wars.

There was another factor. Bad as the situation was for blacks in the Army, it was worse nearly everywhere else. Except in times of severe depression, the Army has historically been unable to enlist enough men to maintain its authorized strength. Yet it never had the slightest difficulty in filling its assigned quota of blacks. Recruiting sergeants did not even bother to talk to blacks; they merely told them to go to a post where a black unit was stationed. There the prospective recruit—who had to travel at his own expense, usually from the Southeast to the western plains—had to wait for an opening in a black regiment, an opening that seldom came because black re-enlistment rates were much higher than the rate among white troops. For three generations after the Civil War, the Army maintained four black regiments, the 9th and 10th Cavalry and the 24th and 25th Infantry. These units compiled an outstanding record in the Indian Wars and the Spanish-American War. For the men who served, the Army offered three square meals a day and shoes on the feet, plus regular—if small—pay. At least the pay was equal to what white soldiers received, and in the Army blacks could wear noncoms' stripes and exercise some authority. In general, none of these benefits were available to blacks in any other sector of American society, so that even as late as 1940, when only one black man had graduated from West Point in the preceding generation, and when the total number of black Regular Army officers was five (of whom three were chaplains), there were still far more potential black recruits than the Army wished to accept.

Thus Ulysses Lee, author of *The Employment of Negro Troops* in the Army's official history, *United States Army in World War II*, has concluded: "The Army and military life had long occupied a position of relatively greater concern and importance to the Negro public than to Americans in general. Soldiering had been an honored career for the few Negroes who were able to enter upon it. In the restricted range of economic opportunities open to them, the military life ranked high."

For black leaders, in the nineteenth as well as the twentieth century, the importance of the Army was that it offered a unique opportunity for black Americans to make a direct, undeniable contribution to the nation. Whites might find it possible to ignore the blacks' role in conquering the wilderness, or to downgrade the black man's labor, but to DuBois and other leaders it seemed inconceivable that anyone could fail to notice and respond positively to the black soldiers' heroism. Yet this is precisely what happened, as it had always happened. Blacks had fought in the Revolutionary War; they remained slaves. Blacks fought against the British in 1812 and helped build the American empire in the Mexican War; they remained slaves. Nearly a quarter of a million blacks joined the Grand Army of the Republic and fought in some of the bloodiest battles of the Civil War to help save the Union (and the Republican Party); in 1876 the Grand Old Party, having given the slaves their legal freedom and nothing more, abandoned them once again to their Southern masters. The 9th and 10th Cavalry helped win the West; in 1907 Oklahoma came into the Union with the most blatantly racist, segregationist state constitution ever written.

DuBois was perfectly aware of the fact that no matter what black men did in the service of the nation, they could not count on postwar white gratitude to advance their position. Yet like the whites, he was willing to rewrite history in order to encourage black participation in World War I. He evidently reasoned that in 1917, given the nature of America's war propaganda (make the world safe for democracy), whites could not ignore their clear responsibility. He therefore urged young black men to enlist and, ignoring harassment and severe limitations on the roles they were allowed to play, to do their best.

Whether the black masses needed any encouragement to serve or not is unclear, nor is it at all certain that they had general, as opposed to their own individual, expectations. In 1917-18, in any case, 404,348 black men did enlist or submit to conscription. Less than 1,500 received commissions, and the great bulk served in the services of supply, in quartermaster, stevedore, and pioneer infantry units. In short, the Army assigned them traditional menial labor roles in which they had no opportunity to distinguish themselves. Another serious blow to black hopes came when the Army announced that it had assigned the four Regular Army black regiments to defensive positions in the continental United States and its island territories. These regiments contained combat-tested troops (most recently with Pershing in Mexico), had experienced leaders, and had expected to lead black volunteers and conscripts in any general war situation, just as their white counterparts in the Regular Army did.

The Army did organize and send to France two black infantry divisions, the 92d and 93d. Both had black officers in junior grades but were otherwise commanded by whites. The 93d Division was not a true division, as it never served together and had no divisional trains or artillery. Its four regiments served separately with the French Army, where they were reorganized according to French methods and used as integral parts of French divisions on the Western Front. They fought with credit in Champagne, the Vosges, and in the Oise-Aisne offensive. After the war the French Government awarded the Croix de Guerre to three of the 93d's regiments and to a company of the fourth. These regiments, therefore, fighting as partially integrated units under the command of relatively unprejudiced French officers, achieved the record DuBois had hoped for. The French had such a high regard for the 93d's regiments that in June, 1918, they asked for all the black units the United States could send to serve in their army. Few disputed the achievement of the 93d Division.

The history of the 92d, on the other hand, became a subject of great bitterness and controversy. Even while it was still in training in the States, black leaders became suspicious of the Army's intentions. In May, 1918, *The Crisis* charged that unless improvements in training, equipment and staffing were made, the division was bound to fail. "Is it possible that persons in the War Department wish this division to be a failure?" the magazine asked. After the war, two black junior officers of the 92d charged that "the Negro division was the object of special victimization, superimposed upon its sacrifice." The evidence they advanced was voluminous. It included the fact that the division had trained in sections and was never assembled in one place until the last days of the war. The Army issued it inferior equipment and assigned "the most ignorant and physically disqualified Negroes in the United States," with 40 per cent of the men illiterate. White enlisted men refused to salute the black officers of the 92d, who were also refused service at most officers' clubs. Whites, meanwhile, argued that the difficulties of the 92d proved the hope-lessness of using blacks in any but the most menial roles, and certainly not as officers.

Critical blacks concentrated on two major grievances. The first was the forced retirement, in June, 1917, of Colonel Charles Young, the highest ranking black Regular Army Officer. Most observers had expected that Young would command the 92d Division in battle. His credentials were impressive; a West Point graduate with an outstanding record, he was one of the few field grade officers with General Pershing in Mexico whom Persh-ing had recommended to command militia in the federal service. Blacks charged that Young was retired "because the army did not want a black general" and to prove the charge quoted white officers who had said as much in public addresses.

The second grievance concerned the men who did serve as the senior officers in the 92d. They were almost all southerners, in accordance with Army tradition, which held that southerners knew best how to handle black men. Some of these officers in-troduced themselves to their units by announcing that they "had once suckled black mammies' breasts." The commander of the division told his troops to make 2d Lieutenant John Alexander their model; Alexander, he pointed out, "knew how to stay in his place."

In his provocative study of *Slavery*, Stanley Elkins suggests that the constant reiteration of the Sambo theme by whites, and their expectations about black behavior (not to mention their treatment of the slaves), did actually produce a Sambo personal-ity. One does not have to agree with Elkins' description of the slave personality to recognize the value of role-playing for blacks —those slaves who came closest to fitting the white man's image of blacks generally received the most rewards. The twentieth cen-tury Army was no exception. Thus, in choosing black junior officers for the 92d, whites tended to pick Regular Army en-listed men who, while lacking even a fair education, had proved that they knew how to keep their place and even grovel when required to do so. Or commissions went to those who satisfied the white image of blacks; thus one man became a lieutenant by singing plantation songs for white officers, while another black officer had been a U.S. Senator's butler.

The Army officially maintained that it made no distinction be-tween black and white troops, other than segregating them. In accordance with then current Supreme Court doctrine, it claimed that it provided separate but equal opportunities, privileges, equipment, leadership, and so on. In practice, of course, blacks suffered discrimination everywhere they turned, from Red Cross and recreational facilities to the weapons they received. Soon enough, blacks complained. In March, 1918, therefore, the division commander, Major General Charles C. Ballou, issued Bulletin #35, urging his men to avoid raising questions of discrimination "NO MATTER HOW LEGALLY CORRECT," and advising them that "the success of the Division with all that success implies is dependent upon the good will of the public. That public is nine-tenths white. White men made the Division, and they can break it just as easily if it becomes a trouble maker."

The Wilson Administration never dared go so far as to break up the division, but it seemed to black observers that the War Department did everything possible to destroy morale. Black officers and correspondents reported that when the 92d got to France, the men were kept out of schools; rather than training they spent their time policing drill fields and barracks; staff officers were constantly shifted; white officers came into the division and were transferred out as quickly as they had obtained desired promotions; the division went into the Argonne engagement without proper briefing, artillery support, rifle grenades, wire cutters, or horses.

Most galling of all, perhaps, were the restrictions on contacts with French civilians. White Americans generally had never liked the idea of giving black men rifles and the same uniforms and pay as white soldiers. They were horrified at the thought of black Americans mingling freely with French civilians, especially girls. The Army therefore prohibited all leaves for the men of the 92d.[2]

Despite all the overt, heavy-handed discrimination, the men of the 92d, like nearly all blacks serving in France, remained loyal. Whites took their loyalty for granted, as whites have done since the founding of the Republic, but the Germans—like the British in the Revolution, the Nazis and the Japanese in World War II, the Chinese in Korea, and the Viet Cong in Vietnam—did not. America's opponents in war have attempted through their propaganda to weaken the U.S. Army by striking at its most obvious shortcoming, racial discrimination. Why fight for racist America?

---

[2] Race riots during the war, and in 1919, stemmed in part from the white fear that black soldiers would forget their place. This was the other side of DuBois' coin, for just as he hoped that black service in the Army would promote racial equality—not least by giving black men self-respect— so did whites fear the same thing and work to prevent it.

they have asked in literature and speeches distributed to black troops. The Army has never found it necessary to mount a concerted campaign to counter its enemies' propaganda, for historically the American black man has been among the nation's most loyal citizens.

The ultimate test of the 92d came in combat. On 26 and 27 September, 1918, elements of the division attempted to drive the Germans from a defensive position in the Argonne Forest. They failed, hardly an unusual experience for fresh troops on the Western Front, and a few men ran to the rear, also hardly unique. The blacks had excuses, and not just ones related to their training and general treatment. Among other shortages, they had no wire cutters, maps, or artillery support. Nevertheless, the division was withdrawn in disgrace from the front, much to General Ballou's disgust, for he felt that having had its baptism of fire it was now ready to render good service. Still, he relieved 30 black officers and court-martialed five for cowardice in the face of the enemy, thereby pointing the finger of blame at the black junior officers. The Army concluded that the experiment of using blacks in combat leadership roles had failed.

Ballou, however, knew better. In 1920, he declared, "It was my misfortune to be handicapped by many white officers who were rabidly hostile to the idea of a colored officer, and who continually conveyed misinformation to the staff of the superior units, and generally created much trouble and discontent." But Ballou did nothing effective to change the Army's official view. Even well-meaning commentators could not rise above their stereotypes. On July 26, 1918, the *Milwaukee Sentinel*, after praising two of the 92d's regiments, wrote, "Those two American colored regiments fought well, and it calls for special recognition. Is there no way of getting a cargo of watermelons over there?" Small wonder that black First Lieutenant Howard Long, who held a master's degree in psychology from Clark University, could say that the trouble with the 92d had been "many of the field officers seemed far more concerned with reminding their Negro subordinates that they were Negroes than they were with having an effective unit that would perform well in combat."

Whatever the objective facts may have been concerning the 92d's combat record, it was what the white man believed that counted. And whites concluded that blacks were cowards, inefficient leaders, and capable only of unskilled labor tasks. Major General Robert Bullard, commander of the Second Army, expressed the view of the War Department in his memoirs (published in 1925), when he declared, "If you need combat soldiers, and especially if you need them in a hurry, don't put your time upon Negroes. . . . If racial uplift or racial equality is your purpose, that is another matter." Since the Army adamantly maintained that its purpose was to fight the nation's wars as efficiently as possible, and certainly not to promote "racial uplift or racial equality," that settled the case. In the next war, blacks would provide labor forces, not combat troops or officers.

DuBois had seen this development early on. By the time the war ended, he realized that his dream of achieving racial justice by serving in the war was doomed. "We did love our country," he said, emphasizing the past tense to heighten his bitterness, "because we deemed it capable of realizing our dreams and inspiring the greater world. [We] all loved and loved passionately not America, but what America might be—the Real America, as we sometimes said."

DuBois went to France in 1919 to prepare a history of the black man in the war and immediately recognized that "the word to acknowledge the Negro stevedore . . . has gone forth, but the American army is going to return to America determined to disparage the black officer and eliminate him from the army. . . ." In May, 1919, he published a series of documents he had uncovered. One was a letter from a senior white officer in the 92d Division requesting the removal of Negro officers before they had been tested in battle; another contained orders giving evidence of discriminatory treatment; a third was a letter written by the 92d's chief of staff to a U.S. Senator proposing that never again should a division with black officers be organized. The Post Office Department banned from the mails the issue of *The Crisis* containing the documents.

Under the circumstances, black Americans could hardly accept the pervasive white view about the performance of black troops in the war. Black leaders were certain that if the facts were revealed they would prove that black officers and men did well when given a chance, that when they failed it was because of faulty white leaders too preoccupied with their own prejudices, and most of all that black soldiers had done far better than they were credited with doing. DuBois and others felt that the Army and the Administration had deliberately decided to withhold credit where it was due, for otherwise there could be no justification for denying full rights and privileges as citizens to blacks who had proven their loyalty to America and their ability as leaders and soldiers on the field of battle.

Black leaders, however, even those of DuBois' stature, hardly had the ear of the War Department. In the twenties and thirties, as Army General Staff officers prepared plans for the next mobilization, it was difficult if not impossible for them to overcome their own prejudices, reinforced as they were by the reports on the 92d Division. The widely held conclusion was that black combat troops in World War I failed to come up to Army standards, so the most efficient way to utilize black soldiers was as common laborers. This was the attitude on the eve of World War II—as indicated in the 1937 Army War College study quoted at the beginning of this essay—and it dominated the black man's participation in the U.S. Army in that war.

Franklin Roosevelt commanded the biggest Jim Crow outfit in history. The Navy and Marine Corps under his command did not even accept black volunteers; not until late in the war, when they were forced to take men from a common Selective Service pool, did they have any blacks at all. In the Army, black strength was always lower than the percentage of blacks in the general population would justify, even though fewer blacks than whites were exempted from the draft because of occupational deferments and even though blacks again found it difficult to enlist when they wanted to do so. When the war began, blacks made up slightly more than 10 per cent of the total population but only 5.8 per cent of the Army. By March, 1945, blacks constituted 8.5 per cent of the Army. At that time, there were 694,000 blacks in the Army, nearly all of them in segregated outfits. Over 400,000 of the blacks were in service (labor) units, while 150,000 were attached to combat units as support troops on a segregated basis. Only 5,073 served as commissioned officers.

At the beginning of the war, novelist Dorothy Canfield Fisher (and many others) wrote Chief of Staff George Marshall urging him to form an integrated volunteer division. She pointed to the symbolic importance such a unit would have as an answer to Japanese propaganda that the war pitted white men against the world's colored people. Marshall replied, in a letter probably drafted by General Walter B. Smith (who at that time handled the "colored problem" for the Chief of Staff) that the use of a volunteer system would interfere with the "scientific and orderly selective processes" used by the Army. "The urgency of the present military situation necessitates our using tested and proved methods of procedure," Marshall declared, "in order to increase efficiency." The reply ignored the fact that the clear lesson of

World War I was that putting blacks into segregated outfits was the least efficient, rather than the "tested and proved," method, but nevertheless it remained the policy. A few black divisions were formed (according to Lee's *The Employment of Negro Troops* primarily because there was no other way the Army could absorb large numbers of black soldiers in a hurry), but in general they suffered the same fate as the 92d Division in World War I. The 92d Division, in fact, was once again involved in considerable controversy about its combat record (in Italy), revolving around issues similar to those in 1918. The 93d Division, which served in the Pacific, was mainly limited to rear echelon labor duties. Overall, the Army once again kept its black units in the shadows.

Although black leaders complained about the misuse and mistreatment of black soldiers, as they had in World War I, Mrs. Eleanor Roosevelt received much more attention in the mass media for her attempts to ensure fair (although segregated) treatment for blacks in training camps. Black hopes were not as high in 1941 as they had been in 1917; within the black community there was something like an air of resignation, a realization that for all the talk about Atlantic Charters and Four Freedoms, Jim Crow and business as usual would be the order of the day back in the States once the war was over. Although the black press and black political organizations did press the War Department to meet at least its minimal responsibilities to the black soldiers, few seemed to feel that they could win their freedom at home by fighting for America abroad. For most American blacks, the Army remained a place to seek limited personal advancement, or at least economic security, but hardly a vehicle for social change.

Still, in the last months of the war in Europe, black soldiers did get a chance to prove themselves. The opportunity came in December, 1944, after the German counter-offensive in the Ardennes. When the Germans began the Battle of the Bulge, Supreme Allied Commander Dwight Eisenhower had only a handful of replacements available in his vast theater. By late December, to all intents and purposes he had none. General John C. H. Lee, commander of the Communications Zone (transportation, supply, etc.) offered a partial solution. He had over 100,000 black soldiers under his command, many of whom were eager to volunteer for infantry duty, especially if they could serve with organized, veteran divisions. After getting approval from Eisenhower's headquarters, Lee sent out an appeal to "a limited number of colored troops who have had infantry training, the privilege of joining our veteran units at the front. . . ." He said Eisenhower planned to assign the men "without regard to color or race to the units where assistance is most needed, and give you the opportunity of fighting shoulder to shoulder to bring about victory."

When General Walter B. Smith, by then Eisenhower's Chief of Staff, read the circular, he exploded. Smith recognized that Lee's proposal represented a major break with traditional Army policy, for it would mix black soldiers into white units, not on a smaller unit segregated basis (which had been done sparingly during the war) but as individuals fitted in where needed. Smith told Eisenhower he regarded Lee's circular as "the most dangerous thing that I [have] ever seen in regard to negro relations." Smith said he had talked to Lee, "and he can't see this at all. He believes that it is right that colored and white soldiers should be mixed in the same company." This ran directly counter to War Department policy, Smith insisted, and however great the emergency Lee's circular had to be withdrawn.

Eisenhower bent under Smith's pressure, but the crisis was so severe that he refused to give in altogether. He rewrote Lee's circular, dropping the promise that blacks could serve shoulder to shoulder with their white countrymen but still offering them an opporunity to fight with the infantry in veteran units. In a message to Marshall explaining his decision, Eisenhower said that if he had more black volunteers than vacancies in black combat units, he would assign the excess men to segregated battalions for temporary attachment to divisions. "This will preserve the principle for which I understand the War Department stands," he declared, "and will still have a beneficial effect in meeting our infantry needs."

Even without the promise of integration, over 4,500 black troops volunteered, many of them sergeants and corporals who accepted a reduction in grade to qualify since only privates were eligible. Since the Ground Force Reinforcement System in Europe was equipped only to train individuals for infantry service, the black volunteers could not be formed into black battalions, nor could they be trained as replacements for existing black combat units, as there were no black infantry units in Eisenhower's theater (only some tank and tank destroyer outfits). Eisenhower therefore had them formed into segregated infantry platoons, with white non-coms, and assigned to the front lines as needed.

The black platoons (nearly fifty in all), fighting as integral parts of white companies, compiled an outstanding record. The report of the Personnel Officer of the 104th Division on his black platoon was typical: "Morale: Excellent. Manner of performance: Superior. Men are very eager to close with the enemy and to destroy him. Strict attention to duty, aggressiveness, common sense and judgment under fire has won the admiration of all the men in the company. The colored platoon after initial success continued to do excellent work. . . . All agree that the colored platoon has a calibre of men equal to any veteran platoon." A few white officers declared that the black troops were too aggressive and occasionally overextended themselves, but when the black units suffered losses and could no longer function as platoons, the remaining men were formed into squads and served in white platoons, without complaint from either side. Although the black man's chance to prove himself came only at the war's end, the black platoons did so well that perceptive, younger Army officers began to wonder if segregation really was the most efficient method of organization.

Not, however, the senior officers. After the German surrender, the black platoons were gradually reassigned to all-black units, usually non-combat, and kept in the occupation army in Germany while the division with which they fought went home for demobilization. The policy caused some resentment, for as one of their white commanders explained to his superior, "These colored men cannot understand why they are not being allowed to share the honor of returning to their homeland with the Division with which they fought, proving to the world that Negro soldiers can do something besides drive a truck or work in a laundry. I am unqualified to give them a satisfactory answer."

The answer was that, with the exception of a relatively few liberals and radicals, white America felt no gratitude toward the black community for its contribution to victory and had no intention of killing Jim Crow. Blacks were not going to achieve full citizenship by driving trucks and unloading supplies for white G.I.s, or even by dying in combat for the nation. By 1945 most black leaders knew that DuBois' 1917 hopes of using the Army as a vehicle for social change in America were forlorn, and that if they were going to get anywhere they would have to use direct political pressure. But the great bulk of the black people lived in the South, where there was not the slightest possibility of changing the status quo through local political action. The only effective weapon blacks had was the vote of the ghettos in northern cities, which could be decisive in a close Presidential election. Black leaders therefore decided to increase their pressure on President Harry S Truman to integrate the Armed Forces, not so much because they felt that integration in the military would lead to integration elsewhere, but rather as part of a concerted campaign to destroy Jim Crow everywhere. What made the military especially attractive as a target, however, was both its size and the fact that as Commander in Chief Truman could end Jim Crow in the Army with a single order. Within the military, blacks did not need congressional support to achieve their goals.

On March 22, 1948, A. Philip Randolph of the Brotherhood of Sleeping Car Porters, and Reverend Grant Reynolds, director of the Committee Against Jim Crow in Military Service and Training, called on Truman. They reasoned that Truman was a politician eager to avoid conflict and escape moral challenges, so they came to threaten. Randolph and Reynolds told Truman that unless he ended segregation in the military, they would lead a massive campaign of civil disobedience, in the Gandhi style. America's black youth, they said, were prepared for sacrifices, suffering, terrorism, even concentration camps, to win their rights. A poll of black college students showed that 71 per cent supported the campaign, and even the moderate Urban League and the NAACP gave Randolph and Reynolds some support.

Truman bent under the pressure. He announced that he was arranging for moderate black leaders to confer with the military and to serve as consultants. His halting step, however, ended in disaster, for Secretary of the Army Kenneth Royal declared he would not consider any change in the Army's segregation policy. Blacks therefore refused to serve as consultants and again threatened Truman with civil disobedience. The Democratic Party, meanwhile, fearful of losing the South in the November elections, indicated that it would adopt only a mild civil rights plank in its platform and do nothing about Jim Crow in the military. Seizing the opportunity, the Republicans—who held their national convention first—pledged support for an anti-lynching bill, equality of opportunity in employment, abolition of the poll-tax, and an end to segregation in the military. Henry Wallace, third party candidate for President on the Progressive ticket, cut further into Democratic strength in black ghettos by condemning Jim Crow "in all forms and all places."

Northern Democrats, led by Hubert Humphrey of the Americans for Democratic Action, were thoroughly frightened. They managed to push through a firm civil rights plank in the party platform. It did not directly attack Jim Crow or pledge social equality, but it did promise equal opportunity and full political participation for blacks. Mild as it was, Humphrey's civil rights plank split the convention. The Deep South walked out and formed the States Rights party.

Freed from the South, in no danger of a white backlash (which did not exist in 1948, when almost everyone thought that the black problem was limited to the South), and desperately in need of the ghetto vote to have any chance at all of victory in the election, Truman acted. On July 26, 1948, he barred racial discrimination in federal employment and declared a policy of equal opportunity in the Armed Forces.

Truman may have hoped to avoid an open, legal assault on Jim Crow (he promised only to end discrimination, not segregation) but when Army Chief of Staff Omar Bradley said that the Army "is not out to make any social reform" and would continue to segregate blacks, the President had to rebuke him publicly. Truman said he wanted segregation ended and, in September, appointed a committee of liberals and blacks to advise the military in its revision of race policies. Truman had done enough—he got the ghetto vote and barely won the election.

Over the next two years the committee Truman appointed investigated the military and sought co-operation for racial integration. The Navy, which had a mere handful of blacks and did not practice formal segregation, promised to enlist more Negroes. The newly-born Air Force, while holding to a quota system in some units, ended most segregation. The Army, with a far larger percentage of blacks, lagged behind. Well into the Korean War the Army retained some all-black units; integration among the forces in Europe did not even begin until the spring of 1952. The performance of individual black soldiers serving in integrated units in Korea was so far superior to anything white leaders had expected, however, and not incidentally better than black performance in segregated units, that the Army brass gradually abandoned its opposition to integration. Some even became enthusiastic proponents when it became clear that white G.I.s accepted the new system. In time, the Army became the most thoroughly integrated service.

After almost 200 years of continuous service in the Army, black soldiers had finally achieved formal equality. But they had not been able to force white America to give them full citizenship because of their service to the nation. Whatever happened in the military, America remained too racist to be deeply influenced by racial developments in the military.

Minority Groups
in Military Organization

CHARLES C. MOSKOS, JR.

A Propositional Inventory

Any effort to make meaningful generalization about human behavior is always formidable. Specification of contexts, availability
of data, evaluation of evidence, all must enter into such an en-
deavor. Fortunately the literature on minority groups in military organization is not insubstantial—at least with regard to
blacks in the Armed Forces of the United States. As a general
rule, I have tried to include only the best supported findings in
this area—findings which have a generally accepted high level of
validity. Nevertheless, there are instances where propositions appear warranted but which do not have definitive empirical proof.

The format is as follows: Six topics are covered: 1) recruitment, 2) assignment, 3) performance, 4) attitudes toward service
life, 5) inter-group relations, and 6) Armed Forces and society.
Within each of these broad topics, propositions are stated in
italicized form. The supporting evidence, discussion, and qualifications are in regular print. All told, twenty-four such propositions are presented. They range from statistical statements (e.g.,
re-enlistment rates), to empirically based concepts (e.g., attitudes toward service life), to interpretive propositions (e.g., the
dynamics of inter-group accommodation).

Recruitment. A much higher proportion of blacks, compared

Reprinted by permission from The Inter-University Seminar on Armed
Forces and Society, Inc. Volume I, pp. 234–43, from *A Survey of Military
Institutions*, ed. by Roger W. Little. Copyright 1969, The Inter-University
Seminar on Armed Forces and Society, Inc.

to whites, fail to meet the entrance requirements for military service. The results of pre-induction examinations given potential draftees over the past two decades show black disqualification rates to be about twice that of whites. For the time period 1950 through 1967, 62.7 per cent of blacks were disqualified compared to 35.6 per cent of whites. Most important, the primary factor in the higher disqualification ratio of blacks is due to failures on the mental tests. Since 1950, for virtually every year, blacks are four times more likely to be disqualified on mental grounds—a paramount indicator of socio-educational handicaps—than are whites. Indeed, with regard to failure for medical reasons only, white disqualification rates are slightly higher than those of blacks.

Although the proportion of blacks failing to meet the entrance standards required for military service is markedly higher than that of whites, *blacks are still more likely to be drafted than whites.* For the years 1961 through 1966, blacks average 14.8 per cent of those drafted, a figure higher than the 11–12 per cent of blacks in the eligible age groups. This discrepancy between the high black disqualification rate and the disproportionate number of blacks drafted is indirect but convincing evidence that blacks have a lower likelihood of obtaining draft deferments—deferments that are more available to whites and that often become *de facto* exemptions. It should also be noted, however, that the proportion of blacks inducted is highest during those years when draft calls are lowest. Put in another way, during times of high draft calls, with the resultant necessity of drawing deeper into the draft pool, the overproportionate induction of blacks tends to decline—but not disappear.

A complete picture of black entrance rates into the military, however, requires more than an assessment of disqualification, induction, and deferment rates. For excepting times of war, voluntary enlistments account for approximately three-quarters of all incoming military personnel. An examination of the initial enlistments in each of the four Armed Services for the years 1961–1966 shows that it is the Army, besides its drawing upon the draft, that also has the highest enlistment rate of any of the Armed Services. Over the six-year period, blacks constituted 10.9 per cent of Army initial enlistments, followed by 9.8 per cent for the Air Force, 7.2 per cent for the Marine Corps, and 4.2 per cent for the Navy. In 1967, blacks accounted for 9.0 per cent of all active-duty personnel, a figure slightly *lower* than the black proportion in the total American population.

An insight into the causes underlying volunteer initial enlistments can be gained by looking at reasons mentioned for entering the armed forces. Based on the 1964 NORC survey, motivations of volunteers were grouped into four categories: 1) personal, e.g., get away from home, mature, travel, excitement; 2) patriotic, e.g., serve one's country; 3) draft-motivated, e.g., choose time of service entry or branch of service; and 4) self-advancement, e.g., learn a trade, receive an education, military as a career. There are only slight differences between whites and blacks with regard to personal and patriotic reasons for service duty. The variation between the races is found almost entirely in their differing mentions of draft-motivated versus self-advancement reasons. Among white volunteers, 39.1 per cent gave draft-motivated reasons compared to 24.5 per cent of the blacks. Conversely, only 20.7 per cent of the white volunteers replied they entered the military for reasons of self-advancement compared with 37.2 per cent of the blacks who gave that reason. These differences between the races diminish only slightly when educational level is held constant. In other words, *the draft serves as a major inducement for whites to volunteer, while the belief that self-advancement will be furthered through military service is much more typical of black volunteers.*

Assignment. The larger the proportion of blacks in an armed service, the more equitable is the distribution of blacks throughout its ranks. This is also to say that the proportion and internal distribution of blacks differ markedly between the military services. In 1967, blacks made up 11.2 per cent of the Army, 9.6 per cent of the Air Force, 9.1 per cent of the Marine Corps, and 4.3 per cent of the Navy. That same year, the ratio of black to white officers was roughly 1 to 25 in the Army, 1 to 50 in the Air Force, 1 to 150 in the Marine Corps, and 1 to 300 in the Navy. Also for 1967, the ratio of black to white senior non-coms (pay grades E-7 through E-9) was approximately 1 to 8 in the Army, 1 to 21 in the Air Force, 1 to 22 in the Marine Corps, and 1 to 28 in the Navy. It is also the case that blacks are disproportionately concentrated in the lower non-com ranks (pay grades E-5 and E-6) in all of the armed services. This is especially so in the Army, where 20 per cent of all staff sargeants are black. In brief, it is the Army, followed in order by the Air Force, Marine Corps, and Navy, which has the largest proportion of blacks in its total personnel and the most equitable distribution of blacks.

On a service-wide basis, blacks have been assigned to all occu-

pations, but are still overrepresented in combat and non-technical positions. Thus, 36.7 per cent of all black servicemen in 1967 were in combat positions or service work compared to 22.7 per cent of all whites. Conversely, of all black servicemen 27.7 per cent were found in technical occupations (e.g., electronics, communication, medical and dental, equipment repairmen) compared to 39.5 per cent of all whites. As is to be expected, the over-concentration of blacks in combat units is all too obviously shown in the casualty reports from Viet Nam. During the 1961–1966 period, blacks constituted 10.6 per cent of American military personnel in Southeast Asia while accounting for 16.0 per cent of those killed in action. In 1967 and the first six months of 1968, however, the proportion of black combat deaths dropped to between 13 and 14 per cent. Yet even in these later figures, black combat deaths were still about 3 percentage points above the proportion of blacks stationed in Southeast Asia, and about 5 percentage points above the total black proportion in the American military.

The disproportionate number of blacks in combat units in the contemporary military contrasts directly with the Army reluctance to use black soldiers in combat units in World War II. Indeed, the likelihood of blacks serving in a combat arm is well over two times greater in the 1960's than it was during the earlier segregated period. The current direction of assignment of black soldiers is testimony to the continuing consequences of differential racial opportunity originating in the larger society. That is, *educational disadvantages that make blacks available for military service cause them to be, at the same time, unavailable for many technical job opportunities in expanding skill areas within the military organization.*

The above findings, however, must be placed within a broader context. While there are many pitfalls in comparing civilian and military occupations, the evidence shows that both black enlisted men and officers have attained higher occupational levels than have blacks in the civilian employment market. *Black servicemen enjoy relatively better opportunities in the armed forces than in the civilian economy in every clerical, technical, and skilled field for which the data permit comparison.* Nevertheless, it must be kept in mind that the social and educational deprivations suffered by the black in American society can be mitigated but not eliminated by the racially egalitarian policies of the armed forces.

Performance. The military performance of integrated black

servicemen contrasts markedly and favorably with that of all-Negro units. Virtually all studies and observers of black service-men are in agreement on this proposition. This in no way denies the valor of individual black servicemen or of particular black units, but it does point to the generally deleterious effects of segregation on black performance. Thus in World War I, the combat record of the all-Negro 92nd Infantry Division came under heavy criticism. During the Second World War, the com-bat record of the 92nd was also blemished. Moreover, there was considerable apprehension within the Army's hierarchy of the fighting qualities of any all-Negro unit. The 25th Infantry Regi-ment was judged so poor that its divisional commander recom-mended the unit be dissolved as quickly as possible.

On the other hand, even during the First World War it was noted that black units operating under French command, in a more racially permissive situation, performed well. In World War II, in an important exception to the segregated utilization of black troops, black volunteers fought in previously all-white units during the Ardennes battle. Both in terms of black combat performance and white soldiers' reactions, the Ardennes experi-ment was an unqualified success. In the Korean Conflict, man-power requirements in the field for combat soldiers resulted in many instances of *ad hoc* integration. As integration in Korea became more standard, observers consistently reported that the fighting qualities of blacks differed little from that of whites. With the advent of full integration, all significant differences between white and black combat performance have disappeared. In both Viet Nam and the Dominican Republic, there was little discernible difference between the races concerning combat moti-vation or military performance. . . .

Attitudes Toward Service Life. Blacks, compared to whites, have consistently more favorable attitudes toward service life. This proposition is supported by several sorts of evidence. For one thing, the service-wide black re-enlistment rate throughout the 1960's was approximately twice that of white servicemen. That black servicemen have a more favorable view of military life than whites is reflected not only in their higher re-enlistment rates, but also by the 1964 NORC survey data. Whether broken down by branch of service, educational level, pay grade, or military occupational specialty, black servicemen compared to whites persistently have a less negative view of life in the Armed Forces. Another survey found few black youth who perceived military life as having negative racial aspects. Rather, military life was seen as offering career advantages, foreign duty, and educational gain. The relatively benign terms in which black men regarded military life, however, speaks not only of the racial egalitarianism of the Armed Forces, but more profoundly, of the existing state of affairs for blacks in American society at large.

Further, despite the demonstrable inequities for blacks in the existing draft system, the fact remains that Selective Service even as it was operating in the 1960's was seen in more favorable terms by blacks than by whites. This anomalous circumstance is illustrated by the following findings from the 1964 NORC survey: among blue-collar workers with no military experience, 41.3 per cent of blacks, compared to 28.5 per cent of whites, view the draft as very fair; among Army enlisted men, whether draftees, first-term or career regulars, blacks are much more favorable in their views concerning the draft's equity; among civilians with military experience, only 3.0 per cent of the black veterans who were drafted, compared to ten times that proportion among whites, said the Selective Service system was unfair.

Intergroup Relations. Commenting on the difficulties of social analysis, the authors of *The American Soldier* wrote that "few problems are more formidable than that of obtaining dependable records of attitudes toward racial separation in the Army." Without underestimating the continuing difficulty of this problem, an opportunity exists to compare attitudes toward racial integration held by American soldiers in two different periods. This is done by contrasting responses to equivalent items given in World War II (1943) as reported in *The American Soldier* with those reported in Project Clear during the Korean Conflict (1951).

The trend is toward increasing acceptance of military racial integration on the part of both white and black servicemen. However, black servicemen are much more supportive of racial integration than whites. Among white soldiers, opposition to integration goes from 84 per cent in 1943 to 44 per cent in 1951. Among black soldiers, opposition goes from 36 to 4 per cent over the same time period. It may be argued that recent developments—separatist tendencies within the black community in the late 1960's— have eclipsed the earlier findings. Nevertheless, the data are still convincing that on the eve of integration, black soldiers overwhelmingly rejected a segregated Armed Forces.

One of the most celebrated findings of *The American Soldier* was the discovery that *the more contact white soldiers have with black troops, the more favorable was their reaction toward racial integration.* "The closer men approached to the mixed (racially) company organization, the less opposition there was to it. That is, the men actually in a company containing a Negro platoon were most favorable toward it, men in larger units in which there were no mixed companies were least favorable, while men in all-white companies within a regiment or division containing mixed companies held intermediate opinions." This conclusion is consistently supported in the surveys conducted by Project Clear during the Korean Conflict. Again and again, comparisons of white soldiers in integrated units with those in segregated units show the former to be more supportive of desegregation.

However, social contact is not enough to change racial attitudes. *The social contact must take place under conditions of equal status and in which mutual interdependence is required for unit cohesion.* These circumstances are not uniformly found in military social organization. Thus, *the more military the environment, the more egalitarian are racial relations.* On the whole, racial integration at informal as well as formal levels works best on duty *vis-à-vis* off duty, on base *vis-à-vis* off base, basic training and maneuvers *vis-à-vis* garrison, and sea *vis-à-vis* shore duty. This is especially demonstrable in the actual combat situation where close living, strict discipline and common danger all serve to preclude racial conflict between whites and blacks. In other words, the behavior of servicemen resembles the racial (and class) separatism of the larger American society, the more they are removed from the military environment.

Whatever the level of military organization, closest friendships normally develop within races among individuals of similar socioeducational background. This is to say that *primary groups within the military organization tend to be racially exclusive.* Nevertheless, even at primary groups levels, the integrated military system exhibits a much higher inter-racial intimacy than exists in the non-integrated civilian society. Moreover, beyond an individual's hard core of friends, there exists a larger number of friendly acquaintances. Here the pattern seems to be one of educational similarities overriding racial differences. . . .

One of the consequences of America's global military posture has been to expose large numbers of servicemen to foreign cultures and societies—even if only in a peripheral manner. While the evidence is not entirely conclusive, it appears that *service abroad is more likely to foster parochial American sentiments rather than engender a more appreciative understanding of foreign societies.* Some of the factors bringing this about are: the serviceman's invidious comparison of material standards of living in foreign countries; language barriers; and primary exposure to the exploitative ambience of the so-called "boomtowns" which ring American overseas bases. However, overseas duty offers the black serviceman an opportunity to witness societies where racial discrimination is usually less practiced than it is in his home country. Thus, *black servicemen are more likely to be favorably disposed toward foreign societies than are whites.* Moreover, there is evidence that black soldiers are much more likely to learn local languages when stationed abroad than are whites.

Armed Forces and Society. The analogy between enlisted men *vis-à-vis* officers in the military and blacks *vis-à-vis* whites in the larger society has often been observed. "It is noteworthy that the phrases which white enlisted men used to express their dissatisfaction with the military system were in many instances exact duplicates of phrases which some of the more vocal Negro civilians have been using for years with reference to their treatment at the hands of white society." It is also the case that the apparent lack of awareness on the part of whites of black attitudes has its counterpart among officers' assessment of enlisted attitudes. In both cases there is a tendency by the subordinate group to conceal its true attitudes, and the tendency on the part of the dominant group to avoid believing what is uncomfortable to believe. It has been less frequently observed, however, that enlisted men's behavior is often similar to many of the stereotypes associated with blacks, for example, laziness, boisterousness, emphasis on sexual prowess, consciously acting stupid, obsequiousness in front of superiors combined with ridicule of absent superiors, etc. *Placement of white adult males in a subordinate position within a rigidly stratified system appears to produce behavior not all that different from the so-called personality traits commonly held to be an outcome of cultural or psychological patterns unique to Afro-American life.*

Nevertheless, the fact remains that although the military was until modern times one of America's most segregated institutions, it has leaped into the forefront of racial equality in the past two decades. What features of the military establishment can account for this about-face? For one thing, *the generally successful racial integration of the Armed Forces is due to the military being to an important degree discontinuous from others of society.* And this apartness served to allow, once the course had been decided, a rapid and complete racial integration. The path of desegregation was further made easier by characteristics peculiar, or at least more pronounced, in the military compared to other institutions. With its hierarchical power structure, predicated on stable and patterned relationships, decisions need [to] take relatively little account of the personal desires of service personnel. Additionally, because roles and activities are more defined and specific in the military than in most other social arenas, conflicts that might have ensued within a more diffuse and ambiguous setting were largely absent. This is to say that *the desegregation of the Armed Forces was facilitated by the pervasiveness in the military of a bureaucratic ethos, with its concomitant formality and high social distance, that mitigated tensions arising from individual or personal feelings.*

At the same time it must also be remembered that the military establishment has means of coercion not readily available in most civilian pursuits. Violations of norms are both more visible and subject to quicker sanctions. The military is premised, moreover, on the accountability of its members for effective performance. This in turn means that satisfactory carrying out of stated policy advances one's own position. It is to each individual's personal interest, if he anticipates receiving the rewards of a military career, to insure that decisions going through him are executed with minimum difficulty. Or put in another way, *whatever the internal policy decided upon, racial integration being a paramount but only one example, the military establishment has unique sanctions to realize its implementation.* . . .

It is also probably true, however, that the military establishment—at least into the foreseeable future—will no longer be immune from the racial conflicts occurring in the larger American society. Incidents with racial overtones will become more frequent. That the black soldier may find he owes higher fealty to the black community than to the U.S. Army is a possibility that haunts commanders. The likelihood of such an eventuality, however, will be serious only if the Army is regularly summoned into action in black ghettos. Sensitivity to broader civil rights issues coupled with racially egalitarian internal practices will most likely be sufficient—barring repeated military intervention in black ghettos—to preclude any widespread black disaffection within the Armed Forces.

The nature of black participation in the military organization has nevertheless become inextricable with broader criticisms of America's politico-military policies. Much attention has been given to the relationship between elements of the black militant movement with the anti-military movement of the late 1960's. Yet the black movement as a whole has remained removed from those white radical groups vociferously attacking the military services. Although it would be premature to offer a final statement on any future interpenetrations between the black movement and anti-military groups, a major turning away of blacks *per se* from military commitment is viewed as highly doubtful. Most likely, and somewhat paradoxically, *there will be more vocal anti-military sentiment within certain black militant groups at the same time that the armed forces continue to be a leading avenue of career opportunity for many black men.*

PART VI

The Military
and
the Draft

The Draft and Alternatives of the Draft

JAMES ALDEN BARBER, JR.

For more than twenty years one of the principal facts of life for young American men has been the prospect of the draft. The urgency of the prospect has varied from time to time, but draft considerations have never entirely disappeared, and a great many personal decisions have been made with the draft as a primary influence. This chapter seeks to explore briefly the history of military manpower procurement in the United States, the system as it presently exists, some of the problems of the system, and finally some of the available alternatives to the present system.

In passing the Universal Military Training and Service Act of 1951, the Congress of the United States declared:

> . . . an adequate armed strength must be achieved and maintained to insure the security of this nation. . . . The Congress further declares that in a free society the obligations and privileges of serving in the armed forces and the reserve components thereof should be shared generally, in accordance with a system of selection which is fair and just, and which is consistent with the maintenance of an effective national economy.

The draft has been used because of the inability of the Armed Forces to obtain voluntary enlistments in the numbers and quality needed to maintain authorized personnel strengths since shortly after World War II. This has been true for a number of reasons, among which should be included the relatively low prestige of a military career in the United States, low rates of pay, dislike for military regimentation, and the interferences with normal family life.

Severe criticism of the present Selective Service System is a relatively recent phenomenon, and it is frequently difficult to sort out opposition to the Vietnam War from opposition to the draft itself. Historically, of course, military conscription has rarely been a very popular procedure. Except in times of national fervor, young men do not usually view the prospect of leaving home and being shot at with any great enthusiasm. Neither criticism of a system of military conscription nor evasion of the draft are entirely new phenomena. A short review of the history of military conscription in the United States may help to put the subject in perspective.

Historical Background

From the time of the Revolutionary War, the United States has traditionally relied upon voluntary recruitment to provide military manpower in time of peace, with the professional forces being augmented in time of war by militiamen, reserves and conscripts. Not until the passage of the Selective Training and Service Act of 1940 was it necessary for the United States to resort to conscription during peacetime. Yet there has been a traditional belief in this country that the able-bodied citizen was under an obligation to be armed and ready to fight when the situation demanded, and the conditions of frontier living often created such a demand. The degree of obligation created by this militia system varied from colony to colony, but in general proved adequate throughout the colonial period. During the Revolutionary War, however, procurement of men on a local basis failed to provide the required number of men to the Continental Army, and Washington requested the Continental Congress to authorize universal conscription in all of the colonies. No immediate action was taken, and the war concluded without such a conscription system coming into effect. A similar system was again considered by the Congress to meet manpower requirements during the War of 1812, but again no such law was passed.

During the Civil War both the North and South found it necessary to resort to conscription early in the war. The Confederacy began conscription in 1862, drafting men for one year's service. The Union followed suit in 1863, drafting men for a period of three to nine months' service. Both systems were poorly conceived and administered, creating widespread abuses and discontent. Exemptions were frequent, and usually discriminatory. In the North an exemption could be purchased for $300, or a substitute hired to serve instead.

The Civil War draft systems fell most heavily upon the poor, and in the North resulted in riots in a number of cities. The worst riot, which occurred in New York City in July of 1863, was partly directed against the draft, partly a result of Irish-American resentment of the use of black workers to break up a stevedore's strike. The riots went on for four days and nights. Several hundred people were killed or wounded, and property damage was estimated at a million dollars. One result of the riots was to seriously weaken Meade's army through the necessity of providing detachments for guard duty in northern cities.

Partly because of the inefficiencies of the conscription system, partly because the bounty paid to volunteers encouraged men to choose voluntary enlistment in preference to being drafted, only a small portion of the armies of either North or South were actually composed of draftees. For the entire war, fewer than 50,000 men were actually drafted into the Union Army. The quality of men recruited to the armies during the war was frequently poor, and rates of desertion were high. As would occur in later wars, Canada became a refuge for fugitives from the draft. From almost any point of view, the system of conscription employed during the Civil War was a monumental failure.

The next time the United States resorted to a draft was in World War I. After a lengthy and sometimes bitter debate Congress passed a draft law in the spring of 1917, which was signed into law by President Wilson on May 18, 1917. Because of the widespread resentment of federal agents during the Civil War, care was taken to decentralize the system, and to rely upon local boards. The system functioned smoothly this time, and almost 3 million men were selected and inducted between the time of the first drawing in July 1917 and the end of the war.

Following World War I the United States returned to the traditional policy of small peacetime forces manned entirely through voluntary recruitment. Some preplanning and organization for future draft contingencies took place, however, and when in 1940 Congress passed the first peacetime draft in United States history an organization was already set up to carry out the draft. Inductions began in November, 1940, more than a year before the United States actually entered World War II as a belligerent. From that time until the draft ended, more than 10 million men were inducted.

Upon the recommendation of President Truman the draft law was allowed to expire on March 31, 1947, with the intention of returning to the long-standing policy of small, voluntary peacetime forces. A small corps of selective service personnel was retained to serve as a basic organization in the event of later requirements for the draft.

After World War II, President Truman tried for nearly four years to get Congress to pass a Universal Military Training Act which would have entailed a period of military training for all young men, but without success. By 1948, however, the combination of the difficulties the services were having recruiting adequate personnel and the military requirements of the cold war led to a reinstatement of peacetime conscription. The 1948 Act was similar to the World War II legislation. Only a very few men were drafted under the 1948 Act prior to the Korean War, since the Armed Services, perhaps because of the implicit threat of the draft, were again able to meet their manpower requirements through voluntary enlistments. The machinery remained operative, however, and within two months of the start of the Korean War large numbers of men were again being drafted. Under the combination of the 1948 Act and the Universal Military Training and Service Act of 1951 which replaced it, something over a million and a half men were inducted into the Armed Forces during the Korean War.

There was no return to a system of purely voluntary recruitment following the Korean War. Although the size of draft calls has varied widely from year to year, from a low of 60,000 men in fiscal 1961 to a high of 564,000 in 1953 during the Korean War, not a year has passed without some men being drafted. For more than twenty years, then, United States military manpower procurement has been a mixed system: mostly volunteer, but with a significant proportion of draftees. It should not be overlooked, however, that many of the volunteers are draft-motivated, and enlist only under the imminent threat of being drafted.

Present Draft Policies

Since mid-1948 the United States has had a draft law on the books, which after 1951 has been renewed by Congress at four-year intervals—usually after only perfunctory debate. Several changes have taken place, however. The system of deferments has changed from time to time, most recently in the direction of sharply reduced deferments. In April 1970 a Presidential Executive Order abolished new occupational deferments, new agricultural deferments and new fatherhood deferments. At the same time President Nixon stated that if he was successful in obtaining congressional authority that he intended to cancel all student deferments issued to young men who entered college after April 23, 1970. The intention in eliminating deferments was to equalize chances of being drafted, and to try to avoid the creation of specially privileged groups.

Perhaps the most dramatic change in the way the draft system works was the institution in December 1969 of a lottery system, again in an attempt to equalize exposure to the draft, and to provide somewhat more accurate information to the individual on his prospects of being drafted.

The Supreme Court has also played a role in altering the way in which the system functions. Conscientious objection on the basis of religious scruples has been long recognized as a basis for exemption from military service. A Supreme Court decision of June 15, 1970, held that conscientious objector status could be obtained through belief in a moral code which was not necessarily founded upon formal religious belief. The result was to broaden the basis for obtaining conscientious objector status, and greatly increase the problems of administration.

By early 1971 the Selective Service System operated about like this: At the age of 18 all adult males are required to register for the draft. In the year in which he becomes 19 the individual receives his lottery number from the national drawing, based upon the day and month of his birth. The lottery number can range from 1 to 366 (in leap years), and draft calls start with the low numbers. Since in recent years only a portion of the eligible individuals have actually been inducted, only those with relatively low numbers are certain to be called, and those with high numbers are unlikely to be drafted except in the case of some situation requiring greatly increased draft calls. Once past the year of primary eligibility, the individual is subject to being drafted only if all of a current year group are drafted first. A number of ways of obtaining deferments still exist, but, as noted above, the intention of the Administration has been to severely curtail these exemptions.

An important factor affecting the way in which the draft has worked has been the changing numbers of individuals actually drafted. At the same time that the number of men eligible to be drafted has increased, the size of draft calls has been decreasing. Anticipated draft calls in fiscal 1971 were only slightly over half the number of men inducted during fiscal 1969. The result has been to reduce the likelihood that any given individual will be drafted, but not to diminish the impact upon the life of those individuals who are drafted, or who consider themselves in imminent danger of being drafted. In some cases it may even increase the individual impact, since the draftee is much more likely to feel that he has been unfairly singled out in comparison with the many who have not been and will not be drafted.

The draft has been subject to more criticism in the last several years than at any time since the Civil War. The law in effect at the time this was written was due to expire in mid-1971, and it was apparent that more debate and deliberation were going to go into the consideration of a new law than had taken place in some time. The following section turns to a consideration of some of the problems with the present system.

Problems With the Present System

Some of the problems presented by the draft have been either remedied or at least improved by recent reforms. Until recently the selection procedure called for calling oldest men first, which meant that an individual was most likely to be called after he had begun to get settled into a career, rather than at an earlier time when career plans were more flexible. This also meant that it was difficult to know exactly when you were likely to be called, making the problems of personal planning more difficult. Changes in deferment rules have also helped to some extent to reduce inequities, although as will be discussed below, a number still remain. Finally, the lottery system tends to make everyone's chances at least roughly the same, reduces the time of prime exposure to only one year, and reduces the amount of discretion provided to the local draft board on who is to be called.

There are, however, other serious problems with the Selective Service System which have not been successfully remedied. One of the most basic of these is the problem of equity, a problem which is almost inherent in a system where only a fraction of those eligible are actually required in order to fulfill the manpower requirements of the Armed Services. The draft, as it operated during World War II, was essentially just a manpower distribution system. All eligible manpower was needed either in the Armed Services or in certain specific deferred civilian employment, and the draft operated to see that both civilian and military sectors got an appropriate share of the available manpower. The present draft problem is a great deal different. The Services have not been successful in filling their manpower requirements completely through voluntary means; but on the other hand they do not require anything like all of the men eligible for the draft. In recent years the result has been that roughly a third of all draft-eligible males have been rejected for physical or mental reasons; about a third have either enlisted or been inducted; and the remaining third have been either deferred, or have simply waited out their period of draft elegibility without being called.

It has been argued that compulsory military service is in effect a kind of tax, in that the government compels individuals to accept military employment at a wage less than would be necessary to hire enough men on a voluntary basis. According to this argument, the tax is equal to the difference between the wages actually paid to servicemen and the wages that would be necessary to meet all requirements with volunteers. From this point of view it is clear that a tax which is levied upon only a limited number of those eligible is fundamentally inequitable. No matter how fair the lottery may be in equalizing the chances of being drafted, the man who actually is drafted winds up with an unequal share of the burden.

This problem promises to become even more serious in the future, because the number of young men becoming eligible for the draft increases yearly. If, as anticipated, military manpower requirements return roughly to pre-Vietnam levels, a decreasing proportion of potential draftees will have to be called each year. This may be fine from the point of view of the individual who is not called, but is likely to increase the feeling of unfairness on the part of the man who is called.

A related problem has to do with the basis upon which men are selected, rejected or deferred under the existing conditions of surplus manpower. In the past, the system has operated so as to reject, in large measure, the least privileged third, while the most privileged third has managed to accumulate far more than their proportionate share of deferments and exemptions. A 1964 Department of Defense Study reported that among men of 27–34 years of age in 1964, only 27 per cent of those with at least one year of graduate school had ever had military service. At the same time more than 70 per cent of male high school graduates had been in the military—but only 30 per cent of those with just a grade school education.[1] Thus the system has tended to reject those who are probably most likely to benefit from the experience of military service, to let those in the most privileged strata largely evade service, and to draw the major portion of military manpower from the broad middle stratum. Whatever else such a system may have to recommend it, it falls far short of equity.

Although Selective Service records show that lower-class youths are the most likely to be rejected for failure to meet mental or physical standards, those who do pass have a high probability of being inducted. The reason is that they are much less likely to be able to find a way of being deferred than is someone from a more privileged background. As a draft counselor was reported to have said:

> The whole Selective Service set up is very cerebral, like a chess game. It's definitely a middle-class, educated person's game, and most poor people in the ghetto don't like to play games like that.[2]

Thus, presumably without intention, there is a degree of social discrimination inherent in the way the Selective Service System operates.

The draft has an impact which goes far beyond its effect on just those individuals who are actually inducted. It is well established that a high proportion of volunteers, in both enlisted and officer programs, are draft motivated. One study found that an average of 38 per cent of enlisted volunteers would not have enlisted if it were not for the draft, and that 41 per cent of junior officers on their first tour of duty were draft motivated. Among enlisted men, the higher the level of education the more important the draft is as a motivating factor: only 23 per cent of those who did not graduate from high school report the draft as a primary motivating factor, compared with 58 per cent of those who have attended at least some college.[3] This has two implications for the possibility of an all-volunteer military: first,

[1] Harold Wool, "Military Manpower Procurement and Supply," in Roger Little (ed.), *A Survey of Military Institutions* (Chicago: Inter-University Seminar on Armed Forces and Society, 1969), p. 57.

[2] Father Elmer L. Sullivan, quoted in *New York Times Magazine*, November 29, 1970, p. 124.

[3] Source; Department of Defense Survey of Active Duty Military Personnel, as of October 1964.

that the problem is a considerably greater one than just recruiting enough volunteers to replace the number of men presently being drafted, since a number of those presently volunteering would not do so in the absence of a draft; and second, that an all-volunteer force will almost certainly be composed on average of individuals with a lower level of education, since those of higher educational levels are more likely to have enlisted only under pressure of the draft.

Another effect of the draft operates through the pressures of the deferment rules. Men who wish to avoid being drafted often take actions to procure deferments which they might not have taken in the absence of the draft. In the past this has led to occupational, educational and marital decisions by men who might well have made other decisions in the absence of the draft. More dramatic, if less numerous, are the individual choices to violate the law and go to jail or to flee abroad. There is no good way to measure the extent of the social distortions thus induced by the draft. Some of these distortions might even be argued to have a beneficial effect through encouraging higher education or channeling more people into the teaching professions—although whether it is a good idea to pressure an individual who doesn't want to be a teacher into being one is at the least an arguable proposition.

Alternatives to the Present System

The Selective Service System, as presently constituted, is widely recognized as needing change, although there is much disagreement over exactly what changes are needed. Several alternatives have been proposed, ranging from the administration proposal for an all-volunteer force to proposals for a national service system. Before examining these proposals, however, it is useful to consider briefly some criteria by which to judge a military manpower procurement system.

Any system of military manpower procurement must somehow balance the often conflicting interests of the individual, the society as a whole, and the Armed Forces. The individual has a claim to be treated equitably and to have his life subjected to no more disruption than is absolutely necessary. From the viewpoint of society as a whole, military manpower procurement should create as little interference as possible with the functioning of other agencies in the society, including education, allocation of manpower to occupations, and the institution of the family. The Armed Forces need a system which provides manpower adequate in numbers and in quality to meet the force levels determined by civilian political authority.

A number of solutions have been proposed in an attempt to remedy the problems of the present system of military recruitment in the United States. The principal proposals have been variations on one of four themes: 1) reform of the present Selective Service System to cure its more serious defects; 2) universal military training; 3) an all-volunteer force; and 4) a system of universal service. In practice all kinds of combinations of these proposals are possible, but in the interest of simplicity it is easiest to discuss them separately.

Reform of the present Selective Service System would continue a process already sketched out, the attempt being to equalize exposure and to correct gross inequities. From the viewpoint of practical politics this is probably the easiest to achieve, since it involves the least radical changes. Further changes in deferment rules might serve to minimize social distortions, and from the viewpoint of the Armed Forces the draft as presently constituted does an effective job of providing adequate manpower, less by direct induction than by the indirect pressures which help support voluntary enlistment and the whole range of officer procurement problems such as ROTC and the Officer Candidate schools. From the viewpoint of the individual, however, in a situation in which there is a requirement for drafting or enlisting only a limited portion of the available manpower pool, there is a fundamental inequality between the man who is compelled to serve and the man who is not. It is difficult to conceive of any modification of the present system which could adequately remedy this defect. A lottery combined with severe limitations on deferments and exemptions can equalize exposure to the draft, but no matter how fair the lottery, there is no evading the fact that some win and some lose, and there is a fundamental difference between being selected and not being selected, making that stage of a young man's life a version of Russian roulette.

A second alternative is a program of universal military training similar to that proposed by President Truman after World War II. This proposal handles the problem of equity in a direct way: everyone is required to serve a period of time in the Armed Forces. One of the principal problems with the proposal is that there is no foreseeable need to have the almost two million young men reaching the age of 19 each year undergo military training. A related problem is the huge expansion in military training facilities that would be required to support such a program, and the numbers of professional active duty personnel who would have to be involved in training duties. UMT is appealing from the viewpoint of individual equity, and at least acceptable from the viewpoint of minimizing social disruption, since it would involve a period of military service as part of the normal course of events for all young men. From the point of view of military efficiency, however, UMT is not particularly promising, and past experience casts serious doubt on its political palatability.

The third proposal, an all-volunteer force, deserves careful consideration, both because it has been advanced as an Administration goal, which gives it a political base, and because it is in the normal American peacetime tradition. As of the end of 1970 the Nixon Administration was committed to a goal of replacing the draft with an all-volunteer force for the military services by 1973. The goal was predicated upon the assumption that any large-scale American involvement in Vietnam would be terminated before that time.

From an individual point of view, an all-volunteer force is equitable, in that only those who choose to serve in the Armed Forces do so. It can be argued, however, that such a system is inequitable in another way, since military service is most attractive to the socially disadvantaged, and the result of a system of voluntary recruitment is to effectively exempt the socially privileged and place the entire burden of service upon those individuals lower in the social scale. As has been noted, the present draft system already tends to fall most lightly upon the most privileged segments of society—but the effect of a purely voluntary system would probably be to exempt them entirely. It is worth considering whether this is entirely healthy in a free society. As presently constituted the military services contain a useful leavening of individuals whose service is draft induced, both in the enlisted ranks and in the officer corps, and these individuals come from a wide variety of backgrounds representative of the society at large. An all-volunteer force, drawn from a more limited background, and less subject to the currents of the society which it is designed to serve, could much more easily become isolated from that society. Students of military sociology by and large believe that civilian control of the military is most effective when the military society is effectively a part of the whole social fabric, and not when the military is an isolated caste.

A further argument against the all-volunteer military force concerns cost. No one really knows how much more an all-volunteer force would cost than the present system, although all agree that it would definitely be more expensive. Responsible estimates of the additional cost of an all-volunteer force range from a Gates Commission low of 3.3 billion dollars annually, up to a high of about 17 billion a year. A counter-argument to the high cost of a volunteer force is that we are in effect paying the cost now, but that the cost is hidden by being extracted from those individuals who are compelled to serve at wages lower than would have been necessary to induce them to serve on a volunteer basis—the hidden-tax argument.

One of the most appealing parts of the all-volunteer argument is that we have always done it in peacetime before, so why shouldn't we do it now? The answer, if there is one, is that always before the United States has been able to luxuriate in geographical isolation, and has not required peacetime military forces of the size we now maintain. Certainly a part of this argument is true: technological advances have clearly obliterated the splendid isolation which America once enjoyed, and there seems no prospect of ever being able to return. On one point there does seem to be considerable agreement: an all-volunteer force is not practical without 1) an end to large-scale hostilities, and 2) either greatly increased military wages, or a substantially smaller military establishment.

The fourth main proposal is to substitute a system of universal service for the present Selective Service System. The fundamental notion behind the proposal is that everyone has an obligation to serve, but that service can take a number of forms, and military service would be just one of a number of available options. The proposal will not be treated at any length here, because the following article by Vincent Davis presents a typical proposal in some detail. The universal service idea is appealing from a number of points of view, and is apparently gaining increased support. The most telling objections are administrative, in that it would be an extremely complex kind of a scheme, and political, in that at least at present no such proposal appears to enjoy any very wide political base. A universal service program would also involve substantial costs, although the argument of its defenders that this would mostly involve only consolidation of costs which are now widely scattered under a number of labels is probably valid. In the long run it would probably prove less costly than the all-volunteer force solution, since in effect everyone would be working for minimal wages during their period of required service. The hidden-tax element would still exist, but since everyone would be required to serve, it would at least be an equitable tax. Further discussion of the concept will be left to Davis' article.

Conclusion

None of the alternative means of reforming the present system of military manpower procurement need be adopted as pure forms. Innumerable variations and combinations are possible, all subject to the test of trying to meet the sometimes competing claims of the individual, the society at large, and the military services themselves. The system as it presently exists is such a mixed system, combining conscription and voluntary enlistment in proportions that vary widely from year to year.

Peacetime conscription, as it has existed in the United States since 1948, is a distinct departure from past American tradition. The reason for the departure from tradition is that we have been maintaining a larger military establishment than ever before in peacetime, and the Armed Forces have been unable to compete effectively enough with the appeals of civilian society to enlist sufficient volunteers to maintain authorized strengths. The global competition with the communists is only a partial explanation for the larger peacetime armed forces: the other part of the explanation is that with the development of long-range weapons that has taken place in the last thirty years the United States is now vulnerable to the possibility of outside attack in a way that never existed at any earlier time in our history. In the absence of some fortunate radical change in world political relations, it is clear that the United States is going to maintain a large standing military establishment for the foreseeable future. The question then revolves around making the military establishment as effective, and as effectively controlled, as possible, and in seeing that military manpower procurement policies are made as compatible as they can be with other social goals.

A fact which should not be entirely ignored is that the present Selective Service System has functioned reasonably well for a considerable period of time—particularly when compared with such unsuccessful instances of conscription as the Civil War drafts. Despite some obvious flaws, the draft has provided a flexible system of manpower procurement which has responded effectively to wide variations in demand. For such a vast system wielding so much power over the lives of individuals, it has been amazingly free of corruption and of the taint of graft. Almost everyone would agree that reform is necessary, but the Selective Service System has not been so bad as it is sometimes painted.

Universal Service: An Alternative to the All-Volunteer Armed Services

VINCENT DAVIS

The first instance in Western literature of an attempt to devise an ideal way to recruit and structure military forces into the fabric of a society was probably Plato's dialog, *The Republic.* This same general effort has continued over the intervening two and a half millenia, either aided or handicapped by changing social, political, and economic conditions.

The effort to devise the most acceptable method for recruiting and organizing armed forces appeared to be an especially acute problem in the United States in early 1970 as the nation faced the new decade and the remainder of the twentieth century. The American people seemed weary from thirty years of alternating hot and cold war and preferred to turn their attentions toward a wide variety of urgent domestic problems. Moreover, many Americans appeared to be caught in the grip of an agonizing concern over fundamental social values, customs, laws, and processes. Numerous forms of established order and established authority were under attack, in some cases violent attack. At times it appeared that the very fabric of society was beginning to unravel. Basic uncertainties led to a sense of national drift, if not paralysis, and made it very difficult to determine

Reprinted with the permission of the author and of the *Naval War College Review,* October 1970.

with any degree of precision just how many Americans could be relied on to give strong support to any particular program or course of action.

Yet, many kinds of urgent international problems remained on the global agenda as the 1960's gave way to the 1970's, and most of these involved the United States, whether Americans liked it or not. It was clear enough that the United States, either by action or by inaction, would play a major role in determining how most of these problems would be dealt with. Some of these problems would conceivably require the application of some kind and degree of military force, and some of this military force would conceivably have to be supplied by the United States. It was interesting to note that not even the most militant critics of the U.S. involvement in Southeast Asia argued that the United States should abolish all of its Armed Forces of all kinds. On the contrary, earlier appeals for "general and complete disarmament" were curiously absent from most of the antiwar and antimilitary expressions of the late 1960's and early 1970. The antiwar and antimilitary critics appeared to pay relatively little attention to the Administration's efforts to reduce the probability of major international violence through the so-called "SALT" talks and equally little attention to proposals for force reductions in Europe and elsewhere. But, if there was a crude and inarticulate public consensus that the United States needed to retain some kind and degree of Armed Forces for the foreseeable future, there was little apparent agreement on 1) how to recruit them, 2) how to organize them, 3) how much would be enough, and 4) how and when they should be deployed in accordance with what national purpose, strategy, and tactics.

These complicated questions are all related to each other. It is impossible to answer any one without some effort to answer the others. By one kind of logic, the last question should be answered first, in an effort to specify a grand national sense of mission and purpose leading to a national strategy in foreign affairs. But grand strategies are difficult to devise and are infrequently formulated in an essentially pragmatic nation which has historically preferred to take one step at a time while leaving open the longer range options. Moreover, grand strategies are all the more difficult to formulate and implement in a period of substantial upheaval and flux on the national and international scenes.

Therefore, another kind of logic would suggest that the first question above should come first in answering the whole set of questions: How to recruit the Armed Forces? But this issue requires a much more complicated analysis than it usually receives.

In general, there are three basic ways to recruit people to serve in the Armed Forces: 1) a conscription system; 2) a volunteer system; 3) as part of a universal service system. In actual practice, conscription systems and volunteer systems can be mixed in various ways. A universal service system is in one sense only a special category of a conscription system, although the universal service system to be described here will differ significantly from most similar proposals offered at earlier times in the United States.

Various combinations of incentives and inducements have historically been used with all three of the general approaches outlined here. Conscription, as the term is used in this essay, is meant to include all forms of forced service—for example, impressment and enslavement—when the force derives from the power of the government which is raising the military services. Conscription of whatever form has typically been used whenever no combination of incentives and inducements was adequate to raise the number and kinds of military services which the government thought was needed.

Conscription has been the basic system used by the U.S. Government since the passage of the Selective Service Act of 1940, although supplemented by some aspects of a volunteer system. Indeed, various versions of a conscription system have always been used in the United States.[1]

The conscription system was subjected to increasingly heavy criticism in the United States in the late 1960's not just from youthful opponents of the Vietnam war, but from many other sectors of American society. Most of the critics focused on the unfairness of the system, with unfairness being measured and answered on several sets of criteria. As an interim measure, the Nixon Administration in 1969 tried to eliminate some of the unfair characteristics of conscription by moving toward a randomized selection procedure. By early 1970, however, the randomized procedures did not appear to be working very effectively in practice, and the Administration tried to move ahead toward its true goal of eliminating conscription altogether by means of replacing it with a so-called all-volunteer system.

President Nixon on 27 March 1969, some two months after his inauguration, appointed former Secretary of Defense Thomas S. Gates, Jr., to head a 15-member commission to study the feasibility of an all-volunteer system. The Gates Commission gave the

[1] For a good history of military conscription as it has been used in the United States, beginning with and since the colonial period, see Gary L. Wamsley, *Selective Service and a Changing America* (Columbus, Ohio: Merrill, 1969), Ch. 2.

President a favorable report on 20 February 1970, recommending that an all-volunteer system be implemented by 1 July 1971. The Commission based its work on the assumption of a standing force level ranging somewhere between 2 and 3 million men, with an estimate that a full 3 million force level would not cost more than $4.6 billion per year over what it would cost to maintain the same level through a continuation of the existing Selective Service (i.e., conscription) System. The Commission's report also provided for a backup conscription system to cover emergency contingencies when a standing force level of 3 million men would be inadequate to meet military needs.

The major arguments in favor of an all-volunteer system as offered by Nixon Administration officials, by the Gates Commission, and by others who supported the idea generally included the following:

(1) Voluntary Armed Services is the basic American tradition except during periods of large-scale war.

(2) The costs of an all-volunteer system would not be nearly as high, on balance, as critics asserted, because significant savings would derive from reduced turnover of personnel, more efficient training, and other features.

(3) Statistics from the Vietnam War showed that draftees suffered far higher combat fatality and injury rates than those who had volunteered for service, suggesting that a conscription system tends to discriminate against draftees and in favor of those who are presumably or potentially professional career military men.

(4) An all-volunteer professional military system would be more efficient than a system relying heavily on frequent infusions of untrained and unenthusiastic draftees.

(5) A conscription system is useful primarily to provide personnel for prolonged wars requiring substantial numbers of ground forces, such as World War II or the Vietnam War, but American involvement in wars of that kind seemed increasingly unlikely in the future.

(6) Higher salary levels and other related inducements under an all-volunteer system would encourage recruits from a broad spectrum of American society, in contrast to the heavy representation from underprivileged minority groups (especially blacks) under the present conscription system.

Critics of the all-volunteer idea tended to rebut all of the arguments enumerated above as well as introducing some further considerations, especially emphasizing the following points:

(1) An all-volunteer system could not be relied on to produce adequate numbers, particularly in high-skill or high-education categories.

(2) The monetary costs of an all-volunteer system would be very high and probably unacceptable politically.

(3) An all-volunteer system would not be sufficiently flexible to meet a wide spectrum of conceivable contingencies, including even relatively small wars which required ground forces.

(4) An all-volunteer system would be composed largely of people from low-income white and minority group backgrounds with limited skills and inferior pre-entry education, because those with better educations from more comfortable sectors of the society would see more attractive futures for themselves in non-military careers.

(5) An all-volunteer system would result in an estrangement of the Armed Services from the broader civilian society, and this would pose serious potential problems of civilian control over the military.

(6) The all-volunteer concept would undermine the traditional importance of patriotism and the duty of every citizen to assume, or to be willing to assume, his share of the burden in protecting a free democratic society.

A simple listing of the pro and con arguments on the issue of an all-volunteer system, however, was not an adequate description of the political reaction to this idea as of the spring of 1970. Although President Nixon himself had given many indications that he strongly favored the all-volunteer concept, the Nixon Administration had not formally submitted a proposal to the Congress which embodied this concept. And although several Senators and Representatives had introduced bills which embodied the concept, the general sentiment in Congress as a whole seemed to be strongly skeptical toward the all-volunteer idea. As for the Department of Defense, obviously the agency of government on which the impact of an all-volunteer system would be most directly felt, it was clear that the Secretary of Defense and the uniformed leaders in the Pentagon did not want to mount an open attack on an idea which they knew to be favored by their Commander in Chief. But it was equally clear that these military leaders maintained many strong reservations concerning the all-volunteer idea.

In summary, the political climate in Washington in the spring of 1970 was highly uncertain with respect to future national policy on techniques for generating personnel for the Armed

Forces. Nobody really liked the existing conscription system, and yet the weight of opinion in Congress and the Pentagon was clearly fearful of a radical abandonment of the system. The President and his Gates Commission clearly wanted a radical abandonment of conscription in order to replace it with an all-volunteer system, and yet the President appeared reluctant to campaign for the all-volunteer concept in view of congressional and Defense Department opposition. Typically, the interim result during this kind of uncertain situation in Washington was that everybody claimed to be giving the matter "further study."

A period of further study is perhaps therefore not a bad time to introduce a third possibility for consideration. This is the idea of a "universal service" system. There is some evidence that this kind of idea is already getting some attention from Pentagon thinkers,[2] but the evidence is thin.

Anyone who introduces a third possibility is implying strong reservations about the other two alternatives: either a continuation of conscription, or the all-volunteer concept. This writer would prefer to make these reservations explicit. The conscription system as it evolved over the thirty years following the passage of the Selective Service Act of 1940 was manifestly unfair on a great many grounds. It resulted in serious social, political, and economic inequities. It was costly, inefficient, and discredited in the eyes of many Americans, including President Nixon as the leader of the Republican Party and many leaders of the Democratic Party. In view of all of the published criticisms of this conscription system, most of which are concurred in by this writer, nothing further needs to be added here on this point.

However, this writer also generally shares in most (although not all) of the criticisms of the all-volunteer concept. It was this dissatisfaction with conscription but also with the all-volunteer idea which led to the search for a third possibility: the "universal service" idea.

One way to approach the case for a universal service system is to offer three further considerations which have received little, if any, attention in the discussions of the all-volunteer concept.

The first of these three neglected considerations is the requirement for a periodic and comprehensive national manpower needs survey, as the basis for a comprehensive national manpower policy. The work of the Gates Commission or any other study which confines itself to the manpower needs of the Armed Forces

2 See Secretary of Defense Laird's remarks as noted in the final two paragraphs of article "Laird Says Volunteer Plan Would Cut Forces a Third," *New York Times*, January 30, 1970, p. 16:2.

is seriously guilty of a piecemeal approach, creating more problems than it will solve. There is ample evidence that the draft has been a primary factor, perhaps even the overriding factor, in the major career decisions of most young American men in recent years, extending back well before the Vietnam War. To offer only one example, Vice Admiral William P. Mack, U.S. Navy, reported that a recent survey of motivations for joining the Naval Reserve showed that "more than 75 per cent of enlisted personnel serving their initial obligation indicated a draft related reason for their initial entry into the Reserve."[3] Generalizing from Admiral Mack's report and other evidence, it is clear that young men with no previous military experience who have joined Reserve components of the U.S. Armed Forces in recent years have been "draft dodgers." But this is not the only kind of decision which young men have made as a result of considerations of the draft. They have similarly made major decisions on career fields, on marriage, and on other important issues as a consequence of this consideration.

The consideration of a potential or actual military service requirement, however, is by no means the only important factor taken into account by young people in making major lifetime and career commitments. Another set of factors relates to the apparent demands for people in various professional and vocational fields. From time to time newspapers and magazines publish charts and reports showing the need for people in various fields, and major career decisions are often made on the basis of such evidence. Unfortunately, however, these reports usually lack the authority of a clear-cut long-range national policy, and serious imbalances result. For example, many reports during the period from approximately 1948 to 1950 claimed that the nation was facing a serious shortage of trained engineers, and many young men elected to pursue engineering studies in their college educations. By about 1953-54, however, new reports indicated a glut of engineers. Similarly in 1969-70, reports indicated a glut of people with Ph.D. degrees in virtually all fields, especially in many scientific and technological and engineering specialties. The glut was obviously a result, in large part, of federal cutbacks in support for many research activities and for agencies such as NASA. But at the same time, there was a serious reported shortage of trained people in most of the health science fields (not researchers, but practitioners) including medical doctors, nurses, social workers, and the like. By projection, it was also possible to

3 William P. Mack, "Reserves of Tomorrow: One View from the Top," *The Naval Reservist*, February 1970, p. 15.

anticipate serious shortages in the mid-1970's of people with appropriate training for dealing with most aspects of the environmental-ecological crisis.

Evidence from almost all of the modern industrialized nations tended to show that, contrary to earlier expectations, the need for many kinds of skilled people tended to grow rather than to diminish. Germany, for example, was forced in the 1960's to import and train unskilled workers from Spain and Italy to offset shortages of skilled labor in West Germany. Japan in early 1970 even decided to resort to the desperate stratagem of encouraging a growth in the Japanese population as a device for acquiring a larger labor force (although most outside observers saw this as creating more problems than it would solve for Japan).

Therefore, the United States can ill afford to produce more skilled talent than it needs in certain categories, thus wasting some of the nation's most precious resource, while lacking adequate talent in other categories. More to the point, it cannot continue to let the military draft system or any other system of manpower allocation for the Armed Forces seriously distort the national manpower profile when viewed against overall needs. It is the ultimate in national irrationality to let one single factor, such as a consideration of whether or not a person will be required to perform military service, become a dominating factor in shaping career and educational commitments.

The second of the three considerations generally neglected in debates and discussions on the all-volunteer concept is the fact of youth as a permanent new factor in American politics. The "Madison Avenue people" and others in advertising, marketing, and sales in American business have long understood that young people constitute a powerful consumer market which does not necessarily take its cues and purchasing preferences from other consumer sectors. This as well as other considerations should have, but did not, lead perceptive policy makers to understand that young people in the approximate age group from 16 to 25 increasingly constituted a formidable political grouping—indeed, a political grouping with its own techniques for internal communication and for certain kinds of group action ranging not only across the nation, but across international boundaries. It would be a serious mistake to think that all youth are accurately represented by the more vocal dissenters and political radicals who began to receive such great publicity in the mid-1960's. But it would be an even greater mistake to think that the younger generation will ever again revert to the docile and inert behavior of earlier young people who were generally content to accept the values and goals of their elders as immutable givens. The new political fact of life has gained increasing recognition in the spreading effort to lower the minimum national voting age to 18. But the new political fact of life has not yet gained recognition in the form of an awareness of the necessity for a comprehensive national youth policy.

Therefore, any proposal for satisfying the manpower needs of the Armed Forces which is not part of a comprehensive youth policy as well as part of a national comprehensive manpower policy is certain to create many more problems than it will solve. Moreover, it is clear that a comprehensive youth policy must be intimately related to a comprehensive manpower policy, because youth constitutes the fundamental input ingredient of the national manpower pool, and also because youthful career decisions are a major determinating factor in shaping the national manpower profile for years to come.

One key element in a national youth policy would be the national manpower needs survey suggested earlier in this essay. Whether this survey should be assigned to the Bureau of Labor Statistics or to the Census Bureau or to some other agency of government is not as important as the requirement that it be taken at frequent intervals, preferably once a year, because the forecasting of manpower needs is not yet an infallible science. The needs change over shorter and shorter cycles as new national policies emerge to cope with unforeseen problems in the rapidly evolving circumstances of a modern industrial society.

Beyond this, however, a viable national youth policy must meet several other conditions. First, representatives of the younger generation must be incorporated in the decision-making process which sets the policy, in order to help create a consensus within the younger generation in support of the policy. Second, the policy must offer stronger kinds of guarantees that the nation commits itself to allow a man to practice his profession or vocation at the same time that the man makes his commitment to the profession or vocation, because: 1) substantial numbers of educated and skilled people who suddenly find themselves out of work because of shifting national policies constitute a serious and indeed intolerable national waste; 2) these unemployed people contribute to a sense of social drift, disorder, and malaise which either paralyzes national will and resolve or which encourages a variety of ill-considered radical solutions; 3) a viable youth policy must allow and encourage sounder foundations for educational and career commitments in the first place, but also opportunities for reconsideration and recommitment in new directions at some later time; 4) the youth policy must offer a viable variety of options in terms of young people's own perceptions of this nation and the global society of which it is a part, as well as in terms of their values and goals.

In short, it is now too late in the history of the American society to think that critical manpower needs can be adequately met by a continuation of the unsystematic and impressionistic procedures used by most young people to decide what to study in college, whether and what to study in postgraduate education, and what professional or vocational careers to enter. They need more hard evidence on which to make their decisions, more assurance that the society supports them in those decisions, but also more opportunities to re-decide in a new direction if an early decision proved unattractive.

Social costs are attached to all decisions, and social costs can be translated into economic costs. Calculations of this kind must also be a part of any effort to combine a comprehensive manpower policy with a comprehensive youth policy. One can start with the obvious observation that merely the process of being born, growing up, and receiving a basic education in any society, from birth to perhaps age 18, will give a person a certain set of general attitudes, values, behavioral patterns, and skills. But this set is seldom identical to the ideal pre-entry requirements for any particular profession or vocation. However, in order to minimize costs (social costs as well as immediate economic costs), most professional and vocational groups will try to recruit their new members usually from among those in the 18-22 age bracket who already appear to have the maximum pre-entry attitudes, values, education, skills, etc., and then to give the recruits further education and training and socialization experiences to offset the gap between the actual and the ideal. The costs (all kinds of costs) to a society for producing members of a professional or vocational group which the society desires to have will vary directly upward with the extent to which the society fails to produce the desired number of potential recruits at the threshold of adulthood who already possess the basic requirements for admission to the group as determined by a consensus between the society and the group.

Let us take a hypothetical example. Suppose that a society wants to maintain a medical profession and that the members of this profession must be generally recruited from the ranks of the overall society. Suppose that this society at large as well as those who are already members of the existing medical profession tend to agree that the new medical recruits should have at least the following characteristics: 1) above-average intelligence, 2) a college-level education with some emphasis on subjects relevant to technical medical skills, 3) habits of personal cleanliness, 4) a commitment to improve the health of all peoples even at some sacrifice to the potential medical doctor's personal convenience. But then, to put it in the extreme, suppose that the society suddenly produces no candidates for recruitment to the medical profession who possess these characteristics. The society will then be forced either to accept lower standards of medical care, perhaps no medical care at all, or to pay a price for meeting the standards. The price it is willing to pay, expressed in the terms of an economist, will be a reflection of its marginal propensity to consume medical care in contrast to its marginal propensity to consume other goods and services. A different angle on this hypothetical situation could be suggested by an analogy between the society which wants to produce medical doctors and the business firm which manufactures a product. If the firm is faced with a steady deterioration in the quality of the raw material which it uses to make the product, the costs of remaining in production will increase, or the quality of the product will suffer, or both. It could even become necessary to go out of business.

These considerations can be easily demonstrated on the following simple chart. Obviously, A and B and C are the same on both lists, therefore, the costs to the society will be the costs first of persuading the desired number of people to enter the proposed vocational or professional field and then the costs of converting D to X and E to Y through education, training, and socialization experiences on the job at the apprentice stage.

Actual *Characteristics*
of Typical Pre-entry Recruit
to a Vocation or a Professional Field

A
B
C
D
E

Ideal *Characteristics*
of Desired Pre-entry Recruit
to a Vocation or a Professional Field

A
B
C
X
Y

This raises the third of the three neglected considerations in debates and discussions on the concept of an all-volunteer military establishment. The simple fact of the matter is that the term "volunteer" is a gross misnomer. Do we speak in terms of having an all-volunteer force of auto mechanics or an all-volunteer group of grocery store managers or an all-volunteer medical profession in the United States? Obviously not. In actuality the so-called all-volunteer concept is an all-vocational or all-professional concept, depending on whether one regards a military career as a vocation or a profession (or perhaps mixing elements of both). When people decide whether to enter the military as a career or medicine as a career or any other career choice, they are, in fact, weighing incentives against costs (again, many kinds of costs and not merely simple direct economic costs). This kind of decision is something quite different from the traditional definition of the verb "to volunteer," which usually means a temporary short-range commitment to serve for a brief period *away from* one's primary career commitment.

Therefore, the kind of combined comprehensive national manpower policy and comprehensive youth policy proposed here should make these career choices much clearer than they have ever been before. It is probably fair to say that very few if any young people who make career decisions in the United States have more than the foggiest notion of what daily life is actually like in their chosen fields, under the unsystematic and impressionistic procedures which have traditionally governed such decisions. Even older men who complete or retire from an early career and then decide on a second career are frequently operating under erroneous impressions. The unavailability of adequate information on incentives, inducements, and various kinds of costs not only at the time of initial entry but at stages in a career, as well as requirements in personal life styles, requirements for periodic advanced education and training, and daily stresses and strains, may well account for the allegedly great number of people who regard themselves as misplaced in their chosen vocations or professions. The personal as well as the overall social costs which are attached to this sense of misplacement are undoubtedly staggering.

It is now appropriate to suggest some of the mechanics of the "universal service" system proposed here. First, it would embrace every single young American on graduation from a secondary or high school or, for those not graduating, at age 18. To answer the first obvious question, it would include females as well as males. To answer the second obvious question, it would tend to embrace the entire national population in the 18-to-20 age bracket, and this is a population of approximately 10.5 million people as calculated by the Gallup organization.[4] Exemptions would be granted in only the most severe situations, for example, as in the case of serious protracted illness or in the case of a grave family hardship. Even those young people with physical handicaps could and should be accommodated in some of the conceivable kinds of programs within the scope of the USS idea as proposed here.

The Universal Service System, or USS, would embrace a number of corps, perhaps including a list which would resemble the following:

(1) Military corps (for assignment, as needed and appropriate, to the several Armed Services),

(2) International development corps (embracing work projects such as have heretofore been performed by some Peace Corps groups),

(3) International teaching corps (embracing teaching duties such as have heretofore been performed by some Peace Corps groups),

(4) Urban services corps (embracing work projects, teaching, and other activities in urban areas such as have heretofore been performed by some VISTA groups),

(5) Rural services corps (embracing work projects, teaching, and other activities in rural regions such as have heretofore been performed by some VISTA groups),

(6) Technical skill corps (embracing teaching and learning activities such as have heretofore been conducted within various federal programs designed to train the hard-core unemployed),

(7) Environmental services corps (embracing a wide variety of conceivable work, teaching, and learning projects, as proposed in a statement by Secretary of the Interior Walter J. Hickel on 5 March 1970).

This listing of possible corps is not necessarily the best way to structure the organizational components of a USS program nor necessarily an exhaustive list of the tasks and services on the na-

[4] For further details on the educational mix of this population group and how this group is presently employed, see the chart on p. 2 of sec. 4, "Profile of the 10 Through 20-Year-Old Potential Voter," *New York Times*, March 15, 1970. Note, however, that the indicated figure of 60,000 with less than 9 years of formal schooling was corrected to the accurate figure of 600,000.

tional agenda. However, it does suggest that the agenda is of far greater magnitude than most people have yet realized. In reply or rebuttal to the possible objection—How would the nation ever be able to manage and get useful work from a USS program involving at least 10.5 million young people between about ages 18 and 20 (and this figure would gradually rise as the overall national population increased)?—the response is simply that even this number of people would not be adequate to the staggering needs.

A related question is the management of the overall USS program. The first step would be to abolish the Selective Service System as it has existed and replace it with a new governing agency which would include representation not just from the Department of Defense, but from most other Cabinet-level agencies as well, plus the U.S. Civil Service Commission and other governmental departments and agencies. The new governing agency should also include direct representation of other sectors of the society at large, most especially including representation from the critical 18-to-20 age bracket.

The new governing agency would receive quotas to be filled from agencies such as the Department of Defense, with its needs for manpower for the Armed Forces. The new governing agency, in consultation with appropriate departments and agencies, would determine quotas for other corps.

The new governing agency could "contract" not only with relevant government departments, but with private groups such as business organizations, labor unions, universities, and colleges to assume some of the managerial and/or training functions. For one example, housing is a major national problem, and part of this problem is a result of many structurally sound apartments and dwellings which have fallen into disrepair and have been abandoned by their owners in most large cities. Let us suppose that 500,000 young people, if given not more than 90 days of training in such basic skills as painting and carpentry, could be utilized with great effectiveness in helping to restore these housing units. The new USS governing body could devise a program, in cooperation with the Departments of HUD and Labor, and then actually contract with appropriate labor unions or repair companies to take specified numbers of young people, train them for not more than 90 days, and then use them (i.e., manage and direct them) on work projects.

A major feature of the program as proposed here is that young people would be given a meaningful choice. Indeed, choices could be specified by major corps programs and by subprograms within the corps. Each young person on attaining the age of 17 could register his or her choice on a card form and submit this to the central office of the USS governing body. By means of a computer, these choices could be matched against quotas for each corps program or subprogram. In cases where more than the allowed quota indicated a particular choice, the final selection could be made on a computer-randomized basis from among all qualified candidates. Of course, certain people would be disqualified for certain corps programs or subprograms on the basis of —for example—physical requirements. A paraplegic would be obviously disqualified from service in the infantry but might be well qualified for many other programs. In any event, the computer selection procedure would give each young person in the program his or her highest choice, consistent with quotas in each corps program or subprogram and consistent with the minimal preentry requirements and qualifications.

All available evidence would suggest that the overwhelming majority of young people would prefer nonmilitary over military programs.[5] Differential incentives and inducements would need to be devised to cope with this problem. For example, the required period of service in the military corps could be set at 18 months, while the required period in the other corps programs could be set at 24 to 36 months. Similarly, post-service benefits could be set according to a differential scale. For example, something like the "GI Bill" benefits could be devised, with 2 to 4 years of post-service education or vocational training for those who served in the military but only half that much for those who served in the nonmilitary corps. Special benefits could be included for those involved in extremely hazardous or potentially hazardous work, such as combat situations for those in the military and those who perhaps volunteered for a civilian-type corps which exposed them to serious diseases.

The USS idea could easily be made to serve other important social purposes. For example, it has been widely publicized that most universities and colleges in the nation are facing dire financial problems, and this includes even the most prominent and well-endowed institutions. It has therefore been widely predicted that vast federal support will be required to keep most of these institutions in existence, even if important and perhaps money-

[5] For one philosophical commentary on this matter, see the essay by Arthur N. Gilbert, "Some Reflections on the Future of War," *The Denver* [University] *Quarterly*, Fall 1969.

saving reforms are achieved in the operations and structures of these schools. But it has also been predicted that the good of the society will require that many more young people receive some form of post-secondary school education, in most cases similar to the kinds now offered by colleges and universities. The USS program could support the great resource represented by the nation's colleges and universities, as well as enhancing the even greater resource represented by its young people, if a federal subsidy to higher education were to be created by means of something like a "GI Bill" with liberal post-service educational benefits including tuition support, no-interest loans for further education after the expiration of tuition support, etc. This would be an investment in the future of the society as well as a benefit in exchange for services rendered. It is clearly only a matter of time before 2 to 4 years of post-high school education or training are as ordinary and routine in the United States as high school education is today. The pressing need to accelerate this process could be met by adding to the USS idea the suggested features resembling the old World War II and Korean War "GI Bill" benefits.

This is not the place to try to spell out all of the possibilities and refinements which could be made a part of the USS concept. But, to suggest one other conceivable inducement, people could be allowed to pair themselves, when submitting their preferences, for all corps programs and subprograms where various kinds of pairings would be appropriate. For example, husband-and-wife teams could be paired, but so also could—for example—two high school boys who were close friends and who would find military service more appealing if they knew they could serve together. Provisions of this kind have existed in the past for twins or brothers and could be extended to include many more kinds of appropriate paired-service situations. As for husband-and-wife teams, it could probably be expected that one result of the USS program would be a sharp decline in pre-service or during-service marriages.

This is also not the place to try to reply to all of the anticipated objections to the USS idea, but one major objection should be dealt with at least briefly, and this is the claim of overwhelming monetary costs. One response is that substantial administrative savings would be achieved, in contrast to the Selective Service System, simply because of the everybody-serves feature. "Selection" is one of the costliest aspects of "Selective Service." For certain, there would be high starting-up costs and other expensive "bugs" to remove from the system in early years. But there are other ways of reckoning costs. For example, it should be noted that the USS concept as embraced here would include many activities already being undertaken in a variety of piece-meal federal programs, and some economics of scale should be realized by comprehensive centralized management. Finally, it is possible and indeed desirable to reckon costs not in comparison to what is already being done, but in comparison to the costs of not trying to do the things suggested by a program. The basic argument here is that a continuation of hastily improvised, piece-meal, and scattergun federal programs which fail to match ac-tivities against a long agenda of urgent social needs and which fail to think in terms of a combined comprehensive manpower policy and youth policy will ultimately cost far more than what-ever the USS idea would cost.

The basic obstacles to the "Universal Service System" idea, however, are not the objections that could be expected from many individuals and agencies and organizations which would have to make major adjustments to it nor the objections that could be expected from executive and legislative branch leaders who are not notably enthusiastic for bold new ideas regardless of the cost factor. Even if all relevant agencies and organizations should rally to the USS idea and even if the Congress should enact it and the President should fully support it, the USS would still face two fundamental obstacles in the path of successful im-plementation.

The first of these obstacles is the general and spreading sense of social disorder and upheaval that increasingly characterized American society in early 1970. As stated on the first page of this essay, it appeared at times that the very fabric of American society was beginning to unravel, and a mood of national drift, if not paralysis, was evident in many quarters. The situation was well described by James Reston:

> In his well-publicized memorandum to the President, Daniel Pat-rick Moynihan said: "In one form or another, all of the major prob-lems facing you derive from the erosion of the authority of the in-stitutions of American society. . . . All we know is that the sense of institutions being legitimate—especially the institutions of government —is the glue that holds societies together. When it weakens, things come unstuck."
>
> Well, they are unstuck now.[6]

[6] James Reston, "The Forgotten Principle," *New York Times*, March 25, 1970, p. 46:8.

Most Americans probably preferred not to look at the disturbing facts, but the evidence was impossible to ignore. Three prominent left-wing student radical leaders appeared on Channel 13
television in New York City on the evening of 23 March 1970
and said that American laws rarely punish the "rich" while dealing harshly with the "poor." The Federal Government during
that same week, as if determined to support the left-wing case,
moved at glacial speed on the possibility of prosecuting the major
oil company responsible for the massive oil leak in the Gulf of
Mexico which was causing millions of dollars in damage and
cleanup costs, although the Interior Department said that the oil
company was in violation of several hundred federal regulations.
Major newspapers generally reported the story as if the oil company was merely the unfortunate victim of an accident rather
than possibly guilty of criminal behavior. Other things happened
during that same week. Postal workers felt compelled to resort
to an illegal strike in order to improve their poverty-level wages
while the President and Congress treated the problem as a political football. The environmental crisis deepened as major cities
around the nation reported no foreseeable solution to the problem of the disposal of daily garbage, trash and sewage. The Administration in Washington conveyed the impression of diminishing enthusiasm for improvements in the condition of minority
groups, especially blacks, while the frustrations of some of these
groups were leading to scattered urban-style guerrilla warfare.
In short, the United States appeared to have lost both the will
and the ability to cope with major crisis-proportion problems.
The ultimate crisis, therefore, was a crisis of confidence and self-
confidence.

Consequently, the second major obstacle facing the successful
implementation of a "Universal Service System" concept was the
way in which the national crisis of confidence expressed itself
among young people in the 16-to-25 age bracket. The left-wing
radicals openly proposed a violent social revolution (for example, on the Channel 13 television presentation referred to
above), but the left-wing radicals were only a tiny minority. On
the other hand, most successful revolutions have been led by tiny
minorities when vast majorities were demoralized and suffered
from a paralysis of will. Substantial evidence indicated that many,
if not most, young people did suffer from serious demoralization.
The evidence included the widespread and growing narcotics
problem among young people in large cities but also in small
towns across the nation, as reported in most major newspapers

and news magazines. The evidence also included a comprehensive scientific study of suicides among college students.[7] This report indicated that, contrary to the belief that most college suicide cases were brilliant neurotic students often on drugs, in fact, most of these cases were fairly average students. Escape through drugs or suicide is not generally characteristic of people who self-confidently face the future with some optimism that major problems can be solved.

The basic term in the "Universal Service System" concept is the word *service*, but people do not respond to the idea of service unless they have some degree of confidence in the social system which calls for their service. Some social systems were and are capable of instilling this. The Mormon Church, for example, successfully requires several years of service from all of its young people, and the Israeli Government successfully requires military service from all (male and female) of its young people. For the United States as a nation to be able successfully to implement a program of universal service, however, many things would have to contribute to a restoration of confidence in the American social system on the part of young people and on the part of Americans as a whole. It should be emphasized that the word "military" does not appear in the term "Universal Service System" as proposed here; it is certainly not the same as the "Universal Military Training" or UMT idea which was proposed after World War II. Nor does the word "national" appear in the term "Universal Service System" here, because most young people want to be able to identify their nation with the broader cause of humanity in general.

The USS proposal would allow this identification between the national interests and the broader interests of mankind. It would help to heal the rift between young people who prefer military forms of service and those who prefer nonmilitary forms. It would offer a wide variety of options as to particular forms of service without any kind of discrimination beyond minimal skill and physical qualifications in certain categories. It would not even suggest invidious distinctions between those who spent their period of required service primarily as learners and those who served primarily as teachers. In other words, the young person from an underprivileged background who spent his required years in learning a skill or acquiring remedial education would be

[7] See "College Suicide Study Discounts Impact of Drugs and Pressures," *New York Times*, March 23, 1970, p. 1:1.

viewed as serving the society just as much as the young person who was assigned a teaching role.

Basic pay would be the same for all and would be very low. While young people from more affluent backgrounds would thus suffer some loss in their standards of living while spending their required service, this would be a basic democratizing experience not wholly unlike that acquired by the millions who served in the Armed Forces in the general mobilization of World War II.

The USS idea would give every young person a break of approximately two years between high school and college or high school and other forms of later education, in contrast to the present system in which most young people never experience anything beyond a classroom or school situation between the ages of 6 and 22 when they are expected to reach major career decisions and commitments. The USS idea would thus allow at least this one significant nonclassroom experience on which to base these major career decisions. Further, if the USS proposal could be combined with the kind of comprehensive manpower policy and program called for earlier in this essay, it would represent a national commitment of important kinds of support for young people entering the adult economy.

In conclusion, the USS idea is complicated. It poses some problems, and it would face many expected obstacles. Appropriate administrative arrangements would not be easy to formulate and implement. Most seriously, it could not work unless it was accompanied by a general restoration of American confidence in national abilities and purposes. Yet, the USS proposal itself could make a substantial contribution to this restoration of confidence if it was part of a larger set of activities and programs at all levels of government and in the private sector of the American social order. On balance, it appears to this writer to be the one best way to recruit young Americans for the massive agenda of military and nonmilitary needs now urgently experienced by the United States and to help once again to instill the idea of service to the American society within the broader context of service to humanity. The USS proposal, if implemented, would result in many kinds of costs, but the conviction here is that the costs of not doing it are likely to be far greater than the costs of giving it an honest try.

PART VII

The Military
and
Domestic Order

The Armed Forces and Civil Disorder

On May 4, 1970, at Kent State University in Ohio, a ragged line
of poorly trained, improperly equipped, inadequately led National Guard troops confronted an unorganized group of milling
students, many of whom were changing classes or going to lunch.
The troops felt threatened, tired, scared. An officer gave an order.
The Guardsmen dropped to their knees, raised their rifles to their
shoulders, aimed, and fired. They wounded nine students and
killed four. Nine of the thirteen victims were shot in the back
or side.

From the professional soldier's point of view, nearly everything about the Guard's operation at Kent State was wrong.
Professionals do not try to disperse a mob by advancing in loose,
disorganized formations—they move forward in a rigid, straight
line with bayonets fixed. Professionals do not introduce violence—they react to it, using an absolute minimum of force to
achieve their objective, which is to break up the crowd. Professionals do not carry live ammunition in their rifles and when
they do load and fire, they aim only at those who are shooting
at them. Most of all, professionals distinguish between a crowd
of aimlessly milling people and an angry mob bent on destruction. But handling a mob in a professional manner requires extensive training, tight discipline, and a real determination to avoid
sacrificing the lives of innocent people. The Guard at Kent
State had none of these qualities, as the Guard generally has
not had them throughout American history.

Yet the Guard remains, as it has been, the chief agency of
the state governments for the suppression of domestic disorder.
Its enemies have changed, from labor organizers and strikers

seeking higher wages and shorter hours, to college students striving to find a way out of seemingly permanent war in Asia. But the tactics have remained the same—throw in the troops at the first opportunity and use whatever force seems necessary to drive the opposition from the field and restore the status quo. The Guard has become the defender of whatever exists partly because the Army and the Marine Corps have shrunk from the task of preserving domestic order, partly because the Guard itself has actively sought the role.

The professional soldiers dislike domestic duty for a variety of reasons. Military men see themselves as the defenders of the nation from foreign enemies using organized armed forces. This is not only their *raison d'etre;* it is the job they want to concentrate on. Diversionary tasks, such as running CCC camps or flood relief programs, or police work, detract from their ability to meet foreign enemies. More importantly, Army and Marine leaders realize that any involvement in domestic disorder is political in nature, an involvement they wish to avoid if only for the reason that their political masters are always changing and they cannot afford to be identified with one side or the other. Finally, professional soldiers abhor a situation that pits them against their fellow citizens, who sometimes are veterans or—as at Kent State—future enlisted men and junior officers, and who are unarmed. Everything about the suppression of domestic disorder, in fact, violates the professional soldiers' code and their view of themselves.

The Guard, on the other hand, has embraced the task of providing massive organized service to victims of natural disasters and maintaining law and order. These are, indeed, almost its only remaining functions. Until the late nineteenth century the Guard's predecessor, the organized militia, was a national joke, and since the development of nuclear-tipped missiles (and the consequent low expectation of a general mobilization for protracted total war), the Guard no longer has a central place in anyone's plans for war against foreign enemies. Its great days came in 1918 and in 1941–45, when all Guard divisions were mobilized and many covered themselves with glory on foreign battlefields. But before World War I and after the Korean War, the Guard was never what it sometimes still claims to be—a force of citizens-in-arms serving as the Army's first line of reserves.

The Guard took on its modern form in reaction to the labor riots of 1877. From the first, it was deeply involved in politics.

It recruited its men, especially officers, from the "better classes." Because it was organized, financed, and controlled by the state governments, it served the interests of those who ran the state or had influence with the governor. In practice, this meant that the Guard was used to suppress "anarchists, internationalists, and nihilists," as one officer described the labor leaders who were the Guard's chief enemies. The Guard began, and grew most rapidly, in the industrial North—Massachusetts, Connecticut, New York, Pennsylvania, Ohio, and Illinois. Its funds came not only from the state governments but also from wealthy businessmen. As an Illinois National Guard colonel told the National Guard Association in 1881, "We have a battalion of five companies of cavalry. . . . It grew out of our riots of 1877, previous to which time we had no cavalry in the State. During the riots it was found necessary to have cavalry, and we hastily organized a battlion of cavalry among our business men who had seen cavalry service during the war. Our cavalry was not equipped by the State. It belongs to the National Guard, but was equipped and uniformed complete by the Citizen's Association of the City of Chicago. This association is composed of business men, who look after the best interests of our city."[1] The best interests of the city meant no interruption of business as usual, which meant no disorders, which meant no strikes. Most domestic disorder between 1877 and 1941 grew out of labor strikes. In the typical case, management responded to demands for shorter hours and higher pay by locking out the strikers and attempting to introduce strikebreakers ("scabs") into the factories. The strikers, in turn, used force to keep the scabs out, and they also often endeavored to damage or destroy the factories in order to bring the owners to terms. The Guard's role in such cases was to restore order (get the factory back in operation), protect property, and defend the right of the scabs to work for whomever they pleased for whatever wages they were willing to accept. Under the circumstances, the Guard became, almost automatically, a strikebreaking organization.

Union leaders, organizers, and members were furious. They taunted the Guardsmen by calling them Cossacks, and the Sheet Metal Workers' Association included in its constitution a provision forbidding its members from joining "the regular army, the State militia or naval reserve." One member declared, "It

---

[1] The similarities between the Illinois National Guard, at least as described here, and Vigilantes or Ku Klux Klans is obvious. The only real difference is that the Guard had official state support and status.

is very superficial to suppose that the effect of the use of soldiers in strikes is to prevent violence. It is the knowledge that they have the militia to fall back upon that induces employers to hold out against just demands."

The Guard insisted that it was impartial, interested only in maintaining law and order. At times, indeed, the Guard did succeed in remaining objective, as in the Pennsylvania coal strike of 1902, which was one of the least violent major strikes in American history. The strikers won a substantial victory after a long, drawn-out struggle. Throughout, the Guard strictly observed the governor's injunction: "The presense of the state troops is not to aid the operators to crush the strike or strikers. They are there simply to prevent rioting and bloodshed."

In most cases, however, the Guard was definitely on the side of the owners and used whatever force was necessary to break the strike. Lurid, but not atypical examples, were Cripple Creek, Colorado, where in 1903 gold miners went on strike, and Lawrence, Massachusetts, where textile workers struck in 1912. In Colorado, the state and its agencies—including the Guard—were nothing more than another arm of private capitalism. "To hell with the Constitution," a senior Guard officer declared as he moved his unit into Cripple Creek. "We aren't going by the Constitution." One of the most dramatic incidents came at Ludlow, Colorado, where on September 23, 1913, the coal miners went on strike. The mine owners hired large numbers of guards, contracted for additional men from the Baldwin-Felts Detective Agency, had at least two machine guns with vast quantities of ammunition, and still demanded that Governor Elias Ammons send in the Guard. On October 28 he agreed to do so. General John Chase, a physician, was Adjutant General of the Colorado National Guard, and he took command. Governor Ammons ordered him to be completely impartial and to disarm both the strikers and the mine guards. Both sides, however, hid large quantities of arms. Chase assumed that he was the commanding general of an occupying force in enemy territory and began seizing, jailing, and holding without charges strikers and their sympathizers.

By April, 1914, Governor Ammons decided the situation was calm enough to warrant the removal of most of the Guard (the state had run out of money and could no longer meet the Guard's payroll). He left in Ludlow a small force of one company of infantry and told Chase to raise a new troop of cavalry in the strike zone. But nearly every man in the area was either on

strike or worked for the owners as a mine guard; Chase nevertheless went ahead and recruited the new unit (Troop A, 1st
Squadron, Colorado National Guard) from among the mine
guards. Many of the new Guardsmen continued to draw pay
as mine guards or mining company employees while they were
in the Guard.

The hostility between the Guard and the strikers was bad
enough before the formation of Troop A; it now became explosive. On April 20, 1914, a pitched battle broke out. The fighting
lasted most of the day. The miners' tent city burned down; in
the rubble, in a crude dugout below one of the tent floors, there
were eleven women and children, dead from suffocation. The
miners charged that the Guard had deliberately fired into tents
where the women and children were known to have sought
safety, and with firing upon strikers trying to rescue people
from the burning tents. The Guard denied everything, but the
country as a whole blamed the Guard for the horror. Still, the
Guard continued to uphold the owners' interests, in Colorado
and elsewhere, throughout the period of labor unrest.

The Guard in the twentieth century is a unique organization,
for it has two sovereign masters. Since the passage of the Dick
Act at the turn of the century, the President can federalize the
Guard and bring it under his personal orders (acting in his
capacity of Commander in Chief of the Armed Forces). The
Dick Act almost completely negated the original purpose of
the militia, for the Founding Fathers saw the militia as a liberal
agency that would act in defense of individual and local liberty
against the power of the Federal Government. The Founding
Fathers, in fact, reflecting their deep suspicion of standing armies,
went to great lengths to insure that the Federal Government
would not have a monopoly on violence. On an individual level,
they guaranteed citizens the right to bear arms; on the organized
level, they encouraged the development of state militia units in
order to provide a counter-power to the U.S. Army.

But the Fathers enjoined the President, in the Constitution,
"to take care that the laws be faithfully executed," made the
President the Commander in Chief, and guaranteed to the states
a republican form of government—a guarantee that only the
Federal Government could conceivably enforce. At this point,
the Fathers were torn—they wanted to maintain the independence
of the militia from the Federal Government, but they did not
want a large standing army, which was the only force available
to the President to execute the laws and guarantee a republican

form of government. So they wrote into the Constitution a clause granting to Congress the power "to provide for calling forth the militia to execute the laws of the union, suppress insurrections and repel invasions." The power to federalize the militia, it should be stressed, belonged to the Congress, not the executive, just as it was the Congress, not the President, that had the power to raise and support armies (the President is limited to commanding them.)

The Federalist Party moved immediately to broaden the President's power. During the debate over ratification of the Constitution, Alexander Hamilton pointed out in *Federalist* No. 28, "There may happen cases in which the national government may be necessitated to resort to force . . . seditions and insurrections are, unhappily, maladies as inseparable from the body politic as are tumors and eruptions from the natural body; . . . the idea of governing at all times by the simple force of law . . . has no place but in the reveries of those political doctors whose sagacity disdains the admonitions of experimental institutions." And in *Federalist* No. 29 Hamilton argued that only if the President had a well-regulated militia at his disposal could the nation avoid the evils of a standing army. "If the federal government can command the aid of the militia in those emergencies which call for the military arm in support of the civil magistrate," he wrote, "it can better dispense with the employment of a different kind of force," thus providing the original rationale behind the use of the militia to execute the laws.

Since the Congress was not in continuous session, since it could seldom if ever act in a hurry, and since the President was ultimately responsible for executing the laws, on May 2, 1792, Congress delegated a part of its power to call out the militia to the President. There were legal limitations on the President's power, but the grant was sufficient to enable Washington to federalize the militia of four states to suppress the rebels in western Pennsylvania who refused to pay federal taxes on whiskey (the Whiskey Rebellion). In 1806, in response to the Burr Conspiracy, Thomas Jefferson persuaded Congress to give him authority to use the Regular Army "against insurrection or enterprise on the public peace or authority." From that time on, the President always had a choice of forces to use—state militia brought into federal service, or the Regular Army. Both were used extensively in the nineteenth century. Lincoln originally called out the militia to suppress the insurrection in 1861, a call the border states refused to honor. Cleveland used regulars to "move the mails" in Chicago late in the century, although his real purpose was to break up a strike among railroad workers there. Federal troops were used elsewhere on strikebreaking missions, although not as extensively as the Guard.

Not until after World War II, however, was the larger issue settled—to whom did the militia (Guard) ultimately belong? The question immediately raised the further problem—where, ultimately, does sovereignty reside in a federal system? Who has the real monopoly of force?

In the fall of 1957 President Eisenhower settled the issue, and thereby set out a new role for the Guard. In direct violation of a federal court order, Governor Faubus of Arkansas called out his state Guard to prevent a few black students from entering Central High in Little Rock. Because of the high feelings among Little Rock white people (not to mention the Governor and, indeed, the Guardsmen), violence threatened. Eisenhower decided to send in Regular Army troops—the 101st Airborne Division—to insure order and the speedy enactment of the court order, but the problem of the Guard remained. Eisenhower solved it at a stroke by directing the Secretary of Defense to use both regular forces and "any or all" of the Arkansas National Guard to eliminate "obstruction to justice" in Little Rock. In short, he federalized the Arkansas Guard, thus removing it from Faubus' command and putting it under his own. By late November, 1957, after two months of duty, the 101st Airborne withdrew; the federalized Guard stayed on duty until the end of the school term. Eisenhower had effectively deprived the state of Arkansas of its organized means of violence and guaranteed a monopoly on organized force to the Federal Government. He had also set a new pattern of using Guardsmen and Regular Army troops side-by-side, a pattern that took on increased significance in the late 1960's during America's ghetto riots. In the words of historian Robert Coakley, "The triumph of the federal authority in Little Rock was as significant, certainly, as that achieved in enforcing the court order. In the era before the Civil War, it is unlikely that any President or even Congress could have succeeded in using a state's militia against the active opposition of its governor to enforce a federal court decree within the borders of his state."

Both Presidents Kennedy and Johnson followed Eisenhower's precedent. In September, 1962, Kennedy federalized the Mississippi National Guard to assist regular troops to quell disturbances arising out of the attempt of James Meredith, a black man, to enter the University of Mississippi, Kennedy did so again in 1963 in Alabama to deal with Governor Wallace's defiance of court orders dealing with integration. In 1965, Johnson federalized the Alabama Guard to assist regulars in protecting civil rights marchers in their walk from Selma to Montgomery. The governor had refused to call out the Guard to protect the marchers.

Eisenhower's action at Little Rock had hamstrung the southern governors. Unlike the governors of industrial or mining states in the earlier period, the southern politicians could not use the Guard to enforce the wishes of the dominant social classes in their state. The Federal Government triumphed.

Since the integration difficulties of the late 1950's and early 1960's, the battleground has shifted from the Deep South to the Northeast and the Far West. The chief threats to law and order have become urban blacks and college students. Guardsmen today, whether federalized or not, will most likely find themselves employed either in a ghetto or on a college campus. Usually, as the following essay by Martin Blumenson illustrates, when the Guard is used in a city riot it will have federal troops by its side, again following the Eisenhower precedent. On college campus duty, the Guard has so far acted by itself, operating under the orders of the state governor, whether it be at the University of California or Wisconsin or Maryland or Ohio State or Kent State or at dozens of other schools. As in its earlier actions during industrial strikes, the Guard on college campuses has not been an impartial force striving to prevent violence, but rather has lined up on the side of the school (and state) authorities against the student rebels. It has had widespread support for its actions from the public at large; even after the death of four innocent young people at Kent State most Americans indicated to pollsters that they felt the Guard had acted properly and the students were at fault.

It is, however, perfectly clear that the Guard lacks the discipline, training, or leadership to meet its responsibilities. At a time when the Guard's major, almost sole, *raison d'etre* is riot control and natural disaster relief, it still spends the bulk of its terribly limited training time preparing for another World War II, which no one believes will ever come. The outlook for the future is not sanguine.

On the Function of the Military in Civil Disorders

MARTIN BLUMENSON

Upon the outbreak of civil disorder, what is the function of the military troops called to help quell the violence? What have been the methods employed by armed forces to uphold the authority of government and the law and to restore order and civil peace? What has been the range of military response to civil disturbance in the United States?

In suppressing domestic violence, military forces have reacted on different levels of intensity. How they have put down lawlessness and rioting suggests their place in American life. . . .

In the heart of the Negro ghetto in Detroit, an early morning police raid on an after-hours drinking establishment on July 23, 1967, triggered the appearance of a group of several hundred Negroes. One person threw a bottle at a police cruiser, others shouted obscenities, and the mob surged down 12th Street breaking windows. Forty-five policemen on duty in the 10th Precinct rushed to the disturbed area and sealed off 16 square blocks. In compliance with a policy formulated by Mayor Jerome Cavanagh and Police Commissioner Ray Girardin, the police followed a "walk soft" strategy. This policy had proved effective the previous summer, when riots had flared in the East Side of the city. Negro leaders had then cooled the situation, and

Reprinted by permission from the Inter-University Seminar on Armed Forces and Society, Inc. Volume II, p. 475–517, of A Survey of Military Institutions, edited by Roger W. Little. Copyright 1969, The Inter-University Seminar on Armed Forces and Society, Inc.

the authorities expected that they would do so again. Feeling
that policemen shooting their weapons into the air and making
other displays of force would only inflame additional violence,
the authorities ordered the police to make no attempt to enter
the turbulent area, to place themselves in evidence on its fringes,
to avoid using weapons or force to restrain crowds, and to
guard public utility installations vulnerable to sabotage.

The relative inaction at the outset, it was later argued, permitted the riot to gain momentum, whereas repressive action
might have stopped the violence.

The small band of demonstrators quickly multiplied, looting
increased, fires broke out, and disorder and destruction fed upon
themselves. The disorder spread over almost 11 square miles.

Although the director of the state police was informed that
the incident was under control, he alerted forces for possible
commitment. The Adjutant General of the National Guard was
at Camp Grayling, 200 miles away, conducting the annual summer encampment training for 4,300 Guardsmen; he alerted a
brigade of the 46th Division for possible movement to the city.
A battalion of 300 troops at the Detroit Artillery Armory was
available for quick commitment.

Optimism in Detroit that the violence would soon diminish
began to dissipate during the afternoon as mobs continued to
loot and to set fires. Around 2 P.M., the Mayor requested state
police assistance, and half an hour later, 360 state policemen were
on their way to the city. About that time, the Guard sent three
helicopters to Detroit for aerial surveillance and four armored
personnel carriers to transport law enforcement personnel
through streets made dangerous by burning buildings.

Shortly after 4 P.M., Cavanagh asked Governor Romney to
commit Guard units in support of civil authorities. Four hours
later, state forces, both police and Guardsmen, began a sweeping
movement through the riot quarters. They used 20-man patrols,
each consisting of 15 soldiers and five policemen, plus a 2½-
ton truck to transport persons apprehended and arrested for
lawless acts. As additional troops arrived that evening, they
saturated the riot area. Nevertheless, around 10 P.M., after the
Governor and Mayor toured the city in separate helicopters,
they began to feel that the riot had assumed major proportions
and that Regular troops would be needed.

The riot area now covered 14 square miles, and by 2 A.M.,
July 24, citizens had reported a total of 5,839 lawless incidents—
arson, looting, and disorder. A new element had also appeared—

sniper fire aimed at firemen. Riflemen were then assigned to
protect firefighters and their equipment. Maj. Gen. Cecil Simmons, commander of the 46th Division involved in the city, after
seeing the looting and hearing the sniping, said: "The laws of
the State will be obeyed. We will use whatever force is necessary." Guardsmen received ammunition, together with instructions to shoot if they were fired upon.

Indecision in Detroit whether Regular troops would really
be needed and hope that state forces alone could handle the situation finally gave way to the conviction, around 7 A.M., July 24th,
that federal troops were required to prevent the rioting from
reaching an uncontrollable stage. The Guard commitment totalled
2,800, the fire department was taxed to its limits, and police were
working virtually around the clock. Sniper activity hampered
efforts to control fires or quell the disorder. Deaths numbered
four or five, wounded 800, arrested more than 1,000 and fires
reported more than 300.

After a series of telephone conversations and telegrams, President Johnson, shortly after 11:30 A.M. agreed to dispatch Regular troops. He sent Cyrus R. Vance as his personal representative,
and General Harold Johnson, the Army Chief of Staff, appointed
Lt. Gen. John C. Throckmorton to command the military forces
and selected portions of the 82d and 101st Airborne Divisions at
Forts Bragg and Campbell for the mission.

Vance and Throckmorton met in Detroit with Romney and
Cavanagh in the midafternoon of July 24th. They learned that
a total of 483 fires had been reported, and that more than 1,800
arrests were straining detention facilities. In addition to the
local and state police on duty, almost 5,000 Michigan Guardsmen were on the streets and about 3,000 more were in immediate reserve.

That evening, as contingents of Regulars arrived at Selfridge
Air Force Base near Detroit, the rioting seemed to calm down.
At a meeting of Negro leaders, Congressman Charles Diggs said
that the crisis called for an immediate deployment of federal
troops, while Congressman John Conyers thought that the situation was improving and that sending in more troops might provoke a flareup. Vance and Throckmorton, who had made a two
hour auto tour of the worst areas, had seen no looting or
sniping, and they judged the fires to be coming under control.
Their impression was that Regular troops might not be necessary.

Then came a dramatic change. Suddenly, shortly after night-
fall, the death toll soared to twelve. In large part it came from

a more aggressive response to disorder by police and Guardsmen. The initial order to shoot to kill if taken under fire had been changed: they were now to shoot to kill in order to halt looters and fleeing felons. Five deaths from shooting rapidly occurred, and the number of reported incidents of arson and looting mounted drastically.

Around 11 P.M., Mr. Vance recommended to the President that Regulars be deployed in Detroit and that the Michigan National Guard be federalized. The President agreed. After touring the city, General Throckmorton assigned responsibility for the area east of Woodward Avenue to the 82d Airborne Division and the area west of Woodward to the Guard. His decision was rooted in two factors. First, it appeared that the incident rate was increasing dangerously in the eastern part of the city. Secondly, Selfridge Air Force Base, where federal troops were arriving, was closer to that portion of the city, while the Artillery Armory used by the Guard was closer to the western part.

The western area of Detroit, which had been hardest hit on July 23d and 24th, continued to be the scene of the most serious disorders, and the Guardsmen, poorly trained in comparison to the Regulars, thus carried the heaviest burden of quelling the disorder. The area assigned to seasoned paratroopers quickly returned to normal and remained relatively quiet. Was this development merely coincidental? Or did it reflect a difference in the reactions of the two military forces?

The Governor's initial order to mobilize the Guard for riot duty carried the statement to "use what force you have to enforce all the laws of the State of Michigan. If this includes firing of weapons, you will fire weapons." This was the basis of the shoot-to-kill order to halt looting and arson.

Throckmorton reversed this order when he assumed command. He later explained why he took this action. First, his instructions from the Department of the Army—he was responsible directly to the Army Chief of Staff—emphasized the use of minimum force required by the mission. Army guidelines for dealing with riots provided, in ascending order of priority, four possible levels of counter-violence: 1) soldiers carrying unloaded weapons with bayonets fixed and sheathed; 2) unloaded weapons with bayonets fixed; 3) riot control chemical agent CS_2 more efficacious than tear gas; and 4) soldiers carrying loaded weapons and ready to use them.

Secondly, having toured the troubled areas between 5:15 and 7:15 on the evening of July 24th he—

. . . saw nothing in that tour that to me would justify having soldiers on the streets with their weapons loaded. . . . I was confronted with a group of trigger-happy nervous soldiers in the National Guard. I had no intention of having any of those soldiers shoot innocent people, or small children. . . . It has been my experience that, regardless of how well trained they are, troops going into combat for the first time, where they are shot at, will be nervous and inclined to be trigger-happy—that it takes two or three days for them to calm down and react more quietly and properly. This did not happen in the case of the airborne [Regular troops] because we have between 35 and 40 per cent veterans from Vietnam in those units. So they have had their baptism of fire, and they are in a position to tell the young, excited soldier to calm down and take it easy. This is not the case in the Guard. It was true, however, that after they had been on duty for a while and realized the conditions and the situation which they were in, that they reacted the same as other troops do after their initial baptism.

Although he called for all soldiers to unload their weapons, to refrain from firing at looters, and to return sniper fire only on command of a commissioned officer, the Guard failed to comply. Five days after the order was issued, Maj. Gen. Charles P. Stone, the Deputy Task Force Commander, found that a large majority of the Guardsmen—he estimated 90 per cent of all he inspected—were still carrying loaded weapons. In many cases, Guardsmen disobeyed because "the order was improperly disseminated and was never made clear to the men on the street. As a result the Guard was involved in a total of eleven deaths, in which nine innocent people died."

General Simmons, the National Guard commander of the Michigan troops employed in Detroit, wished to use more rather than less force. He argued that disorder would surely spread if the rioters learned that there would be no shooting of looters and that the Guardsmen "had their ammunition in their pockets." But Throckmorton stood firm, and Simmons finally complied. Throckmorton, supported by Vance, was acting in the conviction that "force should be used with maximum restraint."

Several months after the disorder was suppressed, officials of the Michigan National Guard still resented General Throckmorton's order to unload weapons. This state of mind was apparent when a member of Congress asked the State Adjutant General a leading question: "When you were denied all of the normal reactions that a law enforcement officer or a soldier would expect to put into effect, you became a bystander. How could you apprehend or stop looting under these conditions, General?"

"I don't know, sir," the general replied. "We disagreed with the policy entirely."

The technique of self-restraint nevertheless seemed to work. After several days of a massive, yet controlled commitment of troops, together with police, in the streets, the riot died down and came to an end on July 27th. The withdrawal of Regulars began on the following day and ended on August 2d. The Guard remained in evidence for four more days.

To some observers, the riot resembled war. It "bordered on mass insurrection, more closely resembling guerrilla warfare than . . . the riots and disorders with which the nation is more familiar." It looked like combat—with "Hit-and-run looters, elusive snipers; the task of operating with (and out of) patrol cars; the problem of being separated from one's officers for sentry duty or to 'ride shotgun' on a firetruck."

And this the Guard was less able to cope with than Regulars. There were "nearly 5,000 Guardsmen in the city, but fatigue, lack of training, and the haste with which they had had to be deployed reduced their effectiveness." Their activities were marked by "slow response, tangled lines of authority, uncertain deployment, insufficient training, disruption of the military units, isolation of individuals." There were no mobs to disperse on darkened streets; there was rather the eerie quiet of a battlefield, shattered by an occasional round of fire. Regulars were accustomed to this sort of situation, and during the five days that 2,700 of them were stationed there, they expended 201 bullets. In contrast, when a Guardsman's rifle went off accidentally, 75 nearby Guardsmen raised their weapons and started firing at residential buildings to defend themselves against unseen and in most instances non-existent snipers.

General Throckmorton, who believed that the best way to quell a disorder is to saturate an area with "calm, determined, and hardened professional soldiers," ordered a return to normal by getting street barricades taken down and weapons unloaded. The situation in Detroit, he said, did not justify the risk of injury or death through inadvertent or unnecessary discharge of weapons.

The Guard troops were least effective in the early stages of the riot, when law enforcement was most badly needed. Far below active Army standards in appearance, bearing, courtesy, and general behavior, they showed inadequate discipline, primarily because of deficiencies in command and control. Some, perhaps many, of those in the Guard only to avoid being drafted for service in Vietnam, were suddenly taken from the safety and routine of training and placed on unknown and dangerous streets. This was more than they had bargained for. Yet they improved markedly as they gained experience and confidence. And this became "readily apparent to the citizens of the riot-affected sections of the city."

Another reason for the relatively poor performance of the Guard troops was their almost exclusively white composition. A social club enjoying local prestige, it has in Michigan in its Army component a total authorized strength of 9,859 but only 127, a total of 1.3 per cent, were Negroes; Negroes in the Air National Guard totaled only 0.9 per cent.

Mr. Vance believed that more Negro Guardsmen would have overcome a barrier to communication with citizens on the streets. The racial nature of the conflict would have been less exaggerated.

General Stone found "no apparent organization" on the part of the Detroit rioters, but rather "a wholesale assault on the law characterized by looting, arson and the destruction of property." The best way to stop the violence, he said, was to saturate the affected area as early as possible with the maximum number of law enforcement personnel, both police and military, and take quick action to arrest persons breaking the law. In order to impress the rioters, "the appearance, smartness, and military discipline must be exemplary. The image they portray has a very decided effect on the rioters and on the confidence they create among the (non-rioting) public."

"If early in the game," General Stone expanded,—

> . . . they [the National Guard troops] had looked like soldiers, and had created the image in the mind of the public, which is so essential in a situation like this—because if you look strong and if you look as if you can do the job, then the public is going to have confidence in you, and the looter or the rioter is going to be afraid to confront you.

Some "hard-line" advocates of counter-violence to suppress disorders persisted in characterizing the Detroit riot as warfare. "And were (you) in charge of the task force in the Detroit war, or whatever you want to call it?" one asked. "I don't like that term, 'civil disturbance,' " another said, "Let's use the right term, 'guerrilla warfare.' "

Although General Stone inadvertently once used the term "combat in cities," the Army opposes this point of view. "I hope this committee," General Ralph E. Haines, the acting Chief of

Staff, said firmly, "does not reject the basic principle in the quelling of civil disturbances which is to use minimum force consistent with mission accomplishment."

The experiences in 1967 led to a more effective reaction to disorders occurring in 1968. Federal troops were used in Baltimore, Chicago, and Washington, D.C., and although the disturbances were as explosive as any in the previous year, they were brought under control more expeditiously. All arose on the evening of April 4th, 1968, out of the emotions stimulated by news of the shooting and death of Dr. Martin Luther King, Jr.

Department of the Army instructions to the three task force commanders were the same. They were to cooperate with and assist municipal law enforcement officers to assume their normal roles. They were to use the minimum force necessary to restore law and order. Weapons were to be fired only when authorized or when absolutely necessary to save life. Riot control chemical agents were to be used before live ammunition. Bullets fired against looters were to be aimed to wound rather than to kill. Weapons were to be carried unloaded, with bayonets sheathed, except upon order. Military forces were to work closely with the police. Troops were to make no unreasonable searches of persons, property, or automobiles. Civilian rather than military authorities were to take lawbreakers into custody.

In a democracy, "the maintenance of law and order is primarily the function of civil authority and . . . law enforcement in a humane and democratic society must always use the minimum force necessary." Using military units to enforce civil law is distasteful and dangerous. But it is preferable to lawlessness and anarchy.

The employment of military forces to quell civil disorders resembles the activities performed by the Army on the western frontier. Throughout the nineteenth century, along the moving edge of civilization, soldiers functioned to suppress lawlessness and to promote law and order. Their purpose was to establish conditions that would permit the civil forces to provide a social order consistent with and required for the peaceful life of law-abiding citizens. Although the scene has in more recent times become urban, the military mission is still much the same—to help the civil authorities protect life and property, preserve social values, and maintain the tradition of individual liberty together with social order.

PART VIII

The Military
and
the Ecology

PART VIII

The Military
and
the Ecology

Ecological Impact
of Military Activities

JAMES ALDEN BARBER, JR.

Apparently alone among the planets of the solar system, the Earth is hospitable to life. Within the biosphere, that is, the narrow band of the atmosphere and the upper reaches of the sea, an infinitely complex system of relationships among living organisms serves to maintain and renew itself, and to maintain the hospitable environment of Earth. But the system is not infinitely resilient, and there is genuine danger that man may, through triggering cumulative and irreversible chain reactions, destroy the ecological system. If this were to happen, the Earth could become just another dead rock circling the Sun.

The last several years have seen increasing awareness of ecological problems, and at least a few halting steps toward doing something about them. It seems generally agreed that man's depredations are exceeding nature's capacity to adapt and regenerate, and that without immediate steps to reduce pollution there will, at a minimum, be a steady deterioration in the quality of the environment.

The military services contribute to environmental degradation in many of the same ways as do industry and private citizens. Military aircraft leave behind them noise, fumes and contrails just as civilian airliners do—and the particular kind of noise pollution created by the sonic boom is exclusively military. Oil spills from Navy ships pollute our coastlines in the same way as do commercial tankers and leaking oil wells. Military bases pump raw sewage into the same waters which are being polluted by industrial wastes and city sewage.

As awareness of the seriousness of the problems of pollution has grown, the military services have begun to respond. The National Environmental Policy Act of 1969 has direct application to the military, and specific requirements under the Act were levied on the services by a Deputy Secretary of Defense Memorandum of 8 August 1970. In part, this requires a detailed statement on the environmental impact of all significant programs. A number of specific actions have been taken to lessen pollution. The Navy, for example, is in the process of shifting over from black oil as a ship fuel to distillate fuels, at least partly because of the cleaner burning and reduced contamination from the distillate fuels. Whether the military response to remedying their own pollution problems will be adequate is yet to be seen. It is, in any case, only one component part of a wider range of serious problems, which are not specifically military problems. The military contributes to the problem, but as just another source of pollution. With only a few exceptions the general problems of pollution are not specifically military ones.

There are, however, some serious ecological problems which are specifically military, and it is these which will be discussed in this section. The military ecological problems to be discussed are: 1) biological and chemical weapons; 2) nuclear radiation; and in the following article, 3) the Army Corps of Engineers.

Chemical and Biological Weapons

A series of events over the last several years has aroused widespread concern about military chemical and biological warfare programs. These events include the use of tear gas and herbicides in Vietnam; the death of thousands of sheep as a result of a nerve gas accident in Utah in March, 1968; an accidental release of nerve gas stored in Okinawa in July, 1969; and a series of controversies over transportation of chemical agents, including the dumping of two train-loads of nerve gas off the Florida coast in August of 1970. The resulting controversy has had the effect of bringing into public view information on one of the previously least publicized areas of military activity.

A wide variety of weapons are included in what the military services call "C.B.W.," or Chemical and Biological Warfare. Chemical warfare includes the use of poison and nerve gases, and depending on which definition is used, sometimes also includes incendiaries and chemical herbicides. Biological weapons, or "germ warfare," include a variety of disease-causing micro-organisms, and sometimes include the poisonous toxins generated by bacteria, such as botulin.

The majority of Department of Defense programs in C.B.W. are carried on by the Army. Although the roots of these programs go back much farther, the stepped-up activity during the 1960's was based upon a 1959 House committee report entitled "Research in Chemical, Biological and Radiological Warfare," which recommended extensive research on chemical and biological warfare agents. This report has been cited by the Army as the basis for its C.B.W. programs.[1]

Several arguments have been offered in justification of the C.B.W. programs. One argument is that of military deterrence: that it is necessary to possess a capability of using such weapons in order to prevent them from being used against us. Another is that since C.B.W. may be used against us anyway, that it is necessary to know what forms of chemical and biological weapons are possible in order to prepare adequate defensive measures. A third argument is that in many cases C.B.W. agents are both more humane and more effective than any alternative weapon. This is the argument that has been used to justify the use of tear gas and herbicides in Vietnam. To these arguments the Army has added the additional defense that there are a variety of beneficial side effects from C.B.W. research: that "Chemical Corps research and development contributes to the national welfare—in a wide range of fields, including medicine, agriculture, commerce."[2]

In a letter to Congressman Richard D. McCarthy dated April 15, 1969, John S. Foster, Jr., Director of Defense Research and Engineering, stated that total U.S. expenditures in the chemical and biological fields for fiscal year 1969, including procurement of incendiary weapons, amounted to $350 million. He added that there was no procurement of lethal chemical agents or biological agents.

Gas

The use by the United States of tear gas in Vietnam has provoked controversy over whether or not such use is prohibited

---

[1] Richard D. McCarthy, "Poison for Peace," *The Commonweal*, June 6, 1969, p. 335.
[2] "Benefits of CBR Research," *Army Digest*, August 1969, p. 13.

by the 1925 Geneva protocol against the use of chemical and biological weapons in war. The Geneva protocol was drafted in response to widespread revulsion against the use of gas during World War I, and is the major international treaty on the subject. Although the United States was an active advocate and a signatory of the protocol, when the protocol was submitted to the Senate for ratification it was impossible to secure approval from an isolationist majority, and as far as the United States was concerned the protocol remained in limbo for forty-five years. On August 19, 1970, President Nixon again sent a request to the Senate for ratification of the protocol, attaching a stipulation that the United States would not be bound by the protocol if another country abrogated the treaty. The President also reiterated the U.S. position that tear gas and defoliants did not come within the agreement's jurisdiction.

Whether the uses of tear gas and defoliants are or are not banned by the Geneva protocol is a matter of legal interpretation for which there is no clear correct answer. It seems indisputable, however, that the use of any form of gas in warfare tends to weaken the more general prohibition. As soon as one kind of exception is made it becomes progressively easier to find reasons for making other kinds of exceptions, and the prohibition breaks down. This is in fact what happened to the Hague Gas Declaration of 1899, as the participants in World War I found loopholes to justify their own use of gas. The Geneva protocol has been one of the most successful of attempts to limit war through international agreement, and it would be tragic to have it weakened through unilateral action. This may already have been implicitly recognized in the White House, which has issued a directive to the Defense Department barring the use of tear gas or defoliants without the President's permission after the end of the Vietnam War.

The tear gas and defoliants used in Vietnam have all been of kinds that are normally nonlethal to humans, but much more dangerous chemical weapons have been developed, tested and stored. The potential lethality of some of these weapons was demonstrated accidentally in March of 1968 when a small quantity of VX nerve gas escaped the Army's Dugway Proving Ground in Utah. The first indication of trouble was the death of large numbers of sheep as far as 45 miles away from the test site. The Army at first denied that any tests had been conducted which could be in any way related to the death of the sheep, but as evidence mounted the Army finally accepted responsibility. On the basis of claims paid, 4,377 sheep were killed outright by the nerve gas, and another 1,877 disabled. Fortunately no humans were injured, apparently either because the sheep, which were continuously outside, were subjected to greater exposure (either directly or through grazing), or because men may have greater resistance to VX than do sheep.

The controversy which followed the Dugway incident made public more information about the Army's chemical warfare program than had been available up to that time. The information included an admission by the Army that open-air testing was being carried on at Dugway, as well as at other locations within the United States. One result of the uproar was to cause the Army to sharply cut back on its testing program and to institute more careful controls over the remaining portions. An Army spokesman reported in October 1969 that chemical agents were stockpiled at eight depots across the country, adding the assurance that the munitions posed no hazards to surrounding communities.[3]

The year after the Dugway incident, in July, 1969, VX nerve gas again hit the headlines when an accidental leak revealed the presence of U.S. nerve gas weapons in Okinawa. This time humans were exposed to the gas, but apparently as a result of prompt treatment no serious injuries resulted. The ensuing international uproar led the United States to withdraw the gas from Okinawa, and when plans to store the gas in a depot in Oregon ran into stiff opposition, the gas wound up stored on Johnston Island in the Pacific.

Transportation of lethal gas within the United States also claimed public attention. The Army had been disposing of obsolete World War I phosgene gas to commercial firms which used it in the manufacture of plastic, but suspended such shipments in the fall of 1969 because of public opposition. In August of 1970 the Army, with Navy assistance, disposed of two trainloads of small rockets filled with nerve gas by sinking an old Liberty ship carrying the rockets as cargo. The sinking took place in 16,000 feet of water about 300 miles off the Florida coast. The event received international attention as well as generating both domestic and international opposition. Responding

[3] The listed sites were Edgewood Arsenal, Edgewood, Md.; Blue Grass Army Depot, Richmond, Ky.; Anniston Army Depot, Anniston, Ala.; Pine Bluff Arsenal, Pine Bluff, Ark.; Pueblo Army Depot, Avondale, Colo.; Rocky Mountain Arsenal, Denver, Colo.; Tooele Army Depot, Tooele, Utah; and Umatilla Army Depot, Hemiston, Ore.

to the outcry, Secretary of Defense Melvin Laird stated on August 16, 1970, that U.S. dumping of nerve gas in the sea would never happen again, and that an alternative means of detoxifying the weapons had been developed.

Biological Weapons

Biological weapons make use of microorganisms or fungus spores to induce illness in men, animals or plants. There are no verified instances of biological weapons having been used in the conduct of war, although their use has been charged from time to time. During the Korean War Communist China charged the United States with spreading disease-infected insects over North Korea and northeastern China. The United States denied the charges, and proposed to the United Nations Security Council that they be investigated by the International Red Cross, but the resolution was vetoed by Russia. In 1953 the General Assembly voted an investigation by the World Health Organization, but both China and North Korea refused entry to conduct the investigation. The communists gained tremendous propaganda mileage out of the charges, but neither then nor subsequently was any evidence produced to indicate that anything other than a complete fabrication was involved.

The United States has, however, along with several other nations, carried out a research and development program on biological weapons. Known to have been tested for their potential as weapons are such diseases as anthrax, undulant fever, plague, psittacosis, Rocky Mountain spotted fever, and Venezuelan equine encephalomyelitis. An Army spokesman stated in December, 1970 that the United States had been making biological weapons since 1962.[4]

Biological weapons, like chemical weapons, have been developed on the basis of the argument that the best way to deter the possible use of a weapon against us is to be able to retaliate in kind. The possibility of such use is not imaginary: among the nations known to have developed biological weapons are the Soviet Union, Communist China, and Poland, and the development of such weapons lies within the capability of virtually every nation. It has been said that any nation which can brew beer or manufacture penicillin can make biological weapons. This

[4] *New York Times*, December 19, 1970, p. 1.

lends credence to the argument that we should be prepared to take necessary self-defense measures against the possible use of biological weapons. It does not, however, strengthen the deterrence argument, which is flawed by the difficulty of identifying positively the source of biological infection, and of knowing for sure whether it is a natural or deliberate epidemic. Further, there is no real reason that a response must necessarily take the same form as a provocation for a deterrent to be effective. Other weapons in the U.S. arsenal ought to be as effective in threatening retaliation against an aggressor as would be the threat of responding to germ warfare in kind.

Actually, biological weapons have several difficulties which make their military value somewhat dubious. For one thing, they have a delayed effect, which may range from a minimum of a few hours to several weeks. Thus they have almost no utility as tactical weapons. Second, they tend to have their most serious effect on the weakest elements of the population, so that they are likely to injure the elderly and the very young in larger measure than those of military age. One argument that has been put forward in favor of biologicals, however, is that they can be relatively humane weapons when they take the form of temporarily incapacitating populations rather than killing them as do more conventional weapons. Although LSD is not a biological weapon, the Army has had a similar concept in mind in experimenting with the chemical as a relatively benign way of causing widespread disorientation and temporary incapacitation in a target population. The argument is not without merit. Potentially, certain kinds of biological weapons might be more benign than other forms of warfare, but it appears at present that the effects are sufficiently unpredictable that such use is hazardous at best. Finally, one of the most serious arguments against the military use of biological weapons revolves around the difficulty of keeping them from backfiring. Short of a massive advance program of inoculation, there is danger of any epidemic started by biological weapons leaping national boundaries and infecting allies and even the nation which initiated the attack. Because of these problems even military men are rather pessimistic about the military utility of biological weapons.

The Geneva protocol specifically includes a prohibition against the use of bacteriological methods of warfare, although the prohibition is not spelled out in detail. In order to clarify the prohibition, in 1969 the British submitted to the Disarmament Conference in Geneva a draft convention designed to reinforce and spell out in greater detail the prohibition against biological warfare. In November of 1969 President Nixon placed the United States on record in support of the British proposal.

There have been no accidents of the magnitude of the Dugway sheep kill associated with the storage and testing of biological weapons in the United States, but there have been accidents. The Army has reported that at its primary center for biological warfare research at Fort Detrick, Maryland, during the twenty-six years of research between 1943 and 1969, three deaths resulted from laboratory infection.[5] It has been charged that the Army has understated the seriousness of accidents, but there has been no evidence of any widespread or serious contamination.[6] Despite the meticulous safety precautions that are observed, however, there has been at least some chance for more serious accidents.

On November 25, 1969, President Nixon clarified and revised United States policy on chemical and biological weapons. The President's statement (White House Press Release dated November 25, 1969) was as follows:

Soon after taking office I directed a comprehensive study of our chemical and biological defense policies and programs. There had been no such review in over 15 years. As a result, objectives and policies in this field were unclear and programs lacked definition and direction.

Under the auspices of the National Security Council, the Departments of State and Defense, the Arms Control and Disarmament Agency, the Office of Science and Technology, the intelligence community, and other agencies worked closely together on this study for over 6 months. These government efforts were aided by contributions from the scientific community through the President's Scientific Advisory Committee.

This study has now been completed and its findings carefully considered by the National Security Council. I am now reporting the decisions taken on the basis of this review.

Chemical Warfare Program. As to our chemical warfare program, the United States:

—Reaffirms its oft-repeated renunciation of the first use of lethal chemical weapons.
—Extends this renunciation to the first use of incapacitating chemicals.

[5] *Congressional Record*, June 4, 1969.
[6] Seymour M. Hersh, *New York Times Magazine*, September 28, 1969.

Consonant with these decisions, the administration will submit to the Senate, for its advice and consent to ratification, the Geneva protocol of 1925, which prohibits the first use in war of "asphyxiating, poisonous or other gases and of bacteriological methods of warfare." The United States has long supported the principles and objectives of this protocol. We take this step toward formal ratification to reinforce our continuing advocacy of international constraints on the use of these weapons.

Biological Research Program. Biological weapons have massive, unpredictable, and potentially uncontrollable consequences. They may produce global epidemics and impair the health of future generations. I have therefore decided that:

—The United States shall renounce the use of lethal biological agents and weapons and all other methods of biological warfare.
—The United States will confine its biological research to defensive measures, such as immunization and safety measures.
—The Department of Defense has been asked to make recommendations as to the disposal of existing stocks of bacteriological weapons.

In the spirit of these decisions, the United States associates itself with the principles and objectives of the United Kingdom draft convention, which would ban the use of biological methods of warfare. We will seek, however, to clarify specific provisions of the draft to assure that necessary safeguards are included.[7]

In accordance with the President's statement, the Army announced in December, 1970 its plans for accomplishing the destruction of all biological and toxic weapons. The destruction, which was to take about one year to complete, was to be accomplished without the necessity of transporting the agents outside the storage sites. The Army, clearly smarting from earlier criticism, made public careful and detailed safety precautions which would accompany the destruction of the biological material.

The official policy of the United States on chemical and biological weapons can be summarized briefly. The U.S. has renounced all biological weapons, even for purposes of retaliation, and will carry on only biological research on defensive measures such as immunization. The United States has renounced first use of chemical weapons; and the Geneva protocol was resubmitted to the Senate for consideration in August of 1970, although as of the time of this writing no action had been taken. We have,

7 The Department of State Bulletin, Vol. LXI, No. 1590, December 15, 1969, p. 541.

however, specifically excepted tear gas, herbicides and incendiary weapons, and although renouncing the first use of lethal gases, the United States apparently intends to maintain a stock of them as a deterrent to their possible use against us.

The Use of Defoliants in Vietnam

Wars are usually destructive of the environment of the country in which they are waged. One of the side effects of the destructiveness of modern weapons of war is the infliction of widespread damage on plant and animal life. In Vietnam, however, because ecological damage has been inflicted as a deliberate tactic, the effect of the war on the environment has become a major issue in some ways separate from the issue of the war itself.

Chemicals which could kill or disrupt the growth of plants were developed during World War II, although they were not employed operationally. Following the war the herbicides were marketed commercially as weed killers. The most important of these were the chemicals 2, 4-dichlorophenoxyacetic acid (2, 4-D) and 2, 4, 5-trichlorophenoxyacetic acid (2, 4, 5-T). These chemicals have been used widely, both singly and in combination, in uses ranging from killing dandelions in lawns to keeping firebrakes clear of brush. The kinds of herbicides which have been used in Vietnam are normally referred to by a color name, taken from the color stripe on the drums in which the chemicals are delivered. Three main types were employed: Orange (also known as Purple in a slightly different compounding) which contains equal parts of 2, 4-D and 2, 4, 5-T; White, which is a compound of 2, 4-D and a persistent herbicide named Picloram; and Blue, composed primarily of cacodylic acid, which is mostly arsenic. All of these have been used commercially within the United States, with the exception of Picloram, which has not been authorized for domestic use by the Department of Agriculture, presumably because its herbicidal effect persists for so long after application.

Defoliants were used by the British during the Malaysian insurgency operations of the 1950's, although on a much smaller scale than they have been used in Vietnam.[8] In Vietnam they were first tried on a small scale between July, 1961 and April, 1962. These preliminary trials were sufficiently successful that it

[8] J. B. Neilands, "Vietnam: Progress of the Chemical War," *Asian Survey*, March, 1970 (Vol. X, No. 3), p. 219.

was decided that the herbicides would be effective in removing cover in areas where Viet Cong ambushes were likely, and to destroy food supplies in Viet Cong-held areas. The magnitude of the program increased year by year, reaching a peak in 1967. Figures on the exact area sprayed with herbicides are not in agreement, but one careful observer has estimated that about 12 per cent of the entire area of Vietnam has been sprayed.[9]

The defoliation and "food denial" programs carried out in Vietnam have been reported by both U.S. and South Vietnamese military sources to have been successful from a military point of view, and it has been argued that the programs are relatively more humane than the use of more lethal weapons. The two principal arguments against the program have revolved around the long-term ecological effects of the widespread use of herbicides, and the possible effects of the chemicals in causing birth defects.

One of the principal ecological dangers of the widespread use of herbicides is that no one really knows what the long-term effects will be. It hasn't been done on such a wide scale before, so that all predictions have to be pretty much based on guess-work and extrapolation from small-scale experiments. Some of the possible dangers pointed out by scientists who have studied the problem are that defoliation may result in a long-term degradation of the fertility of the soil, that it may seriously upset the life cycle of the animals who live and breed in the area, and that it may completely change the character of plant life in the area. One of the fears, for example, is that the destruction of the mangroves around the Mekong River may cause depletion of the shell fish and migratory fish of the area, and that fast-growing bamboo may replace the mangrove, preventing the mangrove from ever being able to reestablish itself. Two scientists who conducted a careful investigation of the ecological effects of the war in Vietnam concluded that the effects were somewhat more severe than had been officially acknowledged, and suggested that although the campaign may have been effective militarily, the political and psychological effects were probably damaging to U.S. aims in the area.[10]

Late in 1969 further serious questions about the herbicides arose when a government-sponsored report raised the possibility that they could cause birth defects. A report from the Bionetics

[9] Thomas Whiteside, "Defoliation," *The New Yorker*, February 7, 1970, p. 32.
[10] Gordon H. Orians and E. W. Pfeiffer, "Ecological Effects of the War in Vietnam," *Science*, May 1, 1970, pp. 544–554.

Research Laboratories in Bethesda, Maryland, indicated that doses of the chemical 2, 4, 5-T were associated with a significant increase in birth defects in experimental animals. The Bionetics study concluded on the basis of the animal experiments that 2, 4, 5-T was "probably dangerous," and that 2, 4-D was "potentially dangerous but needing further study." There have been reports from Vietnam of an increase in birth abnormalities, but the inadequacy of past statistics and the difficulties of obtaining current statistics make it impossible to determine the accuracy of the reports.

Shortly after the findings of the Bionetics study were made known the Defense Department restricted the use of herbicides in Vietnam to "areas remote from the population." In April of 1970 U.S. government agencies banned the use of 2, 4, 5-T within the United States anywhere in the vicinity of homes, lakes, ponds or food crops. At the same time the Defense Department announced that the use of agent Orange (containing 2, 4, 5-T) was being completely suspended in Vietnam, but that agent White would continue to be used in sparsely populated areas.

The peak of herbicide use in Vietnam was reached in 1967, fell off somewhat in 1968 and 1969, and was seriously curtailed in 1970. In the late spring of 1970 the spraying operations were completely suspended, and the C-123 aircraft which had been involved in the operation were diverted to support the operations in Cambodia, hauling out captured communist arms and ammunition. At the time it was assumed that limited spraying operations would be resumed at a later time.

We will not know for decades just how badly the defoliant campaign has damaged the ecology of Vietnam. Chances are strong that much of the damage is permanent, and that valuable resources may be lost forever in an area that badly needs all of the resources it can command. Whether the military advantages of defoliation balance the hostility engendered in the peasants whose land was damaged is a moot point, and will probably never be resolved. The poignant fact is that in trying to defend Vietnam the United States may very well have caused damage so deep and irreversible that it can never be undone.

Nuclear Radiation

Of all of the contaminants which man can release, perhaps the one most directly threatening to man himself is nuclear radiation.

Cosmic rays and ordinary rocks create a background of radiation to which we are all exposed, but in the last few decades this has been augmented by the activities of man. Testing of nuclear weapons in the atmosphere releases large quantities of radiation which tends to spread throughout the world. In most cases this man-made radiation amounts to only a fraction of the normal background radiation, but it can be disproportionately serious because of the way in which certain particularly long-lived radioactive products tend to accumulate in living tissue. Particularly threatening in this regard are strontium-90 and cesium-137. Strontium-90 is similar to calcium, and tends to concentrate in bone. Because it is not excreted from the body, and because it becomes less active only very slowly (having a "half-life" of twenty-eight years) it builds up cumulatively in the body over a period of years. Cesium-137 concentrates particularly in muscle tissue, but also builds up in other tissues, including reproductive organs—which makes it particularly likely to induce genetic changes. Cesium-137 decays at about the same rate as strontium-90, but because the body is slowly able to excrete cesium-137 it does not have quite the same capacity for long-term build-up as does strontium-90.

Worldwide fear of the long-term effects of nuclear fallout was at least partly responsible for the partial nuclear test ban treaty signed in Moscow in 1963. The parties to the treaty (which France and Communist China have refused to sign) agreed to limit nuclear testing to tests in which nuclear fallout would not be present beyond their own national borders. Since the treaty was signed, both the United States and the U.S.S.R. have limited their nuclear tests to underground explosions, although both France and Communist China have conducted atmospheric tests.

Other than the atmospheric tests by the non-signatories, the three continuing sources of nuclear radiation which are of concern are: 1) hazards involved in the manufacture and testing of nuclear weapons; 2) nuclear powered ships; and 3) transportation and storage of radioactive by-products. All of these problems have a military aspect, although several result from civilian activities as well.

The 1963 partial test ban treaty by no means meant the end of testing of nuclear weapons. It is estimated that the Atomic Energy Commission has detonated about 250 underground explosions since the treaty went into effect. Several of these have "vented," resulting in the unintended release of radioactive contamination into the atmosphere. Most of the venting has been minor in nature, but on at least three occasions radioactivity from the leaks has been detectable from outside the United States in violation of the provisions of the treaty. One of the severest cases of venting occurred in December, 1970, when 300 employees of the AEC were exposed to radioactive contamination. All underwent decontamination procedures, and the AEC reported that none had received a sufficiently high dose to cause any danger of radiation sickness. None of the cases of venting has been serious enough to constitute a serious or widespread danger, but they cannot help but raise questions with regard to observance of the provisions of the test ban treaty and the possibility of a more serious accident in the future.

In addition to whatever hazards are involved in nuclear testing, the production of nuclear materials presents its own problems. The process of producing nuclear material in a form suitable for use in either weapons or power plants involves the creation of large quantities of nuclear waste, which presents a disposal problem. The biggest disposal site for nuclear material in the world is at Hanford, Washington, where radioactive by-products are stored in huge underground tanks constructed of concrete and steel. There have been fears that an earthquake or other natural disaster might cause a large-scale leakage from these tanks which could be dangerous. The AEC has started a small program of solidifying atomic wastes at Hanford, but at last report the amount being solidified was no more than just keeping up with the requirements for new storage, rather than reducing the quantity of hazardous liquid storage.

A further nuclear danger, again more potential than actual, has to do with the increasing numbers of nuclear-powered ships, most of them military. All of these ships are carefully designed, operated to the highest standards of safety, and have compiled an enviable safety record—but there does not seem to be any way of completely preventing the possibility of serious nuclear contamination resulting from a damaging collision between ships. It is true, however, that at least two nuclear submarines have been lost at sea, apparently without releasing detectable amounts of nuclear radiation.

In a world just becoming aware of the dangers of drowning in our own wastes, it must be acknowledged that more care is taken with nuclear wastes than almost any other kind. Even here, however, whether the degree of care is adequate in view of the potential hazards is open to question. Much of the criticism has revolved around the fact that in many cases the AEC serves as the promoter of nuclear power, manufacturer of nuclear material, and testing agency for nuclear weapons, as well as being the agency charged with setting and enforcing the standards of safety —in many cases upon itself. It is permissible to be at least a little cynical about how effective an organization is likely to be in policing itself over any long period of time.

Conclusion

Perhaps the principal lesson to be gleaned from the material presented in this chapter is that the military services have proved themselves capable of carrying out some pretty dubious and ecologically hazardous undertakings when such projects have been either ignored by the public or hidden behind a screen of secrecy. But another rather clear lesson seems to be that publicity and public controversy have been extraordinarily effective in obtaining modification of military policies. Examples given here include greatly increased care in the transportation, storage and disposition of chemical warfare materials, limitations on the testing of such material, plans for complete destruction of all biological warfare materials, withdrawal of nerve gas stored on Okinawa, a pledge from the Secretary of Defense that the United States would never dump nerve gas in the sea again, and a sharp cutback in the use of herbicides in Vietnam. Not reported here is an extensive program which has been instituted within each of the military services to bring other kinds of environmental pollution resulting from military activities under control.

The lesson seems to be clear: the most effective way of controlling unwise or dangerous military programs is to make sure that they are regularly exposed to critical public scrutiny, a task in which the press and the Congress would seem to share equal responsibility.

Another way in which military activity affects the environment, but which is of a distinctly different sort than the programs discussed in this chapter, is through the activities of the Army Corps of Engineers. This is discussed in the following selection.

Dam Outrage: The Story
of the Army Engineers

ELIZABETH B. DREW

As times change so do the nation's needs and priorities. But the Army Corps of Engineers just keeps rolling along as it has for decades, working one of the most powerful lobbies in Washington, winning more than $1 billion a year from the Congress to straighten rivers, build dams, and dig canals that frequently serve only narrow interests and too often inflict the wrong kinds of change on the environment. Here the Atlantic's *Washington editor tells how the Engineers do it, and suggests that a changing public opinion may at last force a change in their habits.*

The St. Croix River, one of the few remaining wild rivers in the nation, forms a stretch of the border between Wisconsin and Minnesota before it runs into the Mississippi below Minneapolis. Not long ago, Senator Gaylord Nelson of Wisconsin discovered that the Army Corps of Engineers was considering the construction of a hundred-foot-high dam on the St. Croix. At the same time, Nelson and Senator Walter Mondale of Minnesota were trying to win legislation that would preserve the river in its natural state. Nelson took the unusual step of going before a congressional committee to oppose a Corps project in his own state. "The Corps of Engineers," he said, "is like that marvelous little creature, the beaver, whose instinct tells him every fall to build a dam wherever he finds a trickle of water. But at least he has a purpose—to store up some food underwater and create a livable

Reprinted by permission of the author. Copyright © 1970, by the Atlantic Monthly Company.

habitat for the long winter. Like the Corps, this little animal frequently builds dams he doesn't need, but at least he doesn't ask the taxpayer to foot the bill."

Few politicians publicly criticize the Corps, because almost all of them want something from it at some point—a dam, a harbor, a flood-control project. A combination of Corps diplomacy and congressional mutuality keeps most of the politicians content, and quiet. The overwhelming majority of Corps projects are attractive federal bonuses, given free of charge to communities— some local contributions may be involved in small flood-control or municipal-water-supply projects—and therefore they are highly prized. "They take care of all of the states," said one Senate aide. "If there's water in a faucet in one of them, they'll go in there and build a dam."

There is no question that the civil works program of the Army Corps of Engineers, viewed over its long history, has benefited the country. It has made waterways navigable and provided hydroelectric power and flood control. Communities to which it has brought help have been genuinely grateful. Now, however, it is a prime example of a bureaucracy that is outliving its rationale, and that is what is getting it into trouble. As the Corps, impelled by bureaucratic momentum and political accommodation, has gone about its damming and dredging and "straightening" of rivers and streams, it has brought down upon itself the wrath of more and more people disturbed about the effects on the environment. A secret poll taken by the White House last year showed environmental concerns to be second only to Vietnam in the public mind. This rather sudden general awareness of the science of ecology—the interrelationships between organisms and their environment—has brought projects which disturb the environment and the ecology, as Corps projects do, under unprecedented attack. The Corps' philosophy, on the other hand, was recently expressed in a speech by its chief, Lieutenant General F. J. Clarke. "With our country growing the way it is," he said, "we cannot simply sit back and let nature take its course."

Criticism of the Corps and what its programs are all about is not based solely on environmental issues. The broader question, given the claims on our national resources, is whether it makes sense to continue to wink at traditional public works programs, and the self-serving politics which sustain them. The nation is now committed, for example, to making Tulsa, Oklahoma, and Fort Worth, Texas, into seaports, although each is about 400 miles from the sea, at costs of at least $1.2 billion and $1 billion respectively. There are other questions that might be raised at this point, such as whether subsidizing the barge industry should be a national priority; or whether we want to continue to dredge and fill estuaries and build flood-control projects for the benefit of real estate developers and wealthy farmers. The Army Corps of Engineers and its work have been a very important force in American life, with few questions asked. Yet it is not fair simply to castigate the Corps, for the politicians have made the decisions and the public has gone along. General Clarke had a point when he said that the Corps is being put "in the unhappy and, I can't help feeling, rather unfair position of being blamed for presenting a bill by people who have forgotten that they ate the dinner."

The Corps is part of a growing hodgepodge of federal bureaucracies and programs that work at cross-purposes. The Department of Agriculture drains wetlands while the Department of Interior tries to preserve them. The Corps dams wild rivers while the Department of Interior tries to save them. The Corps and the Bureau of Reclamation in Interior provide farmlands for crops which farmers are paid not to produce. The government spent $77 million to build the Glen Elder Dam in Kansas, a Bureau of Reclamation project which provided land to produce feed grains, for which the government pays out hundreds of millions of dollars a year to retire. The Tennessee Valley Authority is also still building dams, and it does strip-mining.

But of these water programs, the Corps' is by far the largest. Each year Congress gives it more than a billion dollars, and each year's budget represents commitments to large spending in the future. In a deliberate effort to spread the money around, new projects are begun and ones already under way are permitted to take longer to complete, in the end driving up the costs of all of them.

The annual Public Works appropriations bill provides money for, among others, the Panama Canal, the Water Pollution Control Administration and the Bureau of Reclamation in the Interior Department, and various public power administrations, as well as the Corps of Engineers. This year it came to $2.5 billion, of which the Corps received $1.1 billion. The Corps is now at work on 275 projects. The total future cost of these will be $13.5 billion, not accounting for the customary price increases. Another 452 projects have been authorized by Congress, but have not yet been started. The Corps says that the total cost of these would be another $10 billion, clearly an underestimation of some magnitude. For every project to which the country is already committed, the Corps, the politicians, and the local interests who stand to gain have many, many more in mind.

"Destiny . . ."

The Corps' official history traces its beginnings to a colonel who dug trenches "in the darkness of the morning" during the Battle of Bunker Hill, and the subsequent orders of President Washington to establish a corps of military engineers and a school to train them. In 1802, the Corps was established, and West Point was designed to provide its members. The history of the Corps is interwoven with that of the country and its frontier ethic. It is a very proud agency. "They led the way," its history says, 'in exploring the great West. They were the pathfinders sent out by a determined government at Washington. They guided, surveyed, mapped, and fought Indians and nature across the continent. . . . They made surveys for work on the early canals and railroads. They extended the National Road from Cumberland to the Ohio and beyond. They made the Ohio, Missouri, and Mississippi safe for navigation in the Middle West. They opened up harbors for steamships on the Great Lakes." After the war with Mexico, in which "the part played by the Army Engineer officers was impressive . . . the last segment of the great Western Empire was soon annexed. These things were all accomplished by the application of America's greatest power. That is the power of Engineering Character, Engineering Leadership, and Engineering Knowledge. All employed to fulfill our destiny." Following the Civil War, the civil works program of the Corps "was revived to benefit all sections of the reunited nation," and that is how the Corps has been fulfilling our destiny ever since. In 1936 the Corps was given major responsibility for flood control (until then largely a local function).

The major activities of the Corps are the damming, widening, straightening, and deepening of rivers for barge navigation, building harbors for shipping, and construction of dams and levees and reservoirs for flood control. It also works on disaster relief and tries to prevent beach erosion. A project can serve several purposes: building waterways, providing flood control, hydroelectric power, or water supply. As the Corps completed the most clearly needed projects in these categories, it found new purposes, or rationales, for its dams. The newer justifications are recreation and pollution treatment.

Pollution treatment (the government calls it "low-flow augmentation") is provided by releasing water from a dam to wash the wastes downstream. But there are now more effective and less expensive ways of dealing with pollution.

Recreation is provided in the form of still-water lakes behind the dam, for speedboating, swimming, and fishing. But the fish that were previously there often do not continue to breed in the stilled water. And the recreation, not to mention the scenery, of the natural river that used to be there, is gone. A flood-control channel is usually surrounded by cement banks, and the trees are cut down when a levee is built. When the water in a reservoir is let out during the dry months, or for "low-flow augmentation," the "recreation" area can become a mud flat.

These problems arise because the Corps of Engineers' mission has been narrowly defined. Other ways of dealing with transportation, power, and pollution are not in the Corps' jurisdiction, so the Corps is left to justifying what it is permitted to do. What hydroelectric power is left to be developed will make a very small contribution to the nation's power needs. The Corps builds its projects on sound engineering principles. If a highway cuts through a park or a city, or a dam floods more land than it protects, those are the breaks. A "straight" river is an engineer's idea of what a river ought to be. A talk with a Corps man will bring out a phrase like, "When we built the Ohio River . . ."

The Corps argues that having military men conduct civil works "is an advantage of outstanding importance to national defense." Actually, the military men in the civil works section of the Army Corps of Engineers represent only a thin superstructure over a large civilian bureaucracy. Most of the 1,100-man uniformed Corps work solely on military construction. The civil works section of the Corps, in contrast, comprises about 200 military men, and under their direction, 32,000 civilians.

Generally, the career military engineers come from the top of their class at West Point, or from engineering schools. Once they join the Corps, they rotate between military and civil work, usually serving in the civil works division for three-year tours. The civil work is sought after, because it offers unusual responsibility and independence in the military system, and the experience is necessary for reaching the high ranks of the Corps. Through the civil work, a Corps officer can gain a sharpening of political acumen that is necessary for getting to the top. And there is the tradition: "The Corps built the Panama Canal," one officer said, "and every Corps man knows that Robert E. Lee worked on flood control on the Mississippi." It is a secure life, and when he retires, a military corps officer can get a good job with a large engineering firm or become director of a port authority.

The civilian bureaucracy is something else. The Corps, like other government agencies, does not attract the brightest civilian engineering graduates, for it does not offer either the most lucrative or the most interesting engineering careers. The Corps work is largely what is known in the trade as "cookbook engineering." A ready-made formula is on hand for each problem. The Corps' bureaucracy draws heavily from the South, where the engineers who built the first dams and controlled the floods are still heroes.

The military patina gives the Corps its professional aura, its local popularity, its political success, and its independence. The military engineers are, as a group, polite, calm, and efficient, and their uniforms impress the politicians and the local citizens. The engineer who heads one of the Corps' forty district offices, usually a colonel, is a big man in his area; the newspapers herald his coming, and he is a star speaker at the Chamber of Commerce and Rotary lunches. But the military man gets transferred, so smart money also befriends the civilian in the district office. These men stay in the area, and want to see it progress. The Tulsa office of the Corps, for example, has about 1,500 employees, of whom only three are military. The local offices are highly autonomous, for the Corps operates by the military principles that you never give a man an order he can't carry out, and that you trust your field commanders. If a district engineer believes strongly in a project, it is likely to get Corps endorsement. The Corps has mastered the art of convincing people that its projects are desirable, and so the projects are not examined very closely. Corps engineers are impressive in their command of details that non-engineers cannot understand, assiduous in publishing books that show what the Corps has done for each state, and punctilious about seeing that all the right politicians are invited to each dedication of a dam.

And so the Army Corps of Engineers has become one of the most independent bureaucracies in the Federal Government. The Corps' civil works section is neither of great interest to the Pentagon nor answerable to more relevant civilian bureaucracies. It makes its own living arrangements with the Congress, and deals not with the Armed Services Committees of the House and

Senate, but with the Public Works Committees. Theoretically, the Corps reports to the appointed civilian chiefs of the Department of the Army, but these men are usually preoccupied with more urgent matters than Corps projects, and after a spell of trying to figure out what the Corps is doing, or even to control it, the civilians usually give up. "It was," said one man who tried not long ago, "like trying to round up the Viet Cong for an appearance on the *Lawrence Welk Show*."

"I think I understand . . ."

The power of the Corps stems from its relationships with Congress. It is the pet of the men from the areas it has helped the most, who also usually happen to be among the most senior and powerful members, and the ones on the committees which give the Corps its authority and its money. Thus, when the late Senator Robert Kerr of Oklahoma was a key member of the Senate Public Works Committee as well as the Senate Finance Committee, he devoted his considerable swashbuckling talents to winning final approval of a plan to build a navigation system stretching 450 miles from the Mississippi, up the Arkansas River, to Catoosa, Oklahoma, giving nearby Tulsa an outlet to the sea. The $1.2 billion project is said to be the largest since the Tennessee Valley Authority was built. The entire Oklahoma and Arkansas delegations, quarterbacked by a member of Kerr's staff, carried it through. The story goes that President Kennedy, having been advised to oppose the Arkansas River project, met with Kerr to seek his help on a tax bill. Kerr, not a very subtle man, told the President, "I hope you understand how difficult I will find it to move the tax bill with the people of Oklahoma needing this river transportation." "You know, Bob," the President is said to have replied, "I think I understand the Arkansas River project for the first time." After Kerr's death, Senator John McClellan inherited the mantle of chief protector of the project, which reached the Arkansas-Oklahoma border last December, an event that was marked by a grand dedication.

The legislation that authorizes and appropriates the money for Corps projects encourages manipulation and swapping because of the unusual way in which it parcels out the money on a project-by-project basis. It is as if a housing bill had designated X dollars for a development here and Y dollars for a development there.

A very formal document—known around Capitol Hill as "eighteen steps to glory"—explains the procedures by which a project is initiated. In actuality, what happens is that local interests who stand to gain from a Corps project—barge companies, industrialists, contractors, real estate speculators—get together, often through the Chamber of Commerce, with the district engineer and ask for a project. The Corps literature is quite explicit about this: "When local interests feel that a need exists for any type of flood control, navigation, or other improvement, it will be most profitable for them to consult at the outset with the District Engineer. He will provide full information as to what might be done to solve their particular problem, the authorities under which it might be accomplished, and the procedures to initiate the action desired." Then the local groups ask their congressman, who is responsive to this particular segment of his constituency, to secure legislation authorizing the Corps to make a study of the project. Usually the Corps man is already aboard, but if not, he is not very far behind. "Sometimes," said a Congressman who, like most of his colleagues, declined to be named when talking about the Corps, "the Chamber of Commerce will call me, and I'll say get in touch with Colonel So-and-so in the district office and he's over there like a shot; or the Corps will make an area survey and go to the community and drop hints that they might have a dam if they work on it." Frequently the project's promoters will form a group—the Mississippi Valley Association, the Tennessee-Tombigbee Association, the Arkansas Basin Development Association, and so on. The Florida Waterways Association, for example, boosters of the controversial Cross-Florida Barge Canal, has among its directors a realtor, representatives of a consulting engineering company, a dredging company, chambers of commerce, port authorities, newspapers, and a construction company. The associations meet and entertain and lobby. The Lower Mississippi Valley Association is noted for its days-long barge parties. Some twenty- to thirty-odd people from an association descend on Washington from time to time, to testify and to see the right people in Congress and the Executive Branch.

The power to authorize the study of a project, then to initiate it, and to appropriate the money for it is held by the Senate and House Public Works Committees, and by the Public Works Subcommittees of the Appropriations Committees of the two bodies. This is a total of seventy-one men; as is usual with congressional committees, a very few of the most senior men wield the key influence. It all comes down to a chess game played by the same players over the years—the committees, their staffs, and the

Corps. There are always demands for more projects than can be studied, authorized, or financed, and so the Corps and the politicians are always in a position to do each other favors. One study can be moved ahead of another by the Corps if a man votes correctly. One project can get priority in the authorizing or appropriating stages. "Everyone is in everyone else's thrall," said a man who has been involved in the process, "unless he never wants a project."

The Corps has managed to arbitrate the demands for more projects than its budget can include through its highly developed sense of the relative political strengths within the Congress, and by making sure that each region of the country gets a little something each time. "We try to satisfy 10 per cent of the needs of each region," said a Corps official. From time to time, the Corps has been pressed by the Budget Bureau to recommend instead the most feasible projects in the nation as a whole, but the Corps has resisted this impolitic approach. The Secretary of the Army rarely changes the Corps' proposals. The Budget Bureau does examine the Corps' proposals on a project-by-project basis, but it runs a poor third to the Corps and Capitol Hill in deciding what the Corps' program should be. The President, who is but a passerby, cannot establish control over the public works process unless he decides to make the kind of major political fight that Presidents usually do not think is worth it. On occasion, the White House will oppose a particularly outrageous project—or, out of political exigency, support one. Outsiders are unable to penetrate the continuing feedback between the Corps and the congressional committees, and are insufficiently informed to examine the rationale, the nature, and the alternatives of each project.

There may have been a Corps of Engineers project that was rejected on the floor of Congress, but no one can recall it. Every two years—in election years—a rivers and harbors and flood-control authorization bill is passed by Congress, and every year, money is appropriated. It has been calculated that, on the average, the authorization bills have provided something for 113 congressional districts (or more than one fourth of the House of Representatives) at a time, and the appropriations bills for 91 districts. "We used to say," said a man involved in the process, "that we could put our mortgage in that bill and no one would notice, and then the appropriations committees would cut it by 15 per cent." The most recent appropriation carried something for 48 states. On occasion, a senator, Paul Douglas of Illinois for one, or William Proxmire of Wisconsin for another, has spoken out against a particular Corps project, or the "pork-barrel" technique of legislating Corps projects, but they have not been taken seriously. "One hundred fifty-five million dollars has been spent as a starter," Proxmire once argued on the Senate floor in futile opposition to the Cross-Florida Barge Canal, "that is what it is, a starter—to make many more jobs, to make a great deal of money, and a great deal of profit. That is the essence of pork. That is why Senators and Congressmen fight for it and win re-election on it. Of course people who will benefit from these tens of millions of pork profit and jobs are in favor of it. That is perfectly natural and understandable. It will snow in Washington in July when a member of Congress arises and says spare my district the pork. What a day that will be."

Douglas fought rivers and harbors projects for years and then, in 1956, made a speech saying that he was giving up. "I think it is almost hopeless," he said, "for any senator to try to do what I tried to do when I first came to this body, namely, to consider these projects one by one. The bill is built up out of a whole system of mutual accommodations, in which the favors are widely distributed, with the implicit promise that no one will kick over the applecart; that if senators do not object to the bill as a whole, they will 'get theirs.' It is a process, if I may use an inelegant expression, of mutual back scratching and mutual logrolling. Any member who tries to buck the system is confronted with an impossible amount of work in trying to ascertain the relative merits of a given project."

"Growing bananas"

The difficulty in understanding what a given Corps project will do, and what its merits are, comes not from a lack of material supplied by the Corps, but from an overabundance of it. A Corps report on a proposed project—the result of a survey that may take three to five years—is a shelf-long collection of volumes of technical material. Opponents of the project are on the defensive and unequipped to respond in kind.

Most of the projects that Congress asks the Corps to survey are, of course, turned down, because a Congressman will pass along a request for a survey of almost anything. By the time a project moves through the Corps' bureaucracy to the Board of Engineers for Rivers and Harbors in Washington—what the Corps calls an "independent review group"—it has a promising future. The Board is made up of the Corps' various division engineers, who present their own projects and have learned to trust each other's judgment.

The supposedly objective standard for deciding whether a project is worthy of approval is the "benefit-to-cost" ratio. The potential benefits of a project are measured against the estimated costs, and the resulting ratio must be at least one-to-one—that is, one dollar of benefit for each dollar spent (the Corps prefers the term "invested")—to qualify. There is, however, considerable flexibility in the process, and at times the benefit-cost ratios of controversial projects are recomputed until they come out right. This was true of the Trinity River project to make Fort Worth a seaport, the Cross-Florida Barge Canal, and projects along the Potomac River. "There is enough room in the benefit-cost ratio," said a man who has worked with the Corps on Capitol Hill, "for the Corps to be responsive to strong members of Congress who really want a project." It has been remarked that the measurements are pliant enough to prove the feasibility of growing bananas on Pikes Peak.

There is much argument over the Corps' method of arriving at prospective benefits. For example, business that might be drawn by a project is considered among the benefits, even though there is no real way of knowing what business the project will attract and what the effects will be. The lower prices to a shipper of sending his goods by barge rather than by rail is also considered a national benefit; such a benefit may involve the fact that a wheat farmer is growing and shipping more wheat because of the lower prices, even though we do not need the wheat. The windfalls to real estate investors who have been lucky or clever enough to have bought inexpensive land—some of it underwater —in the path of a future project can turn up as a boon to us all in the form of "enhanced land values." The land, which can then be sold and developed for industrial, housing, or resort development, undergoes extraordinary value increases.

There are serious questions about how to estimate future benefits of flood control; the 1955 Hoover Commission report said that they are often "considerably overstated." In any event, in the three decades since the Flood Control Act was passed, annual losses due to floods have increased (in real prices). The apparent explanation is that the construction of flood-control dams, which cannot be built to guarantee protection against all manner of floods, do nevertheless encourage developers to build expensive properties on lands that will still be hit by floods. The protection of buildings which a flood-control dam attracts is counted as a national benefit, even though the buildings might have been built in a safer place, and there are less expensive ways to protect them. Antipollution treatment and hydroelectric power are counted as benefits even though there are cheaper ways of cleaning water and providing power. The benefits and costs are not compared with the benefits and costs of doing these things any other way. Promised benefits appear higher than they will turn out to be because of an unrealistic way of projecting the decline of the value of the dollar. Projected recreation benefits, which have accounted for an increasing proportion of the benefit to the nation from building these projects, are based on an assumption of how much people would be willing to pay for recreation privileges, even though they don't. The Corps lobbies to keep its parks free, in contrast to other national parks. The life of a project used to be estimated at 50 years in adding up the benefits; as fewer projects qualified, the Corps has simply shifted to a basis of 100 years. The cost of the loss of a wilderness, or a quiet river valley, is not deducted, there being no market value for that.

Since more projects are authorized than are given money to be begun, hundreds of them lie around for years, forgotten by all but the sponsors, or the sponsors' sons, and the Corps. If a project becomes too controversial, its backers can simply outwait the opponents. When old projects, sometimes thirty years old, are dusted off, they may be started without reconsideration of either the original purposes or the benefits and costs.

Once a project is begun, its costs almost invariably outrun the estimates. Project proponents, on the other hand, argue that the benefits are consistently underestimated. The Corps is very sensitive about cost "overruns." They say that one must keep inflation in mind, and that such projects get changed and enlarged as they go along. Such changes, undermining the original benefit-cost rationale, do not seem to trouble the Congress. The Trinity River project, estimated at $790 million when it was authorized in 1962, is now expected to cost a little over $1 billion, and construction has not yet begun. The increases are not limited to the controversial projects. A look at project costs in a 1967 Corps report, the most recent one available, shows "overruns" of over 300 per cent.

"The wildest scheme"

Last year, despite a tight budget policy against "new starts," money to begin the Trinity River project was included in Lyndon Johnson's final budget, and was approved by the Congress.

During most of his White House years, Mr. Johnson was sensitive about bestowing federal rewards upon Texas, which had benefited so handsomely from his congressional career. Nonetheless, in the end, he overcame his scruples. The fact that he did can be credited to the persistence, and the excellent connections, of the Texas lobbyists for the project.

The major purpose of the Trinity project is to build a navigable channel from the Fort Worth-Dallas area 370 miles to the Gulf of Mexico. Like many other projects, this one has been boosted for a long, long time. It is said that Will Rogers was brought down to Texas once to make a speech in behalf of the Trinity, which is barely wet during some of the year. "I think you're right," Rogers told the Trinity Improvement Association, "I think you ought to go ahead and pave it." There have been a number of restudies of the feasibility of the Trinity project. At first it was justified on the basis of the shipping of wheat. The current justification assures a great deal of shipping of gravel, although there is some question as to the need to ship gravel from one end of Texas to the other. "It's the wildest scheme I ever saw," said a Texas politician who dared not be quoted. "They have to dig every foot of it. Then they have to put expensive locks in. You could put five railroads in for that price. I'm not carrying any brief for the railroads. You could put in a railroad and make the government pay for every inch of it and call it the United States Short Line and save a hell of a lot of money."

The Trinity River will feed barge traffic into another Texas-based waterways scheme, the Gulf Intracoastal Canal, which, when completed, will run from Brownsville, Texas, on the Mexican border, to the west coast of Florida. From there it will link up with the Cross-Florida Barge Canal, and then another channel all the way to Trenton, New Jersey. This has given the whole network a great deal of backing, which comes together in Washington through the efforts of Dale Miller, a long-time representative of a number of Texas interests. Miller, a white-haired, soft-spoken Texan came to town in 1941 with his ambitious, ebullient wife, Scooter, and took up his father's work in promoting projects for Texas. Miller represents the Gulf Intracoastal Canal Association, the Port of Corpus Christi, the Texas Gulf Sulphur Company, and the Chamber of Commerce of Dallas, for which the Trinity project is "the number-one program." He is also the vice president of the Trinity Improvement Association. ("So I have a direct interest in the Trinity at both ends.")

From the time they arrived in Washington, Dale and Scooter

Miller played bridge almost every weekend with the young Corps lieutenants who lived at Fort Belvoir, just outside Washington, and now they are "good friends" with the important members of the Corps. "We move in military social circles," says Miller. "We have them to our parties, and they have us to theirs." The Millers also moved in Washington's political circles and were close friends of Lyndon and Lady Bird Johnson's, and other powerful Washingtonians. Miller was the chairman of Johnson's inauguration in 1965. But he and his wife had the good sense to maintain bipartisan contacts. Last year they gave a large party that was described in the social pages as "50-50 Democrats and Republicans." Miller says that the coming of a Republican Administration has not hindered his work: "I just put on a more conservative tie, and I'm still in business." He works out of a suite in the Mayflower Hotel, its rooms filled with photographs of Johnson and Sam Rayburn, a harp, and a painting of the Dale Miller Bridge over the Intracoastal Canal in Corpus Christi. "It gives me an opportunity for that wonderful line," says Miller, " 'I'm not too big for my bridges.' "

Miller is also president and chairman of the board of the National Rivers and Harbors Congress, an unusual lobbying organization made up of politicians and private interests who support federal water projects. The chairman emeritus of the Rivers and Harbors Congress is Senator John McClellan. Among its directors are Senators Allen Ellender of Louisiana (chairman of the Public Works Appropriations Subcommittee) and Ralph Yarborough of Texas, and Congressmen Hale Boggs of Louisiana and Robert Sikes of Florida. Other officers of the group represent industries which use water transportation for their bulk cargo—such as Ashland Oil, farmers, and the coal business—and the Detroit Harbor and dredging companies. The resident executive director in Washington is George Gettinger, an elderly Indianan who has been in and out of a number of businesses and was a founder of the Wabash Valley Association, and "learned from my cash register" the value of federal water projects. "Your directors of your churches have businesses," says Gettinger, "your trustees of your universities have businesses. Sure our people make a living in water resources, just like other people. So help me, it's time we sat down and started looking at the benefits that have derived from this program. It's one of the bright spots in solving the population problem. It has settled people along rivers so they don't have to live in the inner city. The ghettos in this country are something it's not good to live with."

Cost Increases on Corps Projects

Name of Project	Cost Estimate at Time Project Was Authorized	Amount Spent Through Fiscal Year 1966	Percentage Overrun
Whitney (Tex.)	$ 8,350,000	$ 41,000,000	391
John H. Kerr (N.C. & Va.)	30,900,000	87,733,000	185
Blakely Mountain (Ark.)	11,080,000	31,500,000	184
Oahe Reservoir (N. & S. Dak.)	72,800,000	334,000,000	359
Jim Woodrull (Fla.)	24,139,000	144,734,000	92
Chief Joseph (Wash.)	104,050,000	46,400,000	39
Fort Peck (Mont.)	86,000,000	156,859,000	82
Clark Hill (Ga. & S. Car.)	28,000,000	79,695,000	185
Bull Shoals (Ark.)	40,000,000	88,824,000	122

In its pursuit of a solution to the urban crisis, the Rivers and Harbors Congress meets every year in Washington, at the Mayflower Hotel. Its members discuss their mutual interests and then fan out about town to talk to politicians and government officials. There is a projects committee which chooses priorities among the various proposed projects. "It asks the federal agencies about the projects," explains Gettinger. "Until the Rivers and Harbors Congress there was no kind of national clearance. Their endorsement has meant so much because it comes from a group that serves without pay." The project committee holds hearings at each convention, and then it adjourns to Dale Miller's suite to decide the public works priorities. As it turns out, the projects that are mainly for navigation receive the most support. "We have no axes to grind," says Miller. "We're just in favor of development of water resources."

The nationwide coalition of interested groups keeps the momentum behind the public works program, and gives the barge industry, probably the program's largest single beneficiary, and an important national industry some seventy-five years ago, the strength to continue to win its federal largesse. Besides working with the Rivers and Harbors Congress, the barge companies have their own trade associations, which have warded off tolls for the use of the federally constructed waterways.

The only major group that opposes most Corps projects is the railroad industry, which inevitably resists federally subsidized competition. On occasion, it succeeds. It is generally believed, for example, that the railroads, working through the Pennsylvania state government, blocked "Kirwan's ditch," a controversial project named after Mike Kirwan of Ohio, the chairman of the House Public Works Appropriations Subcommittee. At a cost of almost $1 billion, "Kirwan's ditch" was to link Lake Erie and the Ohio River.

The railroads also opposed the Trinity River project, but they did not succeed. Trinity had too much going for it: Jim Wright, a Congressman from Fort Worth and a friend of President Johnson's, is a senior member of the House Public Works Committee. Dale Miller, with valuable assistance from Marvin Watson when Watson was the President's appointments secretary and later when he was the Postmaster General, was able to help the representatives of the Trinity Improvement Association get a sympathetic hearing from all the important people, including the President. Balky officials were called into Postmaster General Watson's office to be persuaded of the value of the Trinity project.

Watson, as Miller put it, had "great familiarity with water projects in the Southwest." He had worked for the Red River Valley Association, and the Chamber of Commerce of Daingerfield, Texas, and then Lone Star Steel, which is located just outside Daingerfield. Watson had been a major force in securing, with the help of then Senator Johnson, a Corps water project which left Lone Star Steel with water and several of the surrounding little towns with higher taxes to pay off bonds which they had approved, in the mistaken impression that they too could draw water from the project. (It was later determined that they were too far away, and Watson became a very controversial figure in East Texas.) Watson maintained his efforts on behalf of the Red River Valley projects after he took up official positions in Washington. The Red River navigation project, to build a waterway from Daingerfield, Texas, to the Mississippi River, was authorized in 1968 to go as far as Shreveport.

After many years of success, Dale Miller's projects, like so many others, are now coming under fire because of what they will do to the environment. There is a "missing link" between the Gulf Intracoastal Canal and the Cross-Florida Barge Canal on the long way from Brownsville, Texas, to Trenton, New Jersey. The link has been authorized, but construction is being opposed. A navigation channel from Miami to Trenton already exists. "That doesn't carry a tremendous amount of tonnage," Miller says, "but it carries a tremendous amount of recreational traffic, people in their yachts and everything."

The problem which all developers—which we are—now face is the growing awareness of environmental problems. I mean ecological change. It's a very difficult area because we don't know too much about it—what effects dredging will have on baby shrimp, or marine life. It cuts both ways. We had developed that whole Gulf part of it before anyone raised the question of the effects. Nature is much more resilient than people think it is. In dredging, you may disturb an estuary where baby shrimp and marine life were, but it didn't mean permanent destruction, just change. They were breeding somewhere else in a year. In this missing link we're going to have to satisfy the ecologists in advance, and it's going to be very difficult. I'm convinced that the developers and the preservationists are not as far apart as people think. I think the difference can be reconciled and then we can move even faster. The problem a lot of us have, paraphrasing the little-old-ladies-in-tennis-shoes approach, is that we're not dealing with the knowledgeable and experienced people in ecology, but the bird watchers and butterfly-net people who don't want anything changed anywhere, and you can't deal with them.

As the country runs out of choice land near the cities, the solution has been to fill in the adjacent waterways. Besides what such schemes do to the scenery, it is now beginning to be understood what they do to natural life. Estuaries, or those places where rivers meet the sea, provide a special balance of salt and fresh water that is essential to certain fish, such as oysters and shrimp. They also provide food and habitats for waterfowl. The damming of rivers has also damaged estuarine life. Local governments are often willing to have the estuaries dredged and filled, for this raises the real estate values, and hence the local tax base. One third of San Francisco Bay, for example, has already been filled in, most of it for airport runways, industrial parks, and areas proposed for residential subdivisions. "It is conceivable," said Congressman Paul McCloskey, who had fought for conservation as a lawyer before coming to Congress in 1967, "that by 1990 the filling of shallow waters of the Bay could reduce it to the status of a river across which our grandchildren will be skipping rocks."

In response to criticism of its easiness with granting land-fill permits, and to a recent federal requirement that the Corps consider the effects on fish and wildlife, the Corps has begun to deny some permits. One such denial, however, was challenged in court, and a district judge in Florida ruled that the Corps did not have discretion to deny a permit on any grounds other than that it would impede navigation. The case is still in the courts. The Corps argues, with some validity, that it should not be making zoning decisions for local governments. "This points up the fact," said McCloskey, "that some new national land-use authority must be created which will have the power to put federal zoning on waterways, historic sites, and land areas of particular national significance." Such a policy would protect such areas as the Everglades. [Former] Congressman Richard Ottinger of New York, [who was] interested in conservation before it became fashionable, [pushed] legislation to require that the effects on the environment must be taken into account in any federal program which contributes to construction or issues licenses—the Corps, airport and highway programs, and so on.

"Luxurious areas"

The Corps of Engineers public works program has been, among other things, an income-transfer program, and this is a good time to look more closely at who has been transferring what to whom. The Federal Government has been paying for the Corps program —or rather, all of the taxpayers have. And the Corps program consists in the main of subsidies for irrigation, navigation, and flood control. Some projects have been for the benefit of only one particular industry. Former Senator Douglas has charged, for example, that a project to deepen the Detroit River was for the benefit of the Detroit Edison Company alone, and that a project to deepen the Delaware River from Philadelphia to Trenton was to serve one mill of the United States Steel Corporation, which was quite able to pay for the project itself. An industry or developer builds on a flood plain and then asks the Federal Government to save it from floods. A wild river is converted for use by an industry; subsequently a federal subsidy is given to clean up the industry's pollution of the river. The barge industry is kept afloat because it is there.

Robert Haveman, an economist and author of *Water Resource Investment and the Public Interest*, has shown that the preponderance of Corps projects has gone to three regions: the South and Southwest, the Far West, and North and South Dakota, but mainly to the South, in particular the lower Mississippi River area. Within an area, the rewards are not evenly spread. The major beneficiaries of the flood-control projects which also provide water for irrigation have been the large landholders—in particular, in the Mississippi Delta and San Joaquin Valley. These are the same landowners who are paid the largest federal farm subsidies for not growing the crops which the federal water projects make it possible for them to grow. The Corps is still preparing to produce more farmland, in the name of flood control, in the Mississippi Delta region.

The Corps, in a publication called "The Army Engineers' Contributions to American Beauty," notes: "In Dallas, the flood-control project for channeling the flood waters of the Trinity River through the center of town (once some of the least desirable real estate in the city) is being made into a long-winding stretch of parkway. In Los Angeles and other Pacific Coast cities built below mountain slopes, the development of attractive and sometimes luxurious residential areas has been made possible by Army Engineer projects which curb flash floods."

"An idea"

The Corps established an environmental division a few years ago, to advise on the environmental effects of its projects. This summer it is sponsoring a seminar on how it can better "communicate" with the public. Corps officials have been urging greater environmental concerns on the Corps members, and on their clientele, appealing, among other things, to their self-interest. In a recent speech, Major General F. P. Koisch, director of the Corps' Civil Works Division, told the Gulf Intracoastal Canal Association to listen to the voice of the so-called "New Conservation."

"By and large," he said, "its advocates oppose the old concepts of expansion and development. Yet they are not merely negative, for they are willing to lavish huge sums on programs which embody their own conceptions of natural resource management. Their theories and concepts are not always consistent nor fully worked out. They are less concerned with means than with ends and goals—their vision of a better America. But they do seem to represent an idea whose time has come. So it grows clearer every day that it is up to us, who like to think of ourselves as scientific, practical men who know how to get things done, to make this new idea our own and make it work. . . . This can open a whole new career for the Gulf Intracoastal Canal Association. . . . This business of ecology," says General Koisch, "we're concerned, but people don't know enough about it to give good advice. You have to stand still and study life cycles, and we don't have time. We have to develop before 1980 as much water resource development as has taken place in the whole history of the nation."

"It is a fact," said General Richard H. Groves, his deputy, in a speech, "that our nation is engaged in a struggle to survive its technology and its habits. It is a fact, too, that we are defiling our waters, polluting our air, littering our land, and infecting our soil and ourselves with the wastes which our civilization produces. These are serious problems, but we cannot permit ourselves to yield to an emotional impulse that would make their cure the central purpose of our society. Nor is there any reason why we should feel guilty about the alterations which we have to make in the natural environment as we meet our water-related needs."

In an interview, General Groves said he did not believe that the basic role of the Corps would change. "Certainly, parts of it will. One part that is obvious is control of pollution, control of the ecology, which is more or less the same. There are very heavy pressures that have developed, and nobody in this business can ignore them. We would hope that in responding to these pressures we don't lose sight of the need to keep everything in perspective. The program keeps growing. The program as you know is tied to people, and the people double every forty years. . . . We build the program," he said—and here is the heart of it all—"on the notion that people want an ever-increasing standard of living, and the standard of living is tied to water programs. If you conserve undeveloped areas, you're not going to be able to do it. If you double the population and they double their standard of living, you have to keep going. It's not as simple as the people who take an extreme view say."

Clearly, no rational settlement of the conflict between "progress" and the environment is going to come from dam-by-dam fights between the Corps and the conservationists. The conservationists have been out there all alone all these years, and they have worked hard, but they have lacked a national strategy. In some instances, they have tried to have it all ways: opposing not only hydroelectric projects but also alternatives such as generating power through burning fuels (air pollution) or building a nuclear plant (thermal pollution and radiation hazards). Some conservationists have been interested in "preserving" the wildlife so that they could shoot it. Where engineers have been pitted against engineers, as in the case of the Oakley and Potomac dams, the opponents have been more successful. "The only way to resist," says Representative John Saylor of Pennsylvania, a critic of the Corps for years, "is to know a little more about the Corps than the Chambers of Commerce do." The new approach of trying to build a body of law on the basis of the "rights of the people" against a public works project could be of profound importance.

Some water economists have suggested quite seriously a ten-year moratorium on water projects. There is an ample supply of water, they say. Problems arise where industries use it inefficiently because it is provided so cheaply, and pollute much of it. The answer for the pollution, the experts say, is sewage treatment at the point where the pollution originates.

So one solution to the problems the Corps program creates would be simply to stop it. The Corps and the Public Works Committees and the river associations could give themselves a grand testimonial dinner, congratulate themselves on their good works, and go out of business. There are more effective ways of transferring money—for instance, directly—if that is what we want to do; there are others who need the money more. But such suggestions are not, of course, "practical."

For as long as anyone can remember, there have been proposals for removing the public works program from the military, and transferring the Corps' civil functions, or at least the planning functions, to the Interior Department or a new department dealing with natural resources. President Nixon considered similar ideas, but rejected them in preparing his message on the environment. The Corps likes being where it is, and the powerful Forest Service and Soil Conservation Service, which are secure in the Agriculture Department, and the congressional committees whose power derives from the present arrangements, have habitually and successfully resisted up to now. "The two most powerful intragovernmental lobbies in Washington are the Forest Service and the Army Engineers," wrote FDR's Interior Secretary Harold Ickes in his diary in 1937, in the midst of a vain effort to reorganize them and Interior into a new Department of Conservation. Whatever the chances for reform, it has never been clear who would be swallowing whom as a result of such a change. The closed-circuit system by which public works decisions are made should be opened to other interested parties. Certainly a federal program that is more than a century old should be overhauled. The Corps is now at work on some internal improvements, but bureaucracies are not notably rigorous about self-change, and the water interests do not want change.

If there are to be a Corps and a Corps public works program, then proposals to expand the Corps' functions make sense. Making the Corps responsible for sewage treatment, for example, would give it a task that needs to be done, local governments a benefit which they really need and which would be widely shared, and politicians a new form of largesse to hand around. Antipollution could be spared the pork barrel through a combination of requirements for local action and federal incentives, and through adequate financing. Yet making antipollution part of the pork barrel may be just what it needs. Programs which appeal to greed are notably more politically successful than those that do not. The Corps' engineering expertise, in any event, could be put to use for something other than building dams and straightening rivers. It is the judgment of just about every economist who has studied the public works program that there should be cost-sharing and user charges. There have been proposals for making the beneficiaries of flood-control and navigation projects and harbors pay for them, or at least part of them.

In a period of great needs and limited resources, a high proportion of the public works program amounts to inefficient expenditures and long-range commitments of money on behalf of those who make the most noise and pull the most strings. Despite all the talk about "reordering priorities," the Nixon Administration's budget for the next year increases the money for the Corps. Even if the nation should want to double its standard of living (leaving aside for the moment the question of whose standard of living) and even if the public works programs really could help bring that about, it would be good to know more about the nature and price of such a commitment. At a time when a number of our domestic arrangements are coming under re-examination, this one is a prime candidate for reform. Meanwhile, the changes it is making in the nation are irreversible.

Conclusion

The Military Services and American Society: Relationships and Attitudes

JAMES ALDEN BARBER, JR.

American attitudes toward the military services and the role played by the military in the social and political systems of the United States have deep roots in the American heritage. Most of the military practices of the colonies were inherited from England, who had traditionally taken advantage of her insular position to avoid the large standing armies which existed on the Continent. From England the colonists inherited a distaste for a professional military caste and a distrust of a standing army. These attitudes have permeated American civil-military relations ever since.

Yet much as they might have wished to, the colonists could not afford to ignore military questions. Quarrels with the Indians and competition among the European nations seeking colonies in the new world demanded some kind of military organization. Professional soldiers, such as Captain Miles Standish and Captain John Smith, were hired specifically to accompany the early colonists, to train them in the use of arms and to lead them in battle if necessary. In the early days each settlement was virtually a military colony, with all able-bodied men armed and subject to call on short notice to participate in defense of the colony. Even in the absence of any direct threat, the resulting militia organization tended to remain intact, and often exercised an important influence on local politics. At the same time, the long series of French and Indian wars tended to keep alive the requirement for effective military forces in being. These local militia organizations provided the "Minutemen" and a large portion

of the early forces engaged in the American Revolution, although
the primary load of the war quickly fell upon the centrally
organized Continental Army, composed mainly of short-term
volunteers. George Washington's ordeals with the Continental
Army, most of them revolving around the problems of short
enlistments and shortage of funds, are too well known to require
recounting here, but were significant in setting a pattern that
was to be repeated at intervals over the ensuing century and a
half.

As the text of the Declaration of Independence makes clear,
the colonies rebelled not just against the political policies of the
mother country, but against specific military abuses as well, and
when it came time to frame the Constitution these resentments
were still keenly felt. The Founding Fathers believed that a
standing army was dangerous to the liberties of the people, yet
having just completed a lengthy war, the delegates could not
ignore the requirements of national defense. The solution to this
dilemma, like almost everything else in the Constitution, was to
compromise. The nation was to depend upon a navy and a
small peacetime professional army, with primary reliance placed
upon state militias which could be called into federal service in
time of emergency.

Despite its potential weaknesses, the national military policy
worked, because, with the partial exception of the War of 1812,
the virtually unbreachable moat of the Atlantic Ocean kept any
serious threat from ever materializing. Geographical isolation
was at least as important in the development of our national
military policy as were the traditions inherited from the British.
For a long time the United States was able to sit in safe and
aloof isolation from European quarrels, in smug conviction of
moral superiority to the warmongering Europeans. Even as late
as World War II, the ocean barrier gave the United States the
time necessary to transform a tiny peacetime military establishment into the world's most powerful military instrument. Even
in that largest of wars, the continental United States was never
in serious danger, and the bloody and destructive parts of the
war were fought far from American shores.

The Traditional Pattern
of American Military Policy

From the time of independence to after the Second World War
American policy followed a clear and repetitive pattern from

which there were only occasional departures. Part of the pattern was rooted in the tradition of distrust of the military services, and took the form of careful subordination of the military to civilian authority. The unbroken span of effective control of the military services by civilian authority is one of the most striking facets of American history, particularly when contrasted with the history of civil-military relations in many other nations. With the possible exception of the abortive intrigue within the Continental Army in 1783, there has never been a time when there was even a hint of danger of the American military establishment attempting to use its armed strength in domestic politics.

The second part of the continuing pattern has to do with the tendency of the United States to arm hastily in time of war, and to disarm with even greater haste in time of peace. A few quotations from military historians may give some flavor of the process:

> The military policy of the country from 1829 to 1861 was a projection of that which had obtained in earlier years, i.e., distrust of a standing army, parsimony in military expenditures, and reliance upon the militia or volunteers in an emergency.[1]

> The isolation, rejection and reduction of the armed services after the Civil War have left historians to mark this as the low point of American military history.[2]

> The attitude of normalcy and isolation that permeated the 1920's viewed the army as virtually obsolete as the nation moved further away from the notion that war would ever again come to America.[3]

The system worked effectively, because the ocean moat permitted the United States to virtually pick and choose her wars, and always permitted time to rearm. Unilateral disarmament is an old American tradition, but although we have often congratulated ourselves on our moral superiority on that count, geographical isolation has had more to do with it than has morality.

Americans have tended to view peace as the normal state of affairs, and war as an aberration. As a consequence our wars

[1] Leonard D. White, *The Jacksonians*. (New York: MacMillan, 1954), p. 187.
[2] Samuel P. Huntington, *The Soldier and the State* (Cambridge: The Belknap Press of Harvard University Press, 1959), p. 229.
[3] Raymond G. O'Connor, *American Defense Policy in Perspective* (New York: John Wiley, 1965), p. 215.

have tended to become moral crusades—with moral right always on the American side. Once the evil aggressors were defeated, a return to permanent peace could be expected. If this seemed to the Europeans to be a rather simple-minded and somewhat irritating approach to the whole problem, it was because they had never enjoyed the protection afforded the United States by the ocean moat. To them, war seemed a much more regular and inevitable part of human affairs than it did to Americans, and the moral issues sometimes seemed less clear.

Departure from Tradition

World War II was a watershed in American military policy. United States entry into the war was in the long-standing American tradition: despite an accelerating attempt to prepare the country for war in the two years before Pearl Harbor, the military services were almost pitifully unprepared at the beginning of the war. By the end of the war, of course, the United States was the strongest military power in the world, but all indications were that we would return to the hallowed tradition of unilateral peacetime disarmament. The hopes for a peaceful world under the collective security umbrella of the United Nations contributed to our haste, as did the domestic clamor to bring the boys home. The immediate result was a dissolution of the Armed Forces almost as rapid as had taken place in 1918. Between June, 1945 and June, 1947 the number of men in the Armed Forces dropped from almost twelve million to just over 1.5 million. Yet the reduction of the Armed Forces could not be as drastic as in 1918, for the U.S. had acquired responsibilities in Europe and Asia that demanded a U.S. troop presence, at least for the time being. In addition, we had a monopoly of the atomic bomb, and despite the mothballing of many ships, the U.S. retained the world's most powerful Navy—so that outside of the dominance of the Red Army on the Eurasian continent, the U.S. was by far the most powerful nation in the world during the years following World War II.

No single event can really be taken as marking the beginning of the cold war. Relations between the Soviet Union and the Western allies deteriorated steadily after 1945. In March, 1946 Winston Churchill, in a speech at Westminster College in Fulton, Missouri, marked this deterioration when he said, "From Stettin in the Baltic to Trieste in the Adriatic an iron curtain has descended across the Continent." In 1947 military and economic assistance was given to Greece and Turkey to help them resist communist pressure, as the first commitment under what came to be known as the Truman Doctrine. In 1948 the fall of Czechoslovakia to a communist coup d'etat, the passage of the Marshall Plan for the reconstruction of Europe, and Stalin's imposition of the Berlin Blockade in June, signaled that the cold war was on in earnest. The signing of the North Atlantic Treaty the following year was a major step in the expansion of U.S. commitments which was to end with the U.S. committed in one way or another to the defense of almost the entire non-communist world.

With the expansion of U.S. commitments, and with recognition of the increasing tensions of the cold war, it became clear that something more in the way of a standing military force was called for than ever before in peacetime. After flirting with the idea of Universal Military Training for a while, the Congress in 1948 passed a peacetime draft law to provide a continuing supply of manpower to the military services. The outbreak of the Korean War in 1950 tended to reinforce the pattern that was already being established. By the decade of the 1970's, more than twenty years of relatively high levels of military spending confirmed a new pattern of U.S. military policy entirely different from that which had characterized the previous century and a half.

In the beginning, this high level of military spending was based almost solely on the need for military forces to balance Russian pressures against non-communist nations overseas, a policy which came to be known as "containment." Only gradually did another element creep into military considerations: the possibility of direct damage to the United States itself. The ocean moats had always made any threat of significant damage to the continental United States by an enemy a remote and unlikely consideration—although sufficient to generate popular hysteria from time to time. But with development by the Soviet Union of intercontinental missiles with thermonuclear warheads, the ocean moat became technologically obsolete in the same fashion as the castle moat became obsolete in the face of cannon. No longer could the United States sit safely and smugly behind two oceans to gain the time necessary to create military power virtually from scratch when it was needed. The combination of the vastly expanded commitments which accompanied the cold war, and the new vulnerability of the United

States, led to the large standing military establishment which had always been avoided before.

The New Role of the Military

Traditionally, military policy in peacetime has been almost exclusively a concern of the Executive Branch. The relative unimportance of military issues led to a lack of interest by Congress in much other than insuring that military budgets stayed low. Under these circumstances, as Samuel Huntington has pointed out, the military chiefs of the services tended to act primarily as spokesmen for the Executive Branch in their dealings with Congress.[4] With the advent of the cold war, however, Congress became much more vitally interested in military questions, and began to probe for areas in which professional military opinion deviated from Administration policy. This seemed necessary if Congress was to play an independent part in determining national military policy, for it had no military experts of its own on whom to call in evaluating Administration proposals.

The attempt by Congress to play a more assertive role in determining military policy placed the military leaders of the Armed Services in an uncomfortable position. The military services belong to the Executive Branch of government and are subject to the control of both the civilian Secretaries and the President as Commander in Chief of the Armed Forces. If they confine their testimony before Congress to support of Administration policies and programs, they deny to the Congress the benefit of their independent professional judgment, and are placed in the political role of defending the policies of the Administration. If, on the other hand, they disagree with Administration proposals, they bring their loyalty to their Commander-in-Chief into question. There seems to be no easy way out of the dilemma. Some members of the Joint Chiefs of Staff have chosen to break with the Administration on issues they considered vital. Two examples are Admiral Louis Denfield, who was dismissed as Chief of Naval Operations in 1949 after disagreeing with the Administration during the B-36 controversy, and General Maxwell Taylor, who resigned as Chief of Staff of the Army in 1959 because of what he viewed as inadequate resources for the Army. Others have chosen the course of

---

[4] Huntington, *op. cit.*, pp. 412–418.

publicly defending Administration policy, and have thus placed themselves in the unprofessional position of being political partisans. This has been particularly notable during the Vietnam War.

Despite the attempt by Congress to be more assertive in the formulation of military policy, the principal role remains with the Executive Department. In the main, Congress has been content to criticize military policy as developed by the Executive Department, and to attempt to play a watchdog role. Even in this role, however, Congress often lacks both time and staff resources to do an adequate job of policing an organization as mammoth and complicated as the defense establishment.

One result of the increased size of the military services has been to multiply the layers and kinds of civilian management within the Executive Branch. Where once the chief of a military service had only his own Service Secretary between him and the President, he now has his own Service Secretary, the Secretary of Defense, and an almost uncountable array of Assistant, Deputy and Undersecretaries to contend with, not to mention the civilian operations analysts who, under the MacNamara regime, gained fame as the "whiz kids." This panoply of civilian officials accomplishes more in the way of detailed supervision of military activities than ever before. As Part III (The Military and Foreign Policy) demonstrates, civilians do control the military, but the elaborate bureaucracy through which this control is accomplished is itself a major contributor to the fumblings, inefficiencies and blatant stupidities which sometimes characterize the military establishment.

We have tried in the course of this book to shed some light on the more important issues involved in the relationship of the military services to American society. The subject is so vast that our treatment cannot avoid omissions, yet two topics seem to require at least brief mention here. The first is the question of priorities: given all of the pressing demands upon government and the social inequities crying for reform, what proportion of the public revenue should be devoted to military expenditures? The second has to do with the efficiency and effectiveness of the Armed Forces—or the lack of it.

Part of the problem of priorities has to do with the inherent unanswerability of "how much defense is enough?" The soldier's answer is always, and should always be, on the conservative side. No general ever feels that he has adequate resources to meet all of the contingent threats he can imagine, and as a professional soldier he sees the military dangers to the country written in larger letters than he sees other problems. That is why the Constitution provides for civilian control over the military, and for determination through the political process of what proportions of the national resources will be put to what uses. The balancing of competing claims is inherently a political process, and it is in the arena of politics that the decisions must be made.

The military services are sometimes guilty of exaggerating the military threat to the country and the requirements for their own services. This is not surprising; it is a human tendency to overestimate one's own role, and to see one's own needs in brighter hues than the needs of others. Yet particularly at a time when we are reacting to the tragedy of the Vietnam War there is danger that the response may be to swing too far in the other direction. As pointed out earlier, war has invariably caught the United States in a position of military unpreparedness, and the ocean barrier which has saved us from suffering any major consequences in the past has lost much of its effectiveness. It may be somewhat melodramatic to point out that in the fable the wolf *did* come, but only after the shepherd boy's warnings were ignored. American optimism about the permanence of peace has always proved mistaken before, and the world does not seem markedly more peaceful now than in the past. It appears, therefore, that the U.S. will have to continue to support a sizable military establishment, although not necessarily so large as in recent years. At the same time it is imperative that we actively seek solutions to the problems inherent in a large standing military establishment, many of which we have tried to treat in these pages.

It would be futile to be militarily strong if our society or even our planet were to disintegrate under us for lack of the proper allocation of resources. There is evidence that in the last several years Congress, and to a degree the Administration, have begun shifting resources away from military uses and toward pressing domestic social programs. Figures released by the Office of Management and Budget in early 1971 indicated that the portion of the total federal budget going to defense dropped from about 46 per cent in fiscal 1968 to an estimated 34 per cent in fiscal 1972. At the same time, the portion of the budget devoted to "human resources" increased from about 32 per cent in fiscal 1968 to an estimated 42 per cent in fiscal 1972.

The second problem has to do with the efficiency and effectiveness of the Armed Forces. Large bureaucracies apparently have an almost inevitable tendency toward doing fumbling and inept things, and as has been pointed out at several points in this volume, the Armed Services are no exception. A certain amount of this is probably unavoidable in any large bureaucracy, but much of it is responsive to public scrutiny and concern. Not discussed in any detail in the text is an accumulation of problems which may add up to a coming crisis of major proportions for the military services.

There are increasing indications of a partial breakdown of morale, discipline and professionalism within the military services, at least in part as a result of the war in Vietnam. Fighting a war is always expensive, and when it is long, bloody, unpopular and unsuccessful, it is destructive of military morale, organization and professional integrity. Some of the indications of this breakdown include the practice of "fragging" officers and non-coms in Vietnam (enlisted men throwing grenades into officer and NCO quarters or messes); high AWOL and desertion rates; reported high rates of drug usage among servicemen in Vietnam; and evidence of lack of integrity and repeated attempts to cover up problems at high levels in the military services.[5] Willingness of both officer and enlisted personnel to remain in the Armed Services beyond their initial period of obligated service is at a low ebb. Tragedies like the My Lai incident generally result not from some deliberate and reprehensible policy, but from a breakdown in the military system.

The war in Vietnam has been at least as frustrating for the professional soldier as it has been for anyone else. Never before has an army been subjected to as much detailed, politically directed control, or to such intense strictures upon the military commander's freedom of action. Ironically, in view of the widespread charges of the immorality of the war, no major power has ever before fought a war under such a panoply of self-imposed restraints. This is not to say that the result of the restraints was a more moral war; it may well be that their result was to make the war even more prolonged and brutal than it otherwise would have been. The point is that the professional soldier has had to operate under unprecedented restraints and interferences at the same time that he has become the target of unparalleled criticism, vituperation and even hatred.

Vietnam is not an isolated example, but a specimen of a rela-

[5] General Hamilton H. Howze, U.S. Army (ret.), "Military Discipline and National Security," *Army*, January 1971, p. 11; Colonel Samuel H. Hays, U.S. Army (ret.), "The Growing Leadership Crisis," *Army*, February 1970, pp. 39–43.

tively new kind of undeclared limited war. There have been two major conflicts during the last quarter of a century, both without a declaration of war. The result has been an immense increase in the problems of the military forces involved in those wars, confusing their objectives and multiplying the extent to which political considerations necessarily dictate restrictions, interference and close control. At the same time, lack of clearly understood objectives and the often protracted and indecisive nature of such wars, coupled with the phenomenon of continuous, rapid and highly selective television coverage of the most sensational aspects of the Vietnam War, have seriously undermined public support. As a result, at the same time that the military man has been asked to undertake more confusing and frustating tasks, he has lost the public support that has generally been present in past conflicts.

One of the unfortunate results of the reaction to the Vietnam tragedy has been the tendency to place virtually all of the blame on the military. As Charles Moskos has pointed out, Americans have been developing an inverted version of the "stab-in-the-back" theory by which the German general staff managed to transfer to the civilian Weimar government the responsibility for the loss of World War I.[6] In a curious reversal, the liberal and intellectual communities in the United States seem to be embarked on placing the full responsibility for the debacle of Vietnam upon the military.

The trouble with making the military the scapegoat is that it directs attention away from the real causes of the present dilemma. The chain of events that led us into Vietnam grew directly out of long-term U.S. policy as enunciated vigorously by the most responsible civilian policy makers of our government. To blame the military services for the direction of our foreign policy is to avoid the vital issues. The Vietnam War was the product of the cold war, the policy of containment, and a long chain of policy decisions formulated by civilian advisors and civilian decision makers. This is not to say that the military services are blameless, for they have undoubtedly given mistaken recommendations and over-optimistic assessments in the course of the Vietnam War. But theirs is not, and has not been, the responsibility for making the key decisions, and at least in some cases they have apparently not even been con-

[6] Charles C. Moskos, Jr., "Antimilitarism—Intellectuals' New Anti-Semitism," *Los Angeles Times*, September 6, 1970.

sulted. It may be psychologically satisfying to blame all that is bad in our foreign policy on the man in uniform, but it is an evasion of the real issues, and no more likely to contribute to a solution to our problems than is any other form of scapegoating.

The widespread hostility toward the military services has been at least partially responsible for a lessening of discipline and morale within the services. Opposition to the war in Vietnam came in many cases to take the form of questioning of the legitimacy of dedicating one's life to military service, and the characterization of the armed forces as the embodiment of all that is evil within American society. The situation has led one sociologist to describe the wave of antimilitarism as "the anti-Semitism of the intellectual community," in that it provides an outgroup to blame for everything.[7] This lack of public confidence, and the charge that military service is not a legitimate role in life, undermines the professional ethic, which is based upon the ideal of service to the nation. It is unrealistic to expect a young man to want to serve his country in a role in which he is castigated as a villain.

The same denial of legitimacy to military institutions has contributed to a weakening of discipline within the Armed Forces. In the officer corps it is difficult to maintain the tradition of honor and integrity in the face of widespread belief that military service is evil and immoral. Nor is it easy to create an atmosphere conducive to discipline when the legitimacy of the institution itself is in question. Yet if countless generations of experience are to be believed, nothing is more essential to the effectiveness of a military service than internal discipline. If we need an army at all, we need a disciplined army; yet concerted attacks upon the legitimacy of the military life make the task of creating an atmosphere of discipline, loyalty and integrity more and more difficult.

If we are to have the most effective control over our military forces and our foreign policy, the military services in a democracy should not be isolated from the currents of society. It is easier for a government to follow an adventuristic foreign policy with an army of mercenaries than it is with an army of draftees who come from all levels of the society. Yet there are a number of indications of growing isolation of the armed forces: opposition to ROTC on many college campuses, the attempt to move toward an all-volunteer force and the widespread hostility toward

[7] *Ibid.*

anything associated with the military. This is neither wise nor healthy, and serves only to make it easier to hide or ignore the problems of American policy which should be faced directly.

The traditional American suspicion of the military has probably never been stronger; the credit earned in World War II has been spent, and the Armed Services are being subjected to intense criticism from all sides. Much of the criticism is justified, and because of the military penchant for secrecy, there are undoubtedly things in need of criticism which are hidden from public view. Yet much of the criticism is unjustified. The Armed Forces are not the source of all evil in our society, and they are certainly not to blame for everything that is wrong in our foreign policy.

The essential point is that the military services are not something different from and apart from American society, but are an integral part of the fabric of that society. No less than the broader society itself, the military services desperately need a period of respite, in order to heal their psychic wounds and to restore the shaken standards of military professionalism.

Index

301.59